ENTERPRISE CULTURE

£35.00

INTERNATIONAL LIBRARY OF SOCIOLOGY

Founded by Karl Mannheim

Editor: John Urry
University of Lancaster

ENTERPRISE CULTURE

Edited by

RUSSELL KEAT

and

NICHOLAS ABERCROMBIE

*The Lancaster University Centre
for the Study of Cultural Values*

LONDON AND NEW YORK

First published 1991
by Routledge
11 New Fetter Lane, London EC4P 4EE

Simultaneously published in the USA and Canada
by Routledge
a division of Routledge, Chapman and Hall, Inc.
29 West 35th Street, New York, NY 10001

Phototypeset in 10pt Baskerville by
Mews Photosetting, Beckenham, Kent
Printed and bound in Great Britain by
Mackays of Chatham PLC, Chatham, Kent

British Library Cataloguing in Publication Data
Enterprise Culture.
1. Great Britain. Social values, history
I. Keat, Russell II. Abercrombie, Nicholas
303.372

Library of Congress Cataloging in Publication Data
Enterprise Culture/edited by Russell Keat, Nicholas Abercrombie.
p. cm.
'Originated in a series of seminars organised by the University of
Lancaster's Centre for the Study of Cultural Values . . . 1988–90' –
Pref.
Includes bibliographical references.
1. Free enterprise – Social aspects. 2. Social values.
3. Economic history – 1971– I. Keat, Russell. II. Abercrombie,
Nicholas.
HB95.E57 1990
330.12'2–dc20   90-32993
                                            CIP

ISBN 0-415-05497-4
0-415-04856-7 (pbk)

CONTENTS

v

CONTENTS

vi

FIGURES
AND TABLES

FIGURES

TABLE

CONTRIBUTORS

The contributors are all members of the Centre for the Study of Cultural Values at the University of Lancaster and hold, or have recently held posts in the University.

Nicholas Abercrombie Reader in Sociology. His current interests include the sociological analysis of popular culture, and change in the 'cultural industries' since the Second World War. His publications include *The Dominant Ideology Thesis* and *Sovereign Individuals of Capitalism* (Unwin Hyman, with S. Hill and B. Turner).

Paul Bagguley Formerly Research Officer, Department of Sociology and now Lecturer in Sociology, University of Leeds. He is joint author with the Lancaster Regionalism Group of *Restructuring: Place, Class, and Gender* (Sage, in press), and author of *From Protest to Acquiescence? Political Movements of the Unemployed* (Macmillan).

Robert Crawshaw Lecturer in the Department of Modern Languages and co-ordinator of European Relations for Lancaster University Management School. Following undergraduate studies in French and Italian, he worked in publishing before taking further degrees in comparative literature and linguistics. Recent publications have included articles on language acquisition and a textbook on commercial French.

Norman Fairclough Lecturer in Linguistics. He has written mainly on critical approaches to linguistics and discourse analysis, including *Language and Power* (Longman). He is interested in discourse analysis as an interdisciplinary field of research and has been closely involved in the work of Lancaster University's Centre for Language in Social Life.

Paul Heelas Lecturer in the Anthropology and Sociology of Religion and Deputy Director of the Centre for the Study of Cultural Values. He has a long-standing interest in anthropological and other approaches to the study of varieties of self-understanding. He is co-editor with A. Lock of *Indigenous Psychologies* (Academic Press) and currently researching 'self-ethics of the contemporary West'.

Russell Keat Senior Lecturer in Philosophy, and Director of the Centre for the Study of Cultural Values. His main interests are in social philosophy, including political theory and the philosophy of the social sciences. He is author of *The Politics of Social Theory* (Blackwell and Chicago UP) and, with J. Urry, of *Social Theory as Science* (Routledge).

Paul Morris Lecturer in Religious Studies. His publications include articles on German Jewish theology, politics and religion, and a forthcoming book *Franz Rosenzweig* (Halbon). His current research interests are: modern Jewish religious thought, religious and cultural pluralism and the relationships between religious and political/economic systems, with particular reference to Britain.

Larry Ray Lecturer in Sociology. He has previously published on: Critical Theory; rural social structure in Kenya; and the political economy of health. Recently, he has edited *Critical Sociology*, and *Formal Sociology – the Sociology of Georg Simmel* (both published by Edward Elgar). His current research interests include the sociology of socialist societies.

Hermann Schwengel Teacher of sociology at the Free University of Berlin, having been Visiting Research Fellow in the Centre for the Study of Cultural Values and the Department of Sociology. His current research interests include the Europeanization of politics and the comparative analysis of city development. His recent book, *Der Kleine Leviathan (Atheneum)* is a historical–sociological study of the gains and risks of American political civilization.

Raman Selden Emeritus Professor of English at Lancaster University, and Professor of English at Sunderland Polytechnic. His publications are mainly in literary theory and seventeenth-century English literature. They include *English Verse Satire, 1590–1765* (Allen & Unwin), *Criticism and Objectivity* (Allen & Unwin) and *A Reader's Guide to Contemporary Literary Theory* (Wheatsheaf Books).

Christopher Stanley Lecturer in Law. Trained as a barrister, he has published on organization theory and company law, corporate crime and securities regulation, and the conflict between business practice and legal ethics. Current research concerns the regulation of the corporate form with specific reference to the nature of the corporate legal personality, property rights and the normalization of criminal action by corporations.

Nigel Whiteley Senior Lecturer and Head of the Department of Visual Arts. His most recent book, *Pop Design: from Modernism to Mod* (Design Council) examines the theories and design of pop culture in Britain between 1952 and 1972. He is currently writing a critique of consumer-led design, particularly from the perspectives of green politics and feminism.

PREFACE

The chapters (papers) in this volume originated in a series of seminars organized by the University of Lancaster's Centre for the Study of Cultural Values as part of its 1988–90 research theme, 'The Values of the Enterprise Culture'. The Centre's aim is to examine the cultural values of modern societies from the varied perspectives offered by different disciplines and theoretical traditions in the humanities and social sciences. We hope that this collection will serve to illustrate the potential contributions to the study of contemporary cultural phenomena that can be made in this way.

The chapters are grouped in three sections. Each of these is preceded by a brief outline of their contents, partly so as to avoid an undue number of cross-references in the chapters themselves. The Introduction to the volume is intended to identify the main themes explored in the papers that follow, and to relate them to one another in the context of a broad overview of the nature of enterprise culture. But neither the Introduction nor the volume as a whole lays claim to providing a 'complete' account, even in schematic form. Nor should readers expect to find agreement, at least on fundamentals, amongst the various contributors. Rather, the collection aims to open up a wide range of significant questions and possible lines of analysis.

Contributors were encouraged to be speculative where they saw fit; to write from within their particular disciplines in a way that was reasonably accessible to 'outsiders'; and not to be secretive about their own values and political judgements. We are grateful to them for their efforts in responding to these requests, and for working to a rather demanding time-schedule that would enable this volume to appear whilst the phenomenon it addresses remains in evidence.

Our thanks also to Anne Bottomley, Tom Cahill, Mick Dillon,

Oliver Fulton, Alan Warde and Oliver Westall for their contributions
to the originating seminar series, and to the many others who took
part in the discussions; to John Urry, for his encouragement of the
project; to Chris Quinn for dealing with some unruly tapes and texts;
and to Marion Brocklebank and Roz Platt for typing some of the drafts.

Russell Keat and
Nick Abercrombie
University of Lancaster, 1990

INTRODUCTION

Starship Britain or
universal enterprise?

RUSSELL KEAT

I used to have a nightmare for the first six years in office that, when I had got the finances right, when I had got the law right, the deregulation etc., that the British sense of enterprise and initiative would have been killed by socialism. I was really afraid that when I had got it all ready to spring back, it would no longer be there and it would not come back. . . . But then it came. The face began to smile, the spirits began to lift, the pride returned.

> (Margaret Thatcher, 'The Brian Walden Interview',
> *Sunday Times*, 8 May 1988)

FROM ECONOMIC LIBERALISM TO ENTERPRISE CULTURE

During the course of the 1980s, the idea of an enterprise culture has emerged as a central motif in the political thought and practice of the Conservative government in Britain. Its radical programme of economic and institutional reform had earlier been couched primarily in the rediscovered language of economic liberalism, with its appeals to the efficiency of markets, the liberty of individuals and the non-interventionist state. But this programme has increasingly also come to be represented in 'cultural' terms, as concerned with the attitudes, values and forms of self-understanding embedded in both individual and institutional activities. Thus the project of economic reconstruction has apparently been supplemented by, or at least partly redefined as, one of cultural reconstruction – the attempt to transform Britain into an 'enterprise culture' (see Chapter One).[1]

But what exactly does this phrase mean? It would be wrong to assume that there is a single correct answer to this question; and indeed the elasticity of the concept may itself have an important function in its political usage. But initially I shall suggest a distinction between two main senses (cf. Chapters Two and Three). The first can be identified by considering briefly some of the main elements in the government's programme of economic and institutional reform, namely: the transfer of state-owned industries, public utilities and so on, to the private sector; the removal of various non-market restrictions affecting the provision of financial services, the conduct of the professions, etc.; and the reorganization of publicly funded bodies in areas such as education, health, local government, broadcasting and the arts.

At one level of analysis, these reforms can be seen as involving an extension of the domain of the 'free market', together with an intensification of the competitive forces operating within this domain; and certainly any account of an enterprise culture must attend to the nature and implications of this process. But in pursuing this analysis one must recognize that many of the reforms of publicly funded bodies have not involved their simple 'relocation' in the market domain, with the goods and services they provide becoming straightforwardly purchasable commodities; and indeed, quite often these changes have been accompanied by new and more stringent forms of state control.

What has, none the less, been characteristic of these reforms is that they have encouraged or required the reconstruction of the institutions concerned along the lines suggested by the model of 'the commercial enterprise' – the privately owned firm or company operating in a free market economy. Precisely what this entails has depended upon which particular features of the model are selected or emphasized, and indeed, upon which particular 'images' of the commercial enterprise are entertained by those involved. In many cases, for example, this process of remodelling has led to the introduction of new managerial structures, 'flexible' employment contracts, etc. (see Chapter Eight); and to new forms of financial control, strategic planning and so on.

But perhaps the most striking and noticeable feature has been the adoption both of specific techniques of marketing and advertising, and of the previously alien vocabularies or 'discourses' associated with these. Terms such as 'product differentiation' and 'market niche' become increasingly commonplace; and above all, references to the *consumer*, a term that displaces others – such as 'student', 'patient' or 'client' – more closely tied to the ways in which the specific nature and purposes of these institutions' activities had previously been understood. Meeting the demands of the 'sovereign' consumer becomes the new and overriding institutional imperative.

Thus, 'the commercial enterprise' takes on a paradigmatic status, the preferred model for any form of institutional organization and provision of goods and services; and this is at least one of the primary senses to be given to the concept of an 'enterprise culture'. What is therefore involved in the construction of an enterprise culture is an extremely wide-ranging process of 'de-differentiation' of previously distinct modes of organization, self-understanding and conceptual representation. Just how far this process is intended to go remains unclear. But in practice, at least, it is by no means confined to the institutional contexts noted so far. For example, many 'personal' activities seem increasingly to be based upon a 'commercial' model – running one's life as a small business, as it were. And in phenomena such as the recent subtitling of the Department of Trade and Industry as 'the Department for Enterprise' and the marketing of its 'enterprise initiatives' (see Chapter Two), the political promotion of enterprise culture takes on an emblematically self-referring character.

However, to understand what is implied by such attempts to promote an enterprise culture, a second and quite distinct sense of the term 'enterprise' must be introduced, in which it refers to the kind of action or project that displays 'enterprising' qualities or characteristics on the part of those concerned (primarily individuals, but also collectives). Here one finds a rather loosely related set of characteristics such as initiative, energy, independence, boldness, self-reliance, a willingness to take risks and to accept responsibility for one's actions and so on. Correspondingly, then, an enterprise 'culture' in this second sense is one in which the acquisition and exercise of these qualities is both highly valued and extensively practised.

The current political rhetoric of enterprise gives considerable prominence to such qualities; and it also suggests a close though complex relationship between these and 'enterprises' in the first sense of the term. On the one hand, the conduct of commercial enterprises is presented as a (or indeed *the*) primary field of activity in which enterprising qualities are displayed. And given that these qualities are themselves regarded as intrinsically desirable – as human 'virtues' – this serves to valorize engagement in such activities, and hence, more generally, the workings of a free market economy. On the other hand, however, it is also claimed that in order to maximize the benefits of this economic system, commercial enterprises and their partici- pants must themselves be encouraged to *be* enterprising, i.e. to act in ways that fully express these qualities. In other words, it seems to be acknowledged that 'enterprises are not inherently or inevitably enterprising'; and enterprising qualities are thus given an instru- mental value in relation to the optimal performance of a market economy.

Thus the task of constructing an 'enterprise' culture is (at least) twofold, reflecting these different senses of the term. First, a wide range of institutions and activities must be remodelled along the lines of the commercial enterprise, including its orientation to the demands of the consumer (see Chapters Ten, Eleven and Twelve). Second, the acquisition and exercise of enterprising qualities must be encouraged, so that the increasingly commercialized world will itself take on an appropriately 'enterprising' form. And this latter task will require, *inter alia*, a sustained attempt to neutralize and reverse all those tenden- cies within British society that are supposedly inimical to 'the spirit of enterprise'. For although enterprising qualities are sometimes depicted as 'natural', or even as distinctively 'British', they are also seen as highly vulnerable to various social forces that may stunt or inhibit their development (see Chapter Three).

The educational system is frequently criticized as a major source of such 'un-' or 'anti-enterprising' cultural attitudes – including a certain disdain or contempt for commercial activities – which are often held to be at least partly responsible for the long-run decline of the British economy since the end of the nineteenth century. Corres- pondingly, the overcoming of these antithetical tendencies is sometimes presented as the recapturing of an earlier 'golden age'.[2] Of more recent vintage are the supposedly damaging effects of the welfare state, which is said to have generated a 'culture of dependency' thoroughly at odds with the initiative and self-reliance required of the enterprising individual. The experience of receiving, as of right, a wide range of welfare and unemployment benefits, pensions, housing (and even perhaps education and health care), is held to generate attitudes of passivity and dependency.

The 'dependent self' regards others, and not itself, as primarily

4

responsible for its own wellbeing, and ascribes to various organs and agencies of the state, in particular, the obligation to provide for this. By accepting such obligations the state, for its part, reinforces these attitudes, and *makes* the individual dependent, both materially and psychologically. (A similar line of argument may also be applied to collective entities, including both private and public sector companies, which become dependent through the expectation of and reliance upon state hand-outs, subsidies, rescue operations, etc. And they, too, must therefore be 'weaned' from their dependency.)

Overcoming the culture of dependency, then, requires a major reconstruction of the systems through which the main elements of material wellbeing are provided. Along with increasingly stringent criteria for the receipt of benefits by right, in which the principle of need is modified by a strongly voluntaristic conception of desert, a key strategy is to encourage the commodification of previously state-supplied goods, replacing them by consumer-purchasable products – e.g. private pensions, health insurance, home-ownership, and so on. Individuals become non-dependent and 'responsible' by taking financial responsibility for these matters, as consumers; and the sphere of consumption thus becomes an important training ground for the enterprising self (see Chapter Four).

But more positive measures of cultural engineering are also called for in this overall project of constructing an enterprise culture. It is not enough to make individuals less passive and dependent: they must also be trained in the virtues of enterprise, so that they are fully equipped with the characteristic qualities of the enterprising individual, and can thus contribute to the success of a properly enterprising form of free market economy. Hence, for example, the recent introduction of schemes such as Enterprise in Higher Education, partly following on from the earlier Technical and Vocational Education Initiative (TVEI) in secondary education (see Chapter One). In these and related contexts can be found a more fully articulated vision of the 'enterprising' self than is implied by the ordinary meaning of this term: a mode of self-identity whose main features can be presented, albeit in a somewhat impressionistic fashion, as follows:

First, enterprising individuals are self-reliant and non-dependent. They make their own decisions, rather than wanting or expecting others to make these for them; and they take responsibility for their own lives, so that when things go wrong they do not assume there is always someone else to blame, or whose job it is to put things right. Second, their activities are oriented towards specific goals or objectives; they are concerned to monitor and evaluate their progress in achieving these; and they are motivated to acquire whatever skills and resources are necessary to pursue these goals effectively. Enterprising individuals can always tell one what they are trying to achieve, and how successful they have thus far been in doing so.

Further, such individuals display high levels of energy, optimism, and initiative. They see the world as full of opportunities for making new things happen; they do not hang back and wait to see what others will do before committing themselves to action; and they regard problems as there to be solved or overcome – not as objects of contemplative fascination, nor as occasions for self-doubt or dismay. Finally, enterprising individuals are keen to pursue the rewards that come from success in a competitive world, and are thus highly responsive to the incentives provided by the prospect of such rewards. They greet success on their own part without feelings of guilt or embarrassment; and they view the success of others not with envy or resentment, but rather as spurs to greater efforts of their own.

This picture of the enterprising self clearly leaves considerable scope for diverging interpretations of many of its elements, and for different degrees of emphasis upon each of them – a point whose significance will be explored later on. But first, I shall consider a certain kind of sceptical response that might be made to the conception of an enterprise culture that has now been presented. I shall then outline some possible rejoinders to this that may serve to shift the analysis of enterprise culture beyond the framework in which it has so far been presented, namely as the current political project of the Conservative government in Britain.

ENTERPRISING PRODUCERS AND SOVEREIGN CONSUMERS?

The ways in which the idea of an enterprise culture is represented in its current political rhetoric, and the measures taken in its name, depend for their plausibility on a number of claims or assumptions about which considerable scepticism might be expressed. In particular, they seem to assume an actual or at least achievable relationship between the conduct of commercial enterprises in a free market economy and the display of enterprising characteristics by those involved in the process of production; and also a high degree of control over what is produced being exercised by the freely made choices of 'sovereign' consumers. Yet both these assumptions may well be regarded as highly implausible.

For example, it might be argued that any credence that could be given to the image of enterprising producers belongs at best – and even then only to a very limited extent – to an earlier period of 'competitive' capitalism, with relatively small-scale firms and significant numbers of individual entrepreneurs. By contrast, the conditions of modern capitalist production, with the dominance of large-scale, globally organized companies, the separation of ownership and managerial control, and the hierarchical command structures of their internal organization, make the idea that free market economies depend primarily on the activities of enterprising individuals an absurdity – a typical *petit bourgeois* illusion (see Chapter Six). And in this context, attention might be drawn to the apparent failure of current representations of enterprise culture to notice the problematic relationship between enterprising individuals, and enterprising collectives or organizations – it being naïvely assumed that the latter are composed straightforwardly of the former.

Similar scepticism may be expressed towards the idea that consumers possess any significant form of 'sovereignty' in contemporary capitalist economies. For this to be so, consumer preferences would at the very least have to be generated independently of the plans and activities of producers. Yet in reality, it might argued, the reverse is increasingly the case, given the massive resources available to modern capitalist enterprises in their attempts to shape and control the 'choices' of consumers, including the growing sophistication and effectiveness of marketing and advertising techniques. It is production that determines consumption, and not vice versa: the sovereign consumer is a fictitious being.

Given these apparently striking divergences between the political rhetoric of enterprise culture and the realities of contemporary capitalism, it may then seem natural to regard the former primarily as an ideological disguise for political projects of a quite different kind – for example, to restore the fortunes of capital after its long period of decline; and/or to increase the powers of the state by the weakening of various 'intermediary institutions' (including trade unions), whose autonomy is undermined, *inter alia*, by the extension and intensification of market forces and the introduction of commercially modelled forms of organization.[3] Nor does the success of such projects depend upon the transformation of cultural values: the coercive powers of the state, and the forces of material necessity, are enough to ensure this. And if any reference is needed here to the attitudes and motives of individuals, then fear, greed, opportunism and the like will suffice – human qualities whose actual character is dignified and sanitized by the rhetoric of enterprise.

Despite the force of these sceptical claims; none the less, it may be argued that they partly ignore or misrepresent a number of increasingly significant features of contemporary capitalist societies. Consider first the sphere of consumption (see Chapter Nine). A growing degree of sophistication and discrimination on the part of consumers may be discernible here, with a corresponding resistance to inflated and unsubstantiated claims on the part of producers, and a more actively demanding attitude towards them. Further, the relatively anonymous and impersonal character of mass production and consumption is arguably being displaced by more differentiated and individualized goods and services, thereby providing consumers with a heightened sense of individual autonomy and choice. Flexibility and responsiveness to the consumer are nowadays genuine requirements for the producer, indicating that the preferences of consumers are, to some considerable extent, generated independently and out of the producer's control: hence the increasingly 'demand-' or 'market-led' character of production. And these changes are arguably taking place in the context of a more general shift towards a culture in which consumption is itself seen as a primary mode of self-expression.

Similarly 'anti-sceptical' points might be made in relation to the sphere of production, where a number of recent developments may give some credibility to the image of enterprising producers. For example, according to at least some versions of post-Fordist theory (see Chapter Eight), significant changes are taking place in the internal organization of many firms, especially in the 'leading sectors' of the economy. The hierarchical command structures of 'Fordist' production are being replaced by less centralized systems, often taking advantage of new information technology, which give greater degrees of autonomy to lower-level units, and provide more obvious opportunities for the exercise of independence and initiative by managers and workers, either individually or in small teams. The related contracting-out of specific services and functions has itself contributed to the marked increase in the numbers of the self-employed and of small businesses, whose growth and economic significance have been further stimulated by other factors also. And even the massive trans-national corporations, which in many ways dominate the economies of nation–states, seem increasingly to recognize the truth of the ecologists' slogan 'Think globally, act locally'.[4]

In these and similar ways, then, it might be argued that neither the figure of the sovereign consumer, nor that of the enterprising producer are altogether illusory; and indeed, that they will, in many respects, become less so as these developments in capitalist societies gather momentum. Further, the two figures may themselves be seen increasingly to intertwine. For, with the growth of personal financial services, the use of home computers and their accounting software, the vicissitudes of the housing market, etc., the sphere of consumption itself takes on some of the characteristics of commercial life: working out how to maximize retirement income, treating one's home as a business investment and so on.

Of course, the extent and significance of these changes in production and consumption is open to considerable debate. For example, decentralized organizational structures may actually involve more effective means of control rather than genuinely 'local' autonomy; the self-employed and those working in small businesses are by no means necessarily wedded to the supposed virtues of enterprising individuals; 'market-led production' may have more to do with the power of retailers over producers than of consumers over either; and product-differentiation may do little really to increase the choices or express the individuality of consumers. Furthermore, the effects of all these developments are themselves highly differentiated along lines of class, gender, ethnicity and so on: compare, for example, the situation of the freelance business consultant with that of the door-to-door salesman or woman 'participating' in a youth unemployment scheme; or the skilled male employee in a small high-tech company with the part-time female temporary worker in a contract cleaning firm.[5]

None the less, these changes do have a number of important implications for the understanding of enterprise culture. First, they should serve to dispel the idea that whatever actual manifestations of enterprise culture may be found in contemporary Britain are solely or even primarily the result of the programme of reforms carried out in the name of this political project. For whilst some of these developments have been given an additional impetus by those reforms, they are largely the result of quite independently generated processes. Hence the project of reconstruction may be seen as one that goes 'with the grain' – not of 'human nature' (see Chapter Three), but of autonomously determined developments that are themselves by no means peculiar to Britain (see Chapter Seven). Second, they may also imply that some of the changes experienced in publicly funded institutions now being remodelled along commercial lines are likewise affecting the conduct of 'already' commercial enterprises in the private sector itself; and perhaps that similar pressures would be operating upon the former, even in the absence of politically engineered reforms directed towards them.

Finally, these points suggest a view of the 'ideological' function of the political rhetoric of enterprise which differs significantly from that noted earlier in presenting the sceptical case. Rather than seeing this as a matter of 'disguise', given the apparently radical divergence between rhetoric and reality, it might instead be seen as attempting to provide a particular (and politically 'motivated') *interpretation* of these phenomena. Any such interpretation has to 'make sense': it has not only to *give* them a particular meaning, but also to give one that seems 'reasonable' to those involved, partly in relation to the prior meanings available to or accepted by them. For just as projects of radical reform work best when they are carried along by independently generated forces, so, too, are ideologies most effective when they provide people with a not-altogether implausible interpretation of their lives.

But at the same time, of course, such ideologies are open to challenge by competing, yet equally plausible, interpretations – by different ways of 'making sense'; and it is this feature of enterprise culture that will now be explored.

ENTERPRISE CULTURE AND THATCHERISM

It was noted earlier that even in more fully articulated visions of the enterprising self, let alone in the ordinary sense of the term 'enterprising', there remains a good deal of openness in possible interpretations of the concepts employed. Consider, for example, the idea of taking or accepting 'responsibility' for one's wellbeing. The politically favoured interpretation of this is such as to be paradigmatically expressed in the form of 'financial' responsibility – hence the encouragement of private health insurance schemes. Yet 'taking responsibility for one's health' is given a significantly different – though not unrelated – meaning in, for example, contemporary 'self-help' women's health groups, and more generally in various alternative health movements that challenge the authority of orthodox medicine and its practitioners, and reject 'dependence' upon them.

Again, the concept of responsibility may be understood in relation to highly voluntaristic conceptions of human agency, which deny altogether the relevance of social conditions in determining individual action; and these are often, though not always, associated with the kind of judgemental moralism to be found in many current political articulations of enterprise and the rejection of 'dependency'. Yet there are other conceptions of responsibility that see it instead as a human potential whose realization depends upon a number of specific social conditions and learning experiences, themselves often of a non-individualistic nature, and requiring various collectively provided resources and opportunities.

Thus concepts such as 'responsibility', and many others that are used in the depiction of enterprising selves, might best be regarded as belonging to a number of partly overlapping moral theories or 'discourses', each of which provides them with more specific meanings that are contested by others. Nor is this a matter purely of semantic interest. For the openness and contestability of these concepts may play an important part in how the political demands of an enterprise culture are interpreted and responded to in particular contexts of 'implementation'; and the partly overlapping discourses are themselves often embedded in the specific kinds of practice actually or potentially at work in these contexts.

To take one example – and analogous points could be made about others – the actual implementation of schemes such as EHE and TVEI often draw heavily upon a conception of the individual based in the humanistic psychology of the 1960s, and already operative in a wide range of practices such as non-directive counselling, group therapy and assertiveness training, student-centred learning, certain forms of management training and so on. Here, one finds an 'ethic of the self' (as distinct from 'an ethic of rules', which specifies an authoritatively binding set of permissible and prohibited actions) that is in many respects congruent with the political rhetoric of enterprise: an active, self-motivated individual, accepting responsibility for its own fate, keen to identify clearly its aims and desires, to remove barriers to its fulfilment, to monitor its success in realizing them and so on. Yet its relationship to the ways in which the political mentors of enterprise require such concepts to be interpreted is complex and problematic.

On the one hand, it may be argued that this 'humanistic' self already bears the conceptual marks of its origins in that legendary exemplar of a commercially oriented, consumption-dominated enterprise culture, the USA; and hence, *inter alia*, that it is no surprise to find so many cases in which the practices associated with this conception of the self are now conducted in the form of highly entrepreneurial businesses or freelance consultancies. On the other hand, however, it may be claimed that there is no intrinsic or necessary relation between the two, and hence that these humanistically informed practices may equally well be employed in ways that improve the ability of their participants to engage effectively in a wide range of activities that have little if anything to do with 'enterprise' in a free market economy.[6]

Similar points can be made about the concept of consumer sovereignty. Consider, for example, the increasing tendency for students in higher education to be referred to as 'consumers', both explicitly, and implicitly in the forms taken by publicity materials directed towards them. As yet, at least, they are not 'in fact' consumers in the sense of purchasers of goods and services in a market economy. But to many it may seem that the adoption of this concept serves only to pave the way for a more complete assimilation of educational institutions to commercial enterprises, in which what had previously been received freely, as of right, will be transformed into a purchasable commodity, with all the obvious implications for questions of justice and equality.

Yet at least some who are keen to 'talk' of students in this way interpret the concept rather differently – as implying, instead, the need to make educational institutions more responsive and accessible to those who enter them ('consumer-friendly', like 'user-friendly' computer software) and to reduce the non-accountable authority of teachers and administrators. Thus, by according students the status of consumers, a more extensive and effective set of rights and a greater degree of control may be made available to them than they had previously possessed; and similarly for the recipients of other publicly funded services.

So the appeal to consumer sovereignty may, in practice, be interpreted in ways that connect it with concepts such as accountability and the undermining of certain forms of privilege and authority. But this kind of linkage is politically double-edged. The current political rhetoric of enterprise itself seems often to trade on such links, implying that the extension of the market domain is itself an extension of democracy, via the assimilation of 'sovereign' consumers to 'sovereign' citizens. The supposed identity here is clearly spurious, if for no other reason than that the inequalities of 'consumer-power' generated by the free market are at odds with the supposed equality of democratic citizens. Yet the political function of this implied identity can, at least in principle, be quite easily reversed, so that the appeal to consumer sovereignty is taken to support, not the extension of the free market, but a shift towards more democratic forms of control over institutions that had previously been insufficiently responsive to those whom they supposedly served.

Thus, a central task for current proponents of an enterprise culture is, as it were, to ensure that only the politically favoured interpretations of the various concepts involved in its articulation are accepted in practice. In particular, there is the fundamental need to ensure that the various characteristics of the enterprising self are understood in such a way that it will seem 'natural' to associate them exclusively or primarily with the conduct of commercial enterprises in a free market economy: to prevent, in other words, the two main senses of the term 'enterprise' being prised apart. Correspondingly, therefore, opposition to this project may depend upon the successful articulation of competing interpretations; but also, of course, on the ability to *realize* such interpretations in practice. For what determines the specific outcomes of such 'contests of meaning' is not itself 'immaterial': it is also a matter of the economic, political and other resources that can be mobilized in particular situations.

But what is also suggested by the preceding argument is that such opposition may often involve not so much the complete rejection of 'enterprise culture', but rather the attempt to define an alternative version of this that differs from, yet also resembles, its current political form. For although the discussion so far has based its conception of an enterprise culture largely upon its representation in the political thought and practice of the Conservative government in Britain, there is no reason to limit its analysis to this context alone.

In particular, it has been noted already that various developments in the spheres of production and consumption, which may serve to provide both a degree of plausibility for the rhetoric of enterprise, and also an independently generated momentum for its programme of reforms, are far from peculiar to Britain. One might therefore expect to find, in other similarly affected societies, phenomena that bear at least a family resemblance to those of enterprise culture in Britain – even if this is largely a matter of their emerging in response to a common set of problems that have recently faced modern capitalist economies (see Chapter Seven). But at the same time, one would also expect these analogous phenomena to differ in ways that reflect their specific economic, cultural and political contexts; and this is one amongst several reasons for doubting that these can be explained as 'the export of Thatcherism' (see Chapters Five and Six).

For in Britain, it is 'Thatcherism' (if one accepts the legitimacy of this concept) that has provided the immediate political context for the theory and practice of 'enterprise culture'. Indeed, the two terms are sometimes used more or less interchangeably. Yet this is misleading, not only for the reasons just adduced, but also because the idea of an enterprise culture is only one, albeit a central one, of the organizing elements of this ideological *mélange*, to which must be added, *inter alia*, its moral conservatism and appeal to 'traditional values', its populistic nationalism, and – at least in practice – its empowering of the state.[7] It has often been noted that there are significant tensions between these various elements, though opinions differ as to how far this is a source of difficulty or of strength. For example, the ideal of consumer sovereignty in its pure form sits uneasily with moral conservatism, since the former rules out any judgements being made about the desirability or otherwise of the actual content of consumer preferences, whilst the latter most certainly does not (see Chapter Four).

However, what is also significant is the way in which the conception of an enterprise culture is itself partly shaped by these other elements of Thatcherism, thereby acquiring specific features that might well be absent in other contexts, both actual and possible. For example, criticism of the 'culture of dependency' is often couched in a highly moralistic, desert-based vocabulary with punitive overtones, which correspondingly affects the depiction of its preferred alternative, the culture of enterprise. Relatedly, the sovereign consumer is represented as a 'responsible' agent, who perhaps thinks more of the costs involved in paying than of the pleasures involved in spending – though of course there is no guarantee that this is how actual consumers will view their activities. Further, there are frequent signs of a populistic anti-elitism at work in dismantling the protection against market forces enjoyed by various occupational groups, including the professions. And perhaps most pervasively, there is the individualistic conception of enterprise itself, so that the attribution of enterprising qualities is primarily to individuals rather than collective entities.

But none of these specific features of the Thatcherite representation of an enterprise culture are essential to the concept; and they should perhaps instead be seen as serving to delineate a particular variant or species belonging to a more broadly defined and generic category. Precisely how this should be characterized is open to considerable debate. But arguably, it should be such as to include the possibility of more collectively oriented modes of enterprise; of 'socialist' market systems involving various forms of social ownership, and more narrowly drawn boundaries for the market itself; and of the exercise of enterprising qualities beyond the market domain. It might then be said that just as the project of Thatcherism is both to construct enterprise culture in a specifically capitalist mode, and to reconstruct capitalism in a distinctively enterprising form, the problem facing many of its opponents is how to socialize the former without losing the economic benefits of the latter.

NOTES

1 References to other papers in the volume will be made in the text. Other references will be made in these notes, and are mainly confined to items not cited in the other chapters. I am grateful to all the contributors to this volume for their ideas and suggestions, but would like to emphasize that they by no means necessarily agree with the claims made in this Introduction.

2 The historical work most frequently cited by proponents of enterprise is probably Wiener (1981): see Raven (1989) on how this and similar works have been 'used' politically. Walvin (1987) provides a sceptical account of the historical basis for contemporary appeals to 'Victorian values'; whilst Marquand (1988) argues that Britain's economic problems stem more from its individualist than its collectivist past. Cf. also Perkin (1989), whose interpretation of English social history since 1880 has important implications for the current ideology of enterprise.

3 On the erosion of intermediary institutions see, for example, Gamble (1988) and Grant (1989).

4 Cf. Lash and Urry (1987) on 'the end of organised capitalism'; and Wright (1987) on the recent phenomenon of a burgeoning management literature about 'intrapreneurs' and the like. If 'dialectical' speculations were in order these days, one might postulate the emergence of a third historical stage in the development of capitalism, transcending the opposition between its competitive and corporate predecessors.

5 On self-employment and small businesses, see Curran *et al.* (1986); Hakim (1988); Burrows (forthcoming) and the current work of the ESRC Research Programme on Small Businesses at Kingston Polytechnic. On gender and ethnicity in enterprise, see Westwood and Bhachu (1989); and on 'the rise of retailing', Gardner and Sheppard (1989).

6 For a Foucauldian analysis of 'practices aimed at the self' see Rose (1989). On the politics of humanistic psychology, see Richards (1989), which also presents a psychoanalytic 'diagnosis' of hostility towards dependency. The concepts of autonomy and dependence, and their possibly gendered character, have been much discussed in feminist work; see Grimshaw (1986), Chapters 5 and 6. On TVEI schemes see Gleeson (1987) and the working papers published by the Institute for Research and Development in Post-Compulsory Education, University of Lancaster. (It might of course be argued that substantial investment in training is a more important determinant of economic performance than individual values and attitudes.)

7 On Thatcherism see, for example, Levitas (1986); Gamble (1988); Skidelsky (1988); and for a review of many other discussions, Douglas (1989). One obvious danger of the concept is the tendency to ignore differences *amongst* 'Thatcherites': for example, in the speeches by Lord Young analysed elsewhere in this volume there seems little sign of the kind of 'judgmental moralism' often displayed by Thatcher herself.

REFERENCES

Burrows, R. (ed.) (forthcoming) *Enterprise Culture: Critical Analyses*, London: Routledge.

Curran, J., Stanworth, J. and Watkins, D. (eds) (1986) *The Survival of the Small Firm*, 2 vols. Aldershot: Gower.

Douglas, J. (1989) 'The changing tide – some recent studies of Thatcherism', *British Journal of Political Science* 19: 399–424.

Gamble, A. (1988) *The Free Economy and the Strong State*, London: Macmillan.

Gardner, C. and Sheppard, J. (1989) *Consuming Passion: The Rise of Retail Culture*, London: Unwin Hyman.

Gleeson, D. (ed.) (1987) *T.V.E.I. and Secondary Education*, Milton Keynes: Open University Press.

Grant, W. (1989) 'The erosion of intermediary institutions', *Political Quarterly* 60: 10–22.

Grimshaw, J. (1986) *Feminist Philosophers*, Brighton: Wheatsheaf.

Hakim, C. (1988) 'Self-employment in Britain: recent trends and current issues', *Work, Employment & Society* 2: 421–50.

Lash, S. and Urry, J. (1987) *The End of Organised Capitalism*, Cambridge: Polity Press.

Levitas, R. (ed.) (1986) *The Ideology of the New Right*, Cambridge: Polity Press.

Marquand, D. (1988) *The Unprincipled Society*, London: Jonathan Cape.
Perkin, H. (1989) *The Rise of Professional Society*, London: Routledge.
Raven, J. (1989) 'British history and the enterprise culture', *Past and Present* 123: 178–204.
Richards, B. (1989) *Images of Freud*, London: Dent.
Rose, N. (1989) *Governing the Soul: Technologies of Human Subjectivity*, London: Routledge.
Skidelsky, R. (ed.) (1988) *Thatcherism*, London: Chatto & Windus.
Walvin, J. (1987) *Victorian Values*, London: André Deutsch.
Westwood, S. and Bhachu, P. (eds) (1989) *Enterprising Women: Ethnicity, Economy and Gender Relations*, London: Routledge.
Wiener, M. (1981) *English Culture and the Decline of the Industrial Spirit*, Cambridge: Cambridge University Press.
Wright, P. (1987) 'Excellence', *London Review of Books*, 21 May, pp. 8–11.

Part One

POLITICAL REPRESENTATIONS OF ENTERPRISE

The chapters in this section are concerned with the ways in which the concept of an enterprise culture has been represented by its political proponents in contemporary Britain, and with its relationship to other elements of 'Thatcherism'.

Paul Morris examines a number of different sources for the concept between 1974 and 1989 – the work of the Centre for Policy Studies, the attempts by Brian Griffiths and others to forge links between Christianity and market economics and the contributions of Lord Young of Graffham. He argues that the concept has been a dynamic one, and identifies three main stages in its genesis and development.

Norman Fairclough presents a sociolinguistic analysis of the 'discourse' of enterprise. Focusing initially on various speeches by Lord Young, he explores the shifts and combinations between different meanings of 'enterprise'. Turning to the DTI's promotional literature, he then argues that the 'discourse of enterprise' concerns the form as much as the content of texts, e.g. in their 'positioning' of the reader as consumer/customer.

Raman Selden's chapter also focuses upon speeches by Lord Young and other proponents of enterprise. But he presents a 'deconstructive' reading of them, arguing in particular that their employment of a binary opposition between 'nature' and 'culture' operates in ways that defeat their own purposes. In doing so he defends Derrida's post-structuralist literary criticism against the charge that in political terms it is inherently non-critical.

Paul Heelas analyses the various forms of self-identity involved in Thatcherite attempts at 'character reform'. The enterprising self, he argues, is only one of these: there is also the sovereign consumer, the active citizen and the 'conservative' self. The possible tensions between these and their associated moralities are explored in a way that casts doubt on the psychological plausibility of 'combining' them, and hence on the likely effectiveness of this project of moral reform.

Chapter One

FREEING THE SPIRIT OF ENTERPRISE

The genesis and development of the concept of enterprise culture

PAUL MORRIS

In the last few years, the phrase 'enterprise culture' has entered our political and cultural vocabularies, and is often used in the British context to refer to the whole Thatcherite endeavour.[1] Although it has played a central role in the self-definition and self-understanding of Thatcherism, and in spite of the seemingly endless studies of this political phenomenon, all too little attention has been directed to the analysis of the concept itself. The 'enterprise' of enterprise culture has long been used to refer to the market-responsive initiatives of business and industry in the private sector (and the businesses themselves), and some commentators still understand enterprise culture as indicating these initiatives. In relation to Thatcherism, however, with its attempt to extend the market as the potential model for the provision and consumption of all goods and services, enterprise culture has come to have a more comprehensive meaning.

In this chapter I will examine the origins of this phrase and its development in the thinking associated with the Conservative Party. I begin by examining the three primary sources for the broadening of 'enterprise' to the notion of 'enterprise culture': the Centre for Policy Studies and other think tanks; the link between Christianity and the 'new Conservatism'; and the work of Lord Young. Finally, by way of conclusion, I trace the three principal phases of this evolution from 1974 until the present. My argument is that enterprise culture has been a dynamic concept, having a series of meanings and generating a series of different policies. My method is a 'polite' extension of that used by Frank Hahn – as Margaret Thatcher rarely takes the public opportunity to present her thinking in a developed and systematic manner, one turns instead to those whose thought has been most influential on her, that accords with

21

hers and that does appear in such a fashion (Hahn 1988: 107).

THE 'THINK TANKS' AND
'THINKING THE UNTHINKABLE'

In the aftermath of the first of the two elections that the Conservatives would lose in 1974, Keith Joseph began the formulation of a new meta-narrative that would explain not only these defeats, but British politics in the whole post-war era. He argued that *all* governments since 1945 had been engaged in the pursuit of a 'semi-socialism' – of government intervention and union power – that had 'forced the private sector of the economy to work with one hand tied behind its back' (Joseph 1975: 4). As the antidote to Britain's economic decline, he advocated a free market monetarist model, with the government's role largely reduced to controlling the money supply. In his attempts to master monetary theory, Joseph drew on the resources of the Institute of Economic Affairs (IEA), an independent, right-wing think tank committed to challenging the then prevailing orthodoxy of Keynesian economic theory, particularly in relation to public spending.

In 1974, with official Party approval, Joseph created the Centre for Policy Studies (CPS) to study free market economies. Although the CPS was not intended to offer an alternative to the party's own research department (or '*the* think tank', disbanded by Thatcher in 1983), it quickly established itself as just such a rival. Joseph became its first Chairman and Margaret Thatcher its Vice-Chairman.[2] The Director of the CPS, Alfred Sherman (later a speech writer for Thatcher), intended the Centre to have a degree of independence from the Party and 'to think the unthinkable',[3] that is, to go beyond its original brief and formulate specific policy options for a future Conservative government, unrestricted by the self-imposed limitations of the older economic orthodoxies and in line with its monetarist ethos.

The importance of the CPS in the development of Thatcherism cannot be overestimated, as it was the link, not only between monetarist theory and the later leader of the Conservative Party and Prime Minister, but also between her and a number of her major advisers.[4] In the early years of Thatcher's leadership, the Centre played a most significant role in the ideological formulation of her 'new Conservatism'.

In its foundational document, the Centre for Policy Studies states its aim as being the fostering of the maximum degree of freedom of choice and the establishment of a 'culture for enterprise'. The Centre has steadily extended its areas of concern, recently to include foreign affairs with the establishment of its International Advisory Council. An examination of the Centre's publications gives an indication of its importance in defining the Tories' past and present political agenda. In its (approximately one hundred) paperback publications we can trace the main lines of Conservative policy and the growing self-definition of Conservative ideology. In addition to studies advocating the new Conservative ideology,[5] accounts of Joseph's new meta-narrative[6] and works on monetarism, public sector borrowing and anti-collectivism, the Centre's imprint is also found on a series of pamphlets that recommend specific policies in a number of areas.[7]

Enterprise was understood – in the publications of the CPS from its inception until around 1985 – largely in terms of commercial and industrial initiative and advocacy of the extension of the market model to new areas. These studies consistently stressed the various barriers to be removed in order to allow for the development of the culture of enterprise (negative definitions), rather than defining the characteristics of enterprise itself (positive definitions). Particular emphasis was given to the inhibiting consequences of the British class system, trade unionism and state intervention in areas ranging from rent controls to wage policies. Since 1985, there has been an increased stress on individualism (including personal property and individual responsibility) and the morality of the market in terms of individual choice.[8] This has been coupled with a concern for fostering national values and maintaining the national heritage, especially in relation to the part that education has to play in this process. Recent publications have distanced Conservative ideology from monetarism, with its notion of the neutral market, attacked unbridled consumerism and challenged self-interest in terms of community and shared values. This 'moral' emphasis characterizes many of the Centre's recent publications.

In 1987 the Centre established an Enterprise Policy Unit whose brief is to direct its attention to the creation of a *full* enterprise culture, concentrating on enterprise and educational issues, business concerns and taxation. The Centre, in a joint policy document with the Institute of Policy Research (another right-wing think tank), offers the following definition of enterprise culture: 'Enterprise culture is defined as the full set of conditions that promote high and rising levels of achievement in a country's economic activity, politics and government, arts and sciences, and also the distinctively private lives of the inhabitants.'[9]

In the same document, enterprise is associated with risk-taking in all areas of life. For example, to save, or to refrain from spending the whole of one's current income, is defined as risk-taking, and the shape of the 'enterprise novel' and enterprise art forms and the possible heroes of the enterprise culture are discussed. Enterprise, individual commitment and creativity, it is argued, should be manifest at all levels of 'work and play', in order to ensure that initiative is fostered. The stress is on motivation, creative ambition, religious factors and striving for excellence – factors to be instilled through education. Enterprise is thus considered to be teachable. At present, it is claimed that the characteristics of enterprise (effort, hard work, independence, flexibility and personal responsibility) are a chance legacy from one's parents, and that the absence of any or all of these characteristics can only be overcome when the 'ancient virtues' can be, and are, taught in all British schools. The enterprise culture and the modes of its implementation are now at the heart of the Centre's work.[10]

In addition to the CPS and the IEA, a number of other think tanks, including the Adam Smith Institute (ASI), have played a role in the formation of Conservative policies. The ASI has, in recent years, come to rival the CPS as the most influential policy group 'thinking the unthinkable'. The think tanks have been the bridge, both of personnel and ideas between monetarism and free market theories and specific government policies. What is significant is that more and more of what was 'unthinkable' has become government policy since 1979. There has been the advocacy (often translated into policy) of the continual extension of the spheres in which market forces are deemed appropriate. There has also been a growing consensus on the part of the think tanks that there are barriers to the development of an enterprise culture that are not of an economic nature and thus cannot be removed by means of economic policy. This has led, in recent years, to a second extension of the understanding of enterprise culture, to include considerations of the cultural and social context of policies designed to foster it.

RECAPTURING THE 'HIGH MORAL GROUND'; CHRISTIANITY AND THE ENTERPRISE CULTURE

Margaret Thatcher has always understood her 'mission' as a moral crusade that goes beyond the economic regeneration of Britain to a revival of the spiritual and national values that she associates with

Christianity.[11] She speaks as 'a politician and a Christian', and although she holds that politics and religion are separate spheres, she maintains that there is no tension between them. The two, however, are related in a number of overlapping ways.[12]

As leader of her party and later as Prime Minister, Thatcher has been acutely aware of the widely held view of the moral force of socialism, and has continually claimed the moral superiority of free enterprise over all forms of socialism. She has also consistently argued that a 'free society' can only be based on the moral and spiritual framework provided by religion, and that the state in a Christian society 'is to encourage virtue and not to usurp it' (Thatcher 1989: 66). In particular, she stresses the absolute values of personal moral and social responsibility and the importance of religious education in inculcating these virtues.[13] However, the nature of her understanding of the relationship between a government committed to a market economy and religion, and the arguments for the morality of free enterprise, have undergone significant changes and have developed from the 1970s to the period after 1983. If we compare her 1978 and 1981 lectures to St Lawrence Jewry in the City of London with her 1988 address to the General Assembly of the Church of Scotland, we can discern something of these developments.

In the earlier addresses, Thatcher attacked socialism for falsely offering a utopia in this life, and advocated a strong state to do what religion cannot, namely, to keep sinful man in check and uphold the rule of the law (Thatcher 1989:69). She emphasized that the 'spirit of this nation is a Christian one', in terms of its heritage of belief in the Almighty, tolerance, moral absolutes and the work-ethic (ibid: 131). Christianity teaches individual moral responsibility *and* social welfare, and she insists that 'we must never think of individual freedom and the social good as opposed to each other' (ibid: 124). Creating wealth is a Christian obligation 'if we are to fulfil our role as stewards of the resources and talents the Creator has provided for us' (ibid: 126). In 1988, Thatcher offers considerably more sophisticated arguments for the 'morality of the market' and the relationship between Christian values and the creation of wealth in the free market economy. Christian values (individualism, personal responsibility, freedom from coercion, charity and the moral foundations of the law) are not just incidental to the free market but are its foundation. And *only* in a free market can these Christian absolute moral values be fostered and protected. Such a market's worst tendencies (greed, exploitation, etc.) are policed by Christian values, and these ensure its smooth and efficient operation.[14] The latter argument draws heavily upon elements developed in the writings of Professor Brian Griffiths, appointed as head of the Policy Unit at 10 Downing Street, after Mrs Thatcher had read his works (Griffiths 1982; 1984), which I will now use as an illustration of the association between enterprise culture and Christianity.

The foundation for Griffiths' Christian new Conservatism is a highly developed form of the argument for 'the morality of the market'. He argues, as do the 'non-Christian' proponents of the morality of the market (e.g. Lawson 1988), for a middle ground between the free market libertarianism of Friedman and Hayek and any form of state socialism or Marxism. He contends that adherents of both these 'extremes', in common with the whole post-Enlightenment economic tradition, have been misled by their adherence to unproven and unprovable ideological models of the market. These models, whether based on the machine, biological natural selection or the notion of 'the game', all lead to understandings of the market as amoral and impersonal, and to viewing it as a self-regulating 'system' with a 'natural tendency to equilibrium' by 'unseen hands' (Griffiths 1983; 1984). He challenges the contention that exploitation is inherent in the operation of the market economy, as based on this mistaken view of the 'system'. Griffiths makes a distinction between the fixing of prices, which can operate in this way, in terms of the 'mechanisms' of demand and supply, and the underlying institutions that such mechanisms assume.

He holds that markets operate in real communities and can only function on the basis of a number of already existing communal institutions, in the main, widespread ownership of private property, the acceptance of the rule of law and positive but limited government control. Just as vital, he insists, are the underlying moral virtues of individual responsibility, community and trust. Markets are social relationships and communal institutions dependent upon trust and self-interest. The rejection of this communal trust impedes the operation of the market. He emphasizes the part that 'justice' plays in the market, not in terms of equality of distribution, but in ensuring the non-coercive operation of the economy. For Griffiths, this results in a 'certain kind and degree of inequality in the distribution of income and wealth', which is 'essential' if the market economy is to function. According to him, markets not only require a moral foundation, but they also strengthen the moral dimensions of society by respecting individual freedom of choice and individual economic responsibility. He identifies both the moral dimensions and the underlying virtues necessary for the market, with Christianity, and historically associates its Protestant forms with the development of the market economy. The enemies of the mutually fostering systems of Christianity and the market economy are liberal humanism and its pluralism, the welfare state, the social sciences and Marxism, as all these undermine Christian virtues and threaten the morality of the market.

In *Morality and the Market Place* (Griffiths 1982), he writes of the crises of capitalism and of Marxism and the 'global conflict' between them. He understands both to manifest the 'crisis of humanism as a religion being played out in economic life' (ibid: 29). They are both based, Griffiths contends, on a notion of freedom (a notion incompatible with Christianity) and entail the necessity of a strong state to ensure such a freedom. In the former, freedom dominates, and in the latter (the state's) 'control'. Further, the dominance of either sets a limit to justice and creates coercion. He argues that while capitalism has proved itself more efficient economically and less coercive politically than Marxism, its humanist values cannot generate or sustain the underlying values that are necessary for its continued functioning and the maintenance of its political freedoms. Historically, the values that allowed for the development of capitalism were Christian values, and only these can ensure its continuance. This entails a rejection of the libertarian defence of the 'spontaneous order' (as in Hayek), and the reconstruction of the market economy along Christian lines (ibid: 71–124).

Griffiths holds that there are seven absolutes derived from Christian teachings that provide the basis for this reconstruction: the positive mandate to create wealth; the requirement of private property rather than state or collective ownership; that each family retain a permanent stake in the economy; that the community strive to relieve poverty rather than pursue equality; that government should remedy economic injustice; that materialism be guarded against; and, that accountability and judgement are an integral part of economic life (ibid: 91–9).

Griffiths seeks to establish the legitimacy of business enterprise and the market economy within a Christian framework (Griffiths 1984). He contends that while materialism, injustice and greed are in fundamental conflict with Christian teaching, the creation of wealth to sustain life is not. Particular cultural values are necessary for the operation of the market, and these have been eroded in the recent past

27

(sometimes for Griffiths, the not-so-recent past, as in the case of the separation of income generation and Christian life in the Renaissance). These values are to be fostered by Christian education and the inculcation of Christian values and virtues.

These elements of Griffiths' argument are to be found, almost line by line, in Thatcher's speeches and lectures on the moral foundations of her politics.[15] His argument for the morality of the market, with its Christian basis of the market economy and protection of the necessary Christian values by that economy, has been widely accepted by Christians in this country and has also been one of the major formulations of Thatcherism to be attacked by church leaders and theologians.[16]

This second source of the extension of the understanding of enterprise culture beyond 'business initiatives', is a vital aspect of the concept in its contemporary British context. Britain, as an enterprise culture, is to be a moral community where self-interest is balanced by concern for others, where there is a mandate for wealth generation, and great stress on the absolute moral values that underlie the nation and its market economy.

LORD YOUNG: ARCHITECT OF THE ENTERPRISE CULTURE

David Young, a successful business man and a member of the CPS, was greatly influenced by Keith Joseph, whose assistant he was when the latter was Minister for Industry. Since 1984 he has carved out an independent path, at least in terms of his approaches to the creation of the enterprise culture. The beginnings of his rise to prominence can be dated, not from his directorship of the CPS, but from a turning point in the evolution of the whole concept of enterprise culture, which originates, not with Joseph or Young, but with Nigel Lawson. The public occasion was a lecture entitled, *The British Experiment*, delivered to the City University Business School when Lawson was introduced by the Dean, Brian Griffiths (Lawson 1984).

Lawson began by reversing the received post-war wisdom on the roles of macro- and micro-economic policy. In relation to macro-economic strategies, he claimed that the government's aim should not be to pursue growth and employment, but to control inflation. And regarding micro-economic policy, the government should not suppress price rises but should operate the conditions conducive to growth and employment. Further, both policies need to pursued simultaneously. The penultimate section of the paper ('On to stable prices'), argues that control of inflation and the encouragement of the conditions for business growth are not enough in themselves and that what is required is 'fighting and changing the *culture and psychology* of two generations'. He acknowledged that this could 'not be achieved overnight', but asserted that 'there be no doubt that this is our goal'.

In the last section of the lecture, entitled 'The enterprise culture', he outlines the ways in which 'culture and psychology' are to be transformed. Lawson insists that Britain must create an enterprise culture by 'changing psychology to change the business culture'. Whilst the abolition of controls on wages, prices, dividends, foreign exchange, hire purchase and industrial building are vital, he claims that they are insufficient in themselves. Likewise, progressive reductions in the burden of taxation, further privatization, and protection against monopolies and restrictive practices, are of value, but alone cannot succeed in bringing about a stable economy and a return to full employment. For, he argues, while all these measures should free the market, their effects will be thwarted by the vested interests created by the particular British historico-cultural and psychological realities. What is needed, he contends, is education in enterprise and specific policies to counter these realities.

In October 1984, Lord Young was appointed, as Minister without portfolio, to run the new Enterprise Unit in the Cabinet Office. His brief, largely the result of the implications of Lawson's analysis, was to promote policies for the growth of enterprise and the creation of jobs. The new unit was to 'encourage and develop enterprise in society and the economy' by identifying, analysing and proposing solutions to problems arising from the lack of effectiveness of existing enterprise policies. Particular emphasis was given to aiding the creation of new businesses, the encouragement of small firms and the formulation and co-ordination of enterprise education for 14–18-year-olds.

The Prime Minister requested that the Manpower Services Commission (MSC), under the chairmanship of Lord Young, set up a Technical and Vocational Education Initiative (TVEI) in November 1982. The TVEI scheme was launched nationally and developed from the Enterprise Unit, via the White Papers *Better Schools* (March 1985) and *Education and Training for Young People* (April 1985). Initially it operated in a number of pilot educational authorities and was granted £240 million. A further £900 million was assigned to extend the scheme to 90 per cent of all the educational authorities for the period 1987 to 1997. By September of 1989 over half a million school children will be involved in the scheme in 75 per cent of LEAs.[17] The aim of TVEI is to give students the opportunity to 'develop enterprise, initiative, motivation', 'problem-solving skills and the development of other appropriate personal qualities', 'more responsibility for their learning and the application of their knowledge'.[18]

A new scheme was introduced in 1987 by the MSC (now renamed the Training Agency) under the auspices of the Department of Employment, Enterprise in Higher Education (EHE). The aim of EHE 'is to increase dramatically the supply of more highly qualified people with enterprise'. The initial document outlining the scheme expands 'enterprise' as follows – 'generating and taking ideas and putting them to work, taking decisions and taking responsibility, taking considered risks, welcoming change and helping to shape it [and] creating wealth'.[19] Five-year pilot schemes are currently operating in four universities and a number of polytechnics. The aim is to integrate EHE into all existing degree schemes, so that every student has experience of the 'real economy' and becomes:

> a person who has belief in his own destiny, welcomes change and is not frightened of the unknown, sets out to influence events, has powers of persuasion, is of good health, robust, with energy and willing to work beyond that which is specified, is competitive, is moderated by concern for others and is rigorous in self-evaluation.[20]

Lord Young became Minister of Employment in 1985 and in his Gresham lecture of the same year, he develops the historical background as to why the British should require such enterprise education, whilst insisting that enterprise is a natural quality that only has to be 'set free'.[21] Although British culture evidences past examples of enterpise, for example, the entrepreneurs of the Industrial Revolution, he rejects the view of the historians he calls the creators of the 'dark Satanic mills to grind down the poor'. He insists that the entrepreneurs and their enterprise were thwarted and their impact reduced by British culture, mainly the 'gentrification process'. Young continues by claiming that the enterprising entrepreneurs sent their children to public schools where the teaching of science was resisted and the stress was on classics. Industry and enterprise were seen as vulgar – what he refers to as the 'stigma of utility' – and he quotes *Tom Brown's School Days*, where business is described as 'mere money making'. These sons then went on to Oxbridge, where business and enterprise were, he claims, 'denounced'. He contends that the British education system inculcated cultural values that were hostile to enterprise, and the family firms set up by entrepreneurs were used as 'milch-cows' for gentrification. The lecture was entitled 'The rise and fall of the entrepreneur' - so far, the 'fall', or rather a limping spasm. The 'rise' requires, he argues, the promotion of changes in language so that words like profit and wealth are used positively and not as 'apologetic asides'. Young has also concentrated a number of his attacks on the professions. He advocates a breakdown of professional bodies, from the BMA and the Law Society to the now 'deregulated' opticians, in his war against protectionism. 'Enterprise' is here understood as flexibility, innovation, risk-taking, hard work. The enterprise culture *can* be actively promoted, but only by overcoming the British cultural past.

In his 1986-7 speeches, Young has come more and more to understand enterprise as a natural facility or attribute that is manifest in all 'men', or rather, in all children, but which, in particular cultures, is lost *en route* in education and other cultural institutions. It is important to distinguish - as he always does - between the recovery of enterprise (the industrial and commercial revolutionary spirit) and enterprise culture, as yet unknown in British culture. In more recent speeches, enterprise has become the most central aspect of human personality, not just required for business entrepreneurs but for everyone, particularly the unemployed. A second recent development, manifest in his 1986 Barnett Lecture on the inner cities,[22] and the 1986 Stockton Lecture,[23] is the vital part that enterprise has to play in the forging of 'one nation'. Young contends that the basis of national unity is a cluster of shared values and that only enterprise values can provide this basis. The values of personal responsibility and confidence, together with the desire to improve one's own circumstances, are the foundation for what he calls 'enterprise in the community'. That is, the creation of communities based on self-respect and respect for others, which is manifest in good citizenship. This also works in reverse, he claims, in that fostering community can and does generate individual enterprise, as in the case of tenant-run housing estates and inner-city task forces.

During this period, Young held that the real opponents of attitudinal and cultural change were the legacies of the more recent twentieth-century British past - the collectivities of the welfare state and the unions. Throughout 1986-7, he refers to these collectivities as symptoms of 'the British disease' (class, unions, welfarism, etc.) and advocates their replacement by the 'community of interests in the benefits of enterprise' – 'one nation' and 'one set of cultural values' – in order to integrate British society. 'Enterprise' has now come to be understood as 'the public good' of community activity and individual responsibility.[24] In his 1987 speeches, he goes to great lengths to distinguish enterprise culture from right-wing libertarianism, and asserts that a strong government is essential both to maintain the market as an open (not free) market, and more essentially, to provide stability for calculated risk-taking at all levels, from the individual to the corporation. In his last major speech of 1987, he identifies yet another collectivist enemy, that of 'corporate cultures', and expresses his intention of creating a new enterprise management scheme that is to be anti-corporate culture, with its stifling of individual initiative.[25]

Lord Young was appointed Secretary of State at the Department of Trade and Industry in June 1987, and in January 1988 subtitled the DTI, the Department for Enterprise. In the White Paper of that month, he unveiled his plans for the DTI until 1993. The encouragement of enterprise is given as one of the major goals of the government and the keynote of DTI policies is to foster business and personal enterprise. Since the beginning of 1988, the DTI has launched a series of heavily publicized 'enterprise initiatives', ranging from Europe 1992, the Enterprise Allowance Scheme and the Private and Business Enterprise Programmes, to various training schemes for school leavers and the long- and short-term unemployed. The White Paper marks a new phase in the development of the enterprise culture, in that it seeks a partnership between the DTI and commerce and industry, in order to 'create a climate for enterprise'.[26]

PHASES IN THE DEVELOPMENT OF ENTERPRISE CULTURE

Phase one: the Marxist phase

The call, beginning in the mid-1970s, was for the application of monetarism to the British economy, in order to provide competitive productive performances that would enable Britain to compete and survive in the world with America, Germany and Japan. The term 'culture for enterprise' was used at this stage, although the main term during this period, particularly after 1979, was the 'new Conservatism'. The speeches at this time (particularly Howe's), emphasized a retreat from government interventions in the economy and the reversal of the trend towards corporatism, in order to reinstate the market mechanism as the principal determinant of the economy. Keith Joseph advocated the attempt to launch an 'economic revolution' to restore private enterprise as 'the engine of the economy'. In the 1977 Conservative Manifesto we find the following:

> We want to work with human nature, helping people to help themselves and others. This is the way to restore self-reliance and self-confidence which are the basis of personal responsibility and national success: attempting to do too much, politicians have failed to do those things which *should* be done. This has damaged the country and the authority of government. We must concentrate on what should be the priorities of *any* government.

But in 1979, Mrs Thatcher herself felt that a sharp cut in taxes would produce this culture of enterprise, that would produce the spurt in growth that had eluded Britain throughout the post-war period. The early work at the DTI (and the MSC) and of the CPS shared this very limited interventionist view of government, in its advocacy of the extension of the enterprise sector to include all spheres of activities beyond a public good limited to defence, law and order and protection of the market. Even in the 1983 Conservative Party Manifesto we read: 'The Conservative Party believes in encouraging people to take responsibility for their own decisions. We shall continue to return more choice to individuals and their families. This is the way to increase personal freedom.'

The first phase, which I call, tongue-in-cheek, the Marxist phase – that is, that external structural changes would suffice – where it was felt that economic policies, designed to free the market, would be sufficient to liberate enterprise in Britain to create the culture for enterprise.

Phase two: the Freudian phase

In the second phase, the pursuit of this 'Marxist' strategy was continued, but it soon became apparent that a number of different cultural factors were central in the formation of individuals, and that the individuals making up the market were influenced and informed by cultural elements – that is, that beneath the raw market was another, just as vital, set of factors that ensured its free operation. These were labelled moral or religious or cultural virtues. The CPS became concerned with this 'moral' foundation and the importance of particular cultural values and virtues, and further, it came to identify the rogue cultural values and traditions that were to be overcome and disregarded. Brian Griffiths and others argued for the Christian rather than the secular humanist (their 'enemy') tradition, based on the operation of the free market, and Nigel Lawson recognized the revolutionary need for cultural and psychological change. Again, tongue-in-cheek, I refer to this as the second, 'Freudian', phase – the attempt to change 'man' himself. That is, no amount of structural change by itself could effect the cultural and psychological foundations.

Phase three: 'partnership in cultural engineering'

I refer to this as 'cultural engineering' or applied enterprise culture – that is, the conscious attempt to create the conditions to effect the massive and unprecedented cultural/psychological transformation of British culture that would undo the damage of the twentieth century and release or create the 'spirit' that is to inform our whole way of life. This third phase required and requires a clearer demarcation between enterprise culture and monetarism, libertarianism, corporate culture, welfarism, unbridled hedonism, etc. Coupled with education is the 'enterprise strategy' – a partnership between government and individuals to foster this cultural engineering. This phase is predicated upon the recognition that no amount of external ('Marxist') or internal ('Freudian') tinkering, without the support of the populace, can bring about enterprise culture. Paradoxically, the new recognition of the limitations of government action still entails a far greater exercise of government intervention than was envisaged in 1979 or 1988. In this third, ontological, stage, enterprise culture, it is argued, has finally begun to emerge. Enterprise is now seen to be the basic factor, the most fundamental prime mover. It is present, as the CPS now emphasizes, in every sphere of activity – it can create art or literature or economic wealth, or community or national consensus.

In each of the three phases we have different understandings of enterprise culture, which give rise to different government policies. This third phase, with its unprecedented government intervention in education (at all levels), represents a massive programme to create a supportive public, a partner in cultural engineering, in order to bring about enterprise culture. The claim at the base of this phase-three programme is that national wealth has substantially increased. It is on this claim that the enterprise culture will succeed or fail.

NOTES

1 Although 'Thatcherism' does not present itself as a coherent political doctrine, except in the writings of devout followers and left-wing critics (cf. Hall and Jacques 1983) and appears to be inconsistent and contradictory in terms of both policy and rhetoric, I use the term to refer to the dominant policies and programmes of Mrs Thatcher's government. The adjective 'Thatcherite' is also used in this way.

2 This can be seen as the formal beginnings of what one commentator has called 'one of the most formative political relationships of modern times' (Young 1989: 43).

3 Alfred Sherman in an interview, 'The think tank' on Radio 3, 21 October 1983.

4 Including: Alan Walters (economic adviser 1981–3 and again in 1989); John Hoskyns (economic adviser); Hugh Thomas (foreign affairs adviser, speech writer for Mrs Thatcher and later, Chairman of the CPS). In addition, prominent members of the CPS have been members of government policy groups.

5 See, for example, Thatcher (1977) *Let Our Children Grow Tall* (selected speeches, 1974–6) (see also Thatcher 1986); Joseph (1976) *Monetarism is Not Enough*; Thomas (1979) *History, Capitalism and Freedom*; Lawson (1980) *The New Conservatism* and (1988) *The New Britain*; Howell (1986) *The New Capitalism*; Brittan (1986) *To Spur and Not to Mould*. All CPS publications, London.

6 For example, Pringle (1977) *The Growth Merchants*; Butt (1986) *The Unfinished Task*; Howell (1980) *The Conservative Tradition in the 1980s*. All CPS publications, London. For an examination of the historical value of this meta-narrative, see Raven (1989) 'British history and the enterprise culture' *Past and Present*, 23 May, pp. 178–204.

7 See *Centre for Policy Studies: Publications in Print* (1989) CPS, London.

8 Cf. Griffiths (1985); Lawson (1988) *The New Britain*; Harris (1986) *Morality and Markets*. All CPS publications, London.

9 Internal CPS document (1987).

10 Ibid.

11 See, for example, 'The mission of this government is much more than the promotion of economic progress. It is to renew the spirit and solidarity of the nation' (Thatcher (1979) Cambridge, 6 June); 'Economics are the method. The object is to change the soul' (Thatcher (1989) *Sunday Times* 7 May; Thatcher 1989: 68).

12 Thatcher does make passing references to Judaism and other faiths but as her references to religion are nearly always to particular forms of Christianity, I use the terms interchangeably.

13 Thatcher has, on this basis, been a consistent advocate of the 'reChristianization' of compulsory religious education, now enshrined in the Education Reform Act 1988.

14 An interesting and independent (of Griffiths) element of her 1988 address to the Church of Scotland is the strange limiting of 'morality' to the distribution of wealth and not its creation: 'But it is not the creation of wealth that is wrong but love of money for its own sake. The spiritual dimension comes in in deciding what one does with the wealth' (Thatcher 1989: 252). For a commentary on this address see Raban 1989.

15 For example, her interpretation of the tenth commandment in her Church of Scotland address (Thatcher 1989: 252) can be found in Griffiths 1982: 97–8.

16 See, for example, Harvey (1989: 68–97); Jenkins (1988: 11–22).

17 *Times Educational Supplement*, 25 January 1989.

18 TVEI document L13, MSC, London, 1987.

19 *Enterprise in Higher Education*, MSC document, London, 1987.

20 MSC press release, November 1987.

21 'The fall and rise of the entrepreneur', Gresham Lecture (unpublished), London, July 1985. I would like to thank Peter Makeham for making Lord Young's unpublished speeches available.

22 Barnett Lecture (unpublished), London, 11 March 1986.

23 Stockton Lecture (unpublished), London, 22 April 1986; see also the *CPS Conference Paper* (unpublished), 31 January 1986.

24 'Private enterprise for the public good' (unpublished seminar paper), LSE, 2 March 1988.

25 Unpublished speech, British Institute of Management, London, 16 November 1987; see also, 'Government economic strategy', unpublished speech, Oxford, 28 July.

26 See, for example, *Britain Resurgent* (CPS, London, 1988); unpublished speech, (Manchester, 14 January 1988; speech to the House of Lords, unpublished, 24 February 1988; 'Enterprise – a strategy for Britain' *Politics and Industry*, London, March 1988, pp. 38–9).

REFERENCES

Griffiths, B. (1982) *Morality and The Market Place: Christian Alternatives to Capitalism and Socialism*, London: Hodder & Stoughton, (2nd edn 1989).
—— (1983) *The Moral Basis of the Market Economy*, London: Conservative Political Centre.
—— (1984) *The Creation of Wealth*, London; Hodder & Stoughton.
—— (1985) *Monetarism and Morality: A Response to the Bishops*, London: CPS.

Hahn, F. (1988) 'On market economics' in R. Skidelsky (ed.) *Thatcherism*; London: Chatto & Windus, pp. 107–24.

Hall, S. and Jacques, M. (eds) (1983) *The Politics of Thatcherism*, London: Lawrence & Wishart.

Harvey, A. (ed.) (1989) *Theology in the City*, London: SPCK.

Jenkins, D. (1988) *God, Politics and the Future*, London: SCM.

Joseph, K. (1975) *Reversing the Trend*, London: Rose Books.

—— (1976) *Stranded on the Middle Ground*, London: CPS.

Lawson, N. (1984) *The British Experiment*, Fifth Mais Lecture, London: HM Treasury.

—— (1988) *The New Britain*, London: CPS.

Raban, J. (1989) *God, Man & Thatcher*, London: Chatto & Windus.

Thatcher, M. (1986) *In Defence of Freedom*, London: Aurum Press.

—— (1989) *The Revival of Britain: Speeches on Home and European Affairs 1975–1988* in A. B. Cooke (ed.) London: Aurum Press.

Young, H. (1989) *One of Us: A Biography of Margaret Thatcher*, London: Macmillan.

ADDITIONAL SOURCE

Lawson, N. (1982) *What's Right with Britain?* London: Conservative Political Centre.

Chapter Two

WHAT MIGHT WE MEAN BY 'ENTERPRISE DISCOURSE'?

NORMAN FAIRCLOUGH

This chapter will refer to political speeches given between 1985 and 1988 by Lord Young of Graffham, until recently Secretary of State for Trade and Industry, and to a publicity brochure produced by his department.[1] My primary objective will be to argue that notions like 'enterprise discourse' ought not to be understood too rigidly, and that enterprise discourse itself is a rather diffuse set of tendencies affecting the 'order of discourse' (Fairclough 1989a) of contemporary British society (i.e. the structured whole of its discoursal practices) as part of wider tendencies of cultural change, rather than a well-defined code or 'formation' (in the sense of Pecheux 1982).

The chapter is in four parts. The first will concentrate upon the word enterprise itself in Young's speeches. What emerges is an unstable picture of various senses being structured and restructured in relation to each other according to shifting strategies – a field of potential meaning, and sets of transformations upon that field according to wider political strategies – rather than *a* meaning. In the second part, an analogous picture emerges when I extend the field from the various senses of 'enterprise' to relationships between vocabularies – the vocabularies of enterprise, skills and consumption. The third part of the chapter shifts the focus from changes over time in Young's speeches to changes in social space as enterprise discourse moves across discoursal domains. I will discuss a Department of Trade and Industry publicity brochure, and suggest that features of enterprise discourse that are manifest in the vocabulary of the Young speeches are manifest at a quite different level here, mainly in the subject positions, which are implicitly established for producer and audience in the brochure. This leads me to the conclusion that enterprise discourse is best conceived of as a rather diffuse set of changes affecting various aspects of the societal order of discourse in various ways. The final part of the chapter places this conclusion in a wider theoretical framework for exploring discoursal change in its relation to social and cultural change.

MEANINGS OF 'ENTERPRISE'

The word enterprise occurs in Young's speeches almost exclusively as a non-count noun (enterprise as a count noun has singular and plural forms and takes indefinite articles – an enterprise, enterprises). According to the *OED*, enterprise as a non-count noun can have three senses:

1. 'Engagement in bold, arduous or momentous undertakings' (*OED* gives as examples 'times of national enterprise' and 'men fond of intellectual enterprise').
2. 'Disposition or readiness to engage in undertakings of difficulty, risk or danger; daring spirit' (e.g. 'enterprise supplies the want of discipline', 'his lack of enterprise').
3. (In collocation with 'private' or 'free') 'private business', as a collective noun.

I shall refer to these for short as the 'activity', 'quality' (in the sense of personal quality) and 'business' senses. All these senses are manifest in the Young speeches, but they also show a contrast in the case of the quality sense (and marginally for the activity sense) between qualities specifically related to business activity (e.g. the ability to spot and exploit a market opportunity) and more general personal qualities (e.g. willingness to accept responsibility for oneself). I shall refer to these senses collectively as the 'meaning potential' of enterprise.

A noteworthy feature of the speeches is that 'enterprise' in its business sense is generally but not always used without the modifiers 'private' or 'free'. This increases what one might call the 'ambivalence potential' of enterprise: in principle, any occurrence of the word is open to being interpreted in any of the three senses or any combination of them. (I use 'ambivalence' where a word may be taken to have a combination of two or more senses, in contrast with 'ambiguity' where a word may be taken to have one sense *or* another (or more than one other).) However, while most occurrences of 'enterprise' are indeed semantically ambivalent and involve some combination of the three senses, this potential ambivalence is reduced by the context, including the more-or-less immediate verbal context in which the word occurs. Verbal context has two sorts of effect. First, it may eliminate one or more of the senses. Second, it may give relative salience to one of the senses without eliminating the others. Examples will be given later in the chapter.

The ambivalence potential of 'enterprise' and the possibilities for manipulating it by varying the verbal context constitute a resource that is open to strategic exploitation, and is indeed strategically exploited in the Young speeches. Different speeches highlight different senses, not by promoting one sense to the exclusion of the others, but by establishing particular configurations of meanings, particular hierarchical salience relationships among the senses of 'enterprise', which can be seen to be suited to wider strategic objectives of the speeches. It should be noted that I am not suggesting a self-conscious awareness of the senses of 'enterprise' and of processes of manipulating its meaning potential. Calculation at such a level of detail is perhaps implausible, and it is more likely that calculation at a more general level about how to achieve specific communicative objectives with respect to particular audiences leads to unselfconscious adaptations of meaning resources to these higher purposes. However, the basic strategic exploitation of the ambivalence of the word enterprise in the speeches is a not insignificant element in achieving these higher purposes – notably in contributing to the revaluation of a somewhat discredited private business sector by associating private enterprise with culturally valued qualities of 'enterprisingness'.

The analysis of enterprise I am suggesting in the speeches has implications for conceptions of meaning both in dictionaries and in specific texts: that the 'dictionary meaning' of a word as a relatively stable entity may be better conceived of as a particular hierarchical configuration of senses rather than a set of complementary senses; that context may not 'disambiguate' words in specific texts in the sense of eliminating all but one of their senses, but may, rather, impose hierarchical salience relations between senses; and that in these textual processes the relatively stable equilibria of dictionary meanings may be open to contestation, destructuring and restructuring. (Such conceptions of meaning are implicit in Williams 1976; see also Hodge 1984).

The strategic exploitation of the meaning potential of enterprise that I have referred to is evident in Young's speeches both in the explicit definitions that are given for 'enterprise' (which are quite numerous), and in the ways in which the word is used. Let me briefly comment on definitions before looking in more detail at uses. Almost all of Young's definitions of enterprise give it the quality sense. What differentiates them is the contrast I mentioned earlier between qualities that are specific to business activity and more general personal qualities. In fact there is a scale here rather than a simple opposition, illustrated in examples 1–4 in the following list, which move from the business end of the scale to the general qualities end:

1. By enterprise I mean the ability of an individual to create goods and services that other people will willingly consume. Enterprise meets people's needs and that is the source of jobs. (CPS)
2. Enterprise encompasses flexibility, innovation, risk-taking and hard work – the qualities so essential to the future of our economy and our nation. (FR)
3. . . . early in life we all have an abundance of enterprise, initiative, the ability to spot an opportunity and take rapid advantage of it. So when we are young we are all entrepreneurs. (PEJ)
4. Enterprise . . . means an acceptance of personal responsibility and a confidence and desire to take action to improve your own circumstances. (BL)

There are short-term strategies at work that involve 'enterprise' being variously defined according to the varying communicative objectives, situations and audiences of the speeches – thus definition 2 occurs in a speech whose focus is tackling unemployment, whereas definition 4, just two months later, occurs in a speech whose focus is inner city policy and 'enterprise in the community'. There also appears to be a progressive though uneven shift from the earlier to the more recent speeches towards the general personal quality sense.

When we turn to the actual use of the word enterprise, strategies become more complex because, as I have already said, what is going on is the establishment of hierarchical configurations of senses rather than just the highlighting of particular elements of the meaning potential. The first speech I shall refer to, entitled 'Enterprise and employment' (EE), was delivered in March 1985 to the Bow Group. Here (apart from the title and the one instance of the expression – enterprise culture) is the first occurrence of 'enterprise':

5. Jobs come when enterprise has the freedom and vigour to meet the demands of the market, to produce the goods and services that people want.

The verbal context unambivalently gives the business sense – only persons or collectivities like private business take predicates like 'have (the) freedom (to)'. Note that this is an instance of 'enterprise' in the business sense without the usual modifiers.

In every instance except example 5, the verbal context gives salience to one sense without excluding the others. The following is an example:

6. The task of government (is) to produce a climate in which prosperity is created by enterprise.

Example 6 occurs immediately following a paragraph referring to private business in which example 5 occurs, which gives the business sense salience without excluding the other senses: one could replace 'enterprise' by any of the expressions – private enterprise, enterprising activity, enterprising individuals – without making the sentence semantically incongruous in its verbal context.

In other cases, salience relations are established through the conjunction of 'enterprise' with other expressions (my italics):

7. Attitudes which regard *business, enterprise and the job of wealth creation* as a positive benefit to society.
8. Competition provides the spur to greater efficiency. Incentives provide the spur for *individual initiative and enterprise*.

The conjunction of 'enterprise' with expressions from the business domain in example 7 highlights again the business sense, while the conjunction of enterprise with an expression that signifies a personal quality (individual initiative) in example 8 highlights the quality sense, though the preceding verbal context places it at the 'business qualities' end of the scale. Notice that example 8 is syntactically ambiguous: the word individual can be taken as modifying both nouns, or just the word initiative.

The expression 'enterprise culture', which occurs in this speech and throughout the speeches, and is widely used as a label for core components of government policy and strategy, is itself highly ambivalent, not only because 'enterprise' is ambivalent between the three senses, but also because the relationship between the two elements of such nominal compounds is itself open to multiple interpretations.

The second speech I shall discuss is the Gresham lecture (FR), which was delivered just a few months later in July 1985. Here again, most instances of the use of the word enterprise are semantically ambivalent, though there is one where the verbal context requires the activity sense, but in a narrowly business activity variant:

9. Their (the Quakers') enterprise may be explained by legal restrictions on other activities.

The focus of this speech as the title suggests is 'entrepreneurs', glossed as 'those who give us leadership in business and industry', and the qualities of entrepreneurs are highlighted – 'innovator', 'promoter', 'risk taker', 'desire to create', 'willingness to take responsibility'.

The way in which the senses of enterprise are 'hierarchized' in the speech reflect this wider strategic focus, and we find the quality sense being more salient than in the first speech. This relative salience is in fact syntactically marked in two cases, through the conjunction of the word enterprise with expressions that isolate the quality sense (my italics):

10. . . . the whole thrust of changes in the structure of our economy . . . have been fundamentally harmful to *enterprise – and the enterprising instincts of individuals*.
11. And partly because conscious decisions have been taken to encourage *enterprise* and to encourage *enterprising individuals*.

Notice that the participial adjective 'enterprising', like the noun 'entrepreneur' is associated with the quality sense. Although the quality sense is relatively salient in this speech, it is again the business qualities end of the scale that is most prominent, so that in this speech as in the previous one the structuring of senses of 'enterprise' is business-dominated. At the same time, however, a more general quality sense is implicit in 'enterprising instincts' in example 10 (as well as 'the urge for enterprise'), which prefigure a notion made more explicit in later speeches of enterprise as an inborn human attribute that social circumstances may stifle.

The third and final speech I shall refer to was delivered in November 1987 to the British Institute of Management (BIM). What is striking here in contrast with the previous two speeches is the number of instances where the verbal context reduces ambivalence potential and imposes one of the senses – the quality sense (my italics):

12. The Technical and Vocational Education Initiative, the National Council for Vocational Qualification and Open College strengthened those links and raised the *skills and enterprise of individuals*.

13. Last April I asked chief executives to pledge their companies to recognise the *professionalism and enterprise of their managers* as a key to business success.

14. I hope the same will happen in management education and development so that we can fully use the *talents and enterprise of people*.

The quality sense is imposed in each case by twin properties of verbal context: (a) enterprise is co-ordinated with another noun that signifies personal qualities; (b) enterprise (and the noun it is conjoined with) is modified by prepositional phrases that attribute enterprise – as a quality of course – to (categories of) persons. Furthermore, although the speech is concerned with management education and so very firmly with business, the qualities being referred to are more towards the general personal end of the scale than in the two previous speeches – witness the conjunction of 'enterprise' with the general quality term 'talents' in example 14. This shift in the salience of senses accords with the longer-term strategy I referred to earlier (the third speech came more than 2 years after the second), and with more immediate strategic considerations: the speech refers to the Handy Report on management development, which emphasized the importance of a broad set of qualities acquired in a good general education for managers of the future. However, this is only a relative shift in salience. A significant proportion of instances of the use of the word enterprise remain ambivalent between the three senses, and in some cases the verbal context (in example 15 the conjunction of 'enterprise' with 'wealth creation') still highlights the business sense (my italics):

15. The whole climate for *wealth creation and enterprise* has changed.

The effect is to contain the shift towards the quality sense and the general personal quality end of the scale within a relatively stable strategic conjunction that gives salience to the business sense and the business end of the quality scale.

The trajectory of 'enterprise' in Young's speeches can be summed up as a process of semantic engineering (Leech 1974: 53–62), whose basic move is the activation of the range of senses associated with 'enterprise' within political discourse and, via the formal device of using 'enterprise', in its business sense, without the usual modifiers ('private', 'free')', the creation of the ambivalence potential I have referred to. A particular meaning potential has been ideologically and politically invested (Frow 1985; Fairclough 1989b) and worked for reasons of political strategy. The result is not something static – we cannot capture it by offering a description of 'the meaning of enterprise in the discourse of enterprise'. It is, rather, a field (a meaning potential and ambivalence potential), and sets of transformations within that field associable with longer- and shorter-term strategies.

CONFIGURATIONS OF VOCABULARIES

The metaphor of a field and sets of transformations within it is also an appropriate conceptual framework for thinking about relationships between the word enterprise and other vocabularies in Young's speeches. 'Enterprise' varies from speech to speech not only in how its senses are hierarchically organized, but also in what wider configurations it enters into, and in what position. One formal way into these patterns of variation is to examine the sorts of expression 'enterprise' is syntactically conjoined with. Here is a sample that is fairly representative of the speeches as a whole: enterprise and employment, initiative and enterprise, enterprise and individual responsibility, self-reliance and enterprise, skills and enterprise, professionalism and enterprise, talents and enterprise.

As the discussion has already shown, what 'enterprise' is conjoined with is a part of its verbal context that can highlight one or other of its senses. But there is more to it than that. Just as establishing particular salience hierarchies among the senses of a word can serve strategic purposes, so, too, can establishing wider configurations – between, say, the vocabularies (what some would call the 'discourses') of enterprise and skill on the one hand, or between the vocabularies of enterprise and individual responsibility on the other. The former combines the vocabularies (and narratives) of 'enterprise' with those of a particular vocationally oriented conceptualization and wording (and ideology) of education and training and of their relationship to work and other dimensions of social life. The latter combines the vocabulary and narratives of 'enterprise' with those of a particular personal morality. These represent contrasting (though potentially complementary) directions of potential alliance for those whose aim is to build an enterprise culture that are matters for important longer-term strategic decisions as well as shorter-term strategic exploitation. They are aspects of the 'intertextuality' of enterprise discourse, the nature of the links between its texts and other categories of text (Kristeva 1986).

The following extract, which is an abbreviated version of a longer passage from Young's NEDC 25th Anniversary Speech (PEJ), gives an extended illustration of strategic configurations of this sort. The italics are mine, and I have numbered the paragraphs for ease of reference.

1. In the schools we have the Technical and Vocational Education Initiative. The main aim of this programme and the big changes in examinations and the curriculum we have introduced, is to *sustain and develop enterprise*. That is the way to encourage and enable young people to use *their growing skills and knowledge* to solve real problems in today's world.

2. For school leavers there is YTS. . . . At heart, the Youth Training Scheme too is about *enterprise*: about *encouraging and helping young people to make and take opportunities, to take responsibility and to welcome change*. A broad foundation of *skills* for the modern world so that our young school leavers can be masters of change and not its victims.

3. Then standards. By 1991 there will be in place the new National Vocational Qualification with at least 5 levels. Those qualifications will be based on *competence what people can do and can show they can do, not academic knowledge alone*.

4. From this September, the Open College will come into every home through the medium of television and radio. The College . . . is unashamedly nailing its colours to the mast of *enterprise, employment, training, skills and competence*.

5. Our system will build on the twin foundations of *competence and enterprise*. There is no room in a modern world for the old divide between 'education' and 'training'. Nor is there any room for

the outmoded and outdated distinction between 'academic' and 'vocational'. We are about *competence, the ability to perform and the capacity to be in charge of your own destiny.*

6. And our system must be built on *individual choice and enterprise*, on commitment and enthusiasm, not coercion.

7. To that end, in our system, *the customer, you as employer or individual must be the driving force.*

Examples 1 and 2 show a configuration of vocabularies of enterprise and skill – notice that the relatively greater salience of the former in the configuration is implicit in its appearance before the latter in each paragraph. Example 2 shows, however, that what is going on is not just the placing of two autonomous vocabularies in relation to each other, but some merging: 'enterprise' is glossed in a way that is familiar from Young's definitions of it (to make and take opportunities, to take responsibility and to welcome change) – but these quality senses of enterprise are then referred to as skills. Example 3 sets up a contrast between 'competence' – part of the vocabulary of skills – and 'academic knowledge' and the conjunction of 'enterprise' with 'competence' as well as 'skill' in 4 underscores the implicit opposition between 'enterprise' and 'academic knowledge'. Example 5 is the key paragraph for the configuration of vocabularies of enterprise and skill. Its first sentence explicitly foregrounds the pairing of 'enterprise' and 'competence', and its last sentence effects a further merger between the vocabularies: this time, 'competence' is glossed with a conjunction of an expression that belongs to the vocabulary of skill (ability to perform) and another that belongs to the vocabulary of enterprise (the capacity to be in charge of your own destiny). Examples 6 and 7 add a new vocabulary to the configuration – that of consumption – with its myths and narratives ('the customer is king', and so forth). This is formally marked in the conjunction: individual choice and enterprise. The total configuration that results is the linguistic facet of a major strategic conjunction in government policies: between a promotion of 'enterprise' in the workplace and beyond, consumerism and a vocationally geared education system.

The vocabulary of consumption shows up in a more explicit and self-conscious form in a speech given to the Birmingham Chamber of Commerce in February 1988 (BCC), shortly after the launch by the Department of Trade and Industry of an 'enterprise strategy', which gives private enterprise a major role in creating the 'enterprise culture'. The following is an abbreviated version of a passage from the speech:

> My recent White Paper – 'DTI – The Department for Enterprise' – shows how we are changing our policies and our organisation to work with business; to accept that we too have customers; that you are our customers; and that, in the end, customers are king.
> First, we are expanding our network of contacts with business at a local level.
> In other words we are getting closer to our market, to our customers. We are promoting and marketing DTI's services to you actively. Our use of TV adverts signals a major change in the relationship between business and DTI.
> If we are running schemes FOR business and encouraging activities BY business we have to make sure that what we have to sell TO business is clearly marketed, easy to understand and easy to use. If government is to provide services to business then they must be customer led.

The DTI is cast in the role of marketer and advertiser of the services it has to 'sell' to business, which is cast in the role of customer. I shall shortly discuss how this metadiscoursal representation of DTI practice compares with its actual promotional practice.

TRANSFORMATIONS OF ENTERPRISE DISCOURSE

I have illustrated both for the senses of 'enterprise' and for relations between vocabularies, a conception of 'enterprise discourse' as a field containing a certain potential, and sets of strategically motivated transformations within that field. So far I have stayed with Young's speeches, but it is now time to point out that the transformations that characterize enterprise discourse are not only transformations in time within a particular discoursal domain, but also transformations 'in space' across discoursal domains. Enterprise discourse may originate and evolve initially in political speeches, but it is transposed from the domain of political discourse into many others: the media and the various discourses of its various sectors; the educational domains – schools, further education, higher education; training of management and other personnel in industry and the health service; and so forth.

Given this complex distribution, enterprise discourse might be expected to show up in divergent ways and forms in different domains.

Part of what is involved here is the question of how it combines with discourses already in place in these various domains – does it replace them, or come to constitute with them complex new forms of merged discourse? There is also the question of resistance: how, if at all, is enterprise discourse opposed in the various domains among which it is distributed, and what are the outcomes of struggle between opposing discourses? This may be, for example, a matter of struggle over the meaning of 'enterprising' by perhaps applying it to activities distant from business, or of drawing upon an alternative vocabulary (e.g. focusing upon cultivating creativity rather than enterprise in education), or constituting alternative subject positions in discourse.

There are, furthermore, variations in what one might call the level of explicitness of enterprise discourse. In Young's speeches, as I have pointed out, the word enterprise is frequently given explicit definition. This is the most explicit level, the metadiscoursal level where aspects of enterprise discourse are overt discourse topics. At a second level, the discoursal level, enterprise discourse is still overtly present in describable features of texts – this is the case with the use of 'enterprise' in the Young speeches. At a third level, what we might call the subdiscoursal level, enterprise discourse is an implicit interpretative resource that one needs to draw upon to arrive at coherent interpretations of the text. I shall exemplify the subdiscoursal level shortly.

I shall illustrate just a small part of this complex set of issues in one piece of Department of Trade and Industry publicity produced in 1988: a 32-page brochure about the 'enterprise initiative', a new label for the services offered by the DTI to business. The enterprise initiative is part of the 'enterprise strategy' launched at the beginning of 1988, which the extracts from BCC in the previous section relate to (see p. 48). I want to focus upon how elements of enterprise discourse function at a subdiscoursal level in the constitution within this text of subject positions for the DTI itself and for the business people the brochure is addressing. All texts express the social identities of their producers and address the assumed social identities of their addressees and audiences. But mass-readership public texts, especially where there are clear instrumental goals as in the case of advertising, actively construct imaginary identities for their producers and audiences, and create subject positions for the latter, which they may or may not compliantly occupy.

The bulk of the brochure is constructed as a series of double-page spreads each detailing one of the 'initiatives' (counselling, marketing, etc.) which cumulatively make up the enterprise initiative. The 'design initiative' is reproduced in Figure 2.1 as an example.

Figure 2.1 The design initiative

---

the
Design
initiative

Look behind any successful business and you'll find good design. While knowing your market can help you find the product or service your customers want, only good design can translate it into something they will want to buy.

Design helps you meet your customers' needs for performance and reliability and meets your needs on ease of manufacture and cost.

Good design helps to position your product and your firm in the market. It doesn't matter if you're manufacturing luxury goods or serving the mass market. The story is the same.

Even if your design is up to scratch now, it will have to evolve to meet changing demands and new opportunities.

If you're not presenting the right image, you're not fulfilling your potential.

How can the Design Initiative help?
The Design Initiative, managed for DTI by the Design Council, offers expert advice on design from product concept to corporate image. Amongst other things they can help you with:-
- product innovation and feasibility studies
- design for efficient production
- mechanical and electrical engineering design
- materials selection and use
- industrial design and styling
- ergonomic and product safety considerations
- packaging and point of sale material
- corporate identity

Who pays what?
DTI will pay half of the cost of between 5 and 15 man-days of consultancy. In Assisted Areas and Urban Programme Areas DTI will pay two thirds (see map on page 32). You pay the rest.

The next step
If you would like to find out more about the Design Initiative contact your nearest Regional Office, Scottish Office or Welsh Office from the list on page 30.

It is typical in having a heading, an 'orientation' section (bold and underlined) that sums up the initiative, then the bulk of the text divided into short headed sections, and a small cartoon and a large photograph (not reproduced in Figure 2.1).

I shall focus upon the orientation sections. Here are four of these, taken from the marketing, design, quality and business-planning-initiative texts. I have numbered them for ease of reference.

1. The essence of good marketing is to provide your customers with what they want. Not to spend time and money trying to persuade them to take what you've got. So, whether you're selling at home or abroad, it's important to understand both the market and your competitors.

2. Look behind any successful business and you'll find good design. While knowing your market can help you find the product or service your customers want, only good design can translate it into something they will want to buy.

3. It doesn't matter how much time and effort you put into marketing, design and production. If the product or service doesn't live up to your customers' expectations, you're wasting your time.

4. Long-term planning is not a luxury confined to the larger companies. It is essential for any business which is to survive and compete in today's market place.

These orientations have consistent features that cue, so to speak, implicit subject positions for the DTI and the businessperson, and an implicit relationship between them. They consist largely of categorical, bald assertions about matters of business practice that the business people addressed would be assumed to have special knowledge of. The assertions are categorical and bald in the sense that they are not modulated by markers of tentativeness, indirectness, modality, hedging and so forth (Brown and Levinson 1978). They imply an expert–client relationship between the DTI and the businessperson.

But that is not the end of the story. Even given an expert–client relationship, the expert has various options open to him or her in terms of the forms in which advice and information are given. The forms opted for here appear to be rather face-threatening. Notice for instance the negatives in 1 and 4 in the list, which imply propositions that are likely to hold for many readers (some businesses spend time and money trying to persuade customers to take what they've got; some smaller companies think long-term planning is a luxury). Similarly, many readers will meet the conditions to be wasting their time in the terms of 3. Moreover, a number of propositions in these orientations are likely to be anything but news to most business readers – the first sentence of the first orientation in the list, for example, is surely a crashing truism for business – yet potential readers are given no credit (by adding the word 'obviously' for instance) for what they already know.

One might therefore expect many business readers to find these orientations irritating and insulting, and it would be interesting to do some research on readings to see if this is so. However, I suspect this would not be a general reaction. The categorical and uncompromising style of the orientations may, I think, carry implicit meanings about social identity additional to the expert–client meanings. It is perhaps an attempt at translating values of the enterprise culture that appear at the discoursal level in association with quality senses of the word enterprise in the Young speeches, into a style of writing (and by implication a style of speech – one finds something similar in the DTI's television advertising), which establishes a social identity for an 'enterprising person'. The particular enterprising qualities for which this style is a sort of metaphor are those of self-reliance – as Young says in the Birmingham Chamber of Commerce speech (BCC), the emphasis in the enterprise initiative is upon 'self-help'. A self-reliant person is a person who does not need to be pampered, can face up to things, can be told things straight. The orientations have, I suspect, a double function in these terms: they give the DTI an 'enterprising' identity, and at the same time offer to business people a model for what is becoming a culturally valued identity. If this is so, irritation on the part of business readers may well be overridden.

What about the relationship between DTI practice in this brochure and the new role announced for the DTI by Young in BCC – that of a promoter selling its services to its business customers? There are parts of the brochure that set up subject positions and social identities akin to those of commodity advertising, casting readers in the role of consumers and the DTI in that of advertiser. This involves a reversal of the authority relations of the expert–client relation: in the latter, it is the DTI as expert that's in the authoritor position, whereas in the former it is the businessperson as consumer who is the authoritor and there are correspondingly manifest efforts to persuade him or her. Here is an example from the part of the brochure that deals with the 'consultancy initiatives':

> Over the past few years, we've helped hundreds of small businesses to enlist the help of specialist consultants. We're convinced that it's the most cost effective way for a firm to help itself. So convinced, in fact, that we're planning to support around a thousand consultancies each and every month.
> The (Enterprise) Counsellor will keep an eye out for the untapped resources, inefficient work systems and unrealized potential. You will get impartial (and, of course, confidential) advice based on the Counsellor's considerable experience. Only then will he or she recommend how the Consultancy Initiatives can best help you.

In the first paragraph we find a selling stratagem widely used by advertisers: we believe in x, and our belief is backed up by the resources we have put into x, showing that you, too, can feel secure in believing in x. Even the syntactic pattern – 'We're convinced/confident/etc. that x', 'So convinced, etc. that we are going to/ have y'(ed.) – is an advertising formula, and the use of 'we' to portray a business hierarchy or bureaucracy as a warm community is an advertising device. In the second paragraph, 'keep an eye out' portrays the Counsellor as trustworthy friend; 'of course' both credits the addressees with relevant knowledge (compare the orientations), and claims a rapport between the DTI and addressees; the modification of 'experience' with 'considerable' can be there only to boost addressees' confidence; and the topicalization of 'then' with 'only' in the last sentence implies meticulous care on the Counsellor's part.

What appears in Young's speeches as a strategic configuration of vocabularies, then, appears in the DTI brochure as a strategic configuration of pairings of subject positions for the DTI and the businessperson addressee: expert/client, and advertiser/consumer. There is also another pairing that is more traditional in publicity about government services, which we might refer to as provider/recipient. This pairing is evident, for instance, where the regulations governing availability of services are being set out. Also from the 'consultancy initiatives' text:

> *Who qualifies?*
> If you're an independent firm or group with a payroll of fewer than 500, the Enterprise Initiative offers financial support for between 5 and 15 man-days specialist consultancy in a number of key management functions.

In respect of subject positions, then, the brochure is an amalgam of both traditional and novel practices.

As this example has, I hope, begun to indicate, as one shifts the domain of reference from particular well-defined bodies of texts such as the Young speeches through relatively if loosely homogeneous entities like 'political discourse', to the complex and heterogeneous set of relations between types of discourse in what we might call the 'order of discourse', the discoursal ramifications of enterprise culture become increasingly diffuse. One can, at least in part, associate the notion of enterprise discourse with fairly circumscribed if shifting vocabularies, for instance, in the Young speeches. While one does find a transposition of such vocabularies across the order of discourse, however, the shifting across levels of explicitness I have tried to indicate here suggests a shaping of the order of discourse by enterprise culture that is much less easy to pinpoint. Detailed research into specific discoursal effects in a range of domains is clearly indicated as a concrete means of exploring the progressive political and ideological investment of an order of discourse in the course of social and cultural change.

CONCLUSION

Let me conclude this chapter by trying to place the view of enterprise discourse that I have been moving towards in a wider theoretical framework. I have been suggesting that enterprise discourse is not a well-defined closed entity, but rather a set of tendencies – transformations within fields that, at least at the level of transformations across discourse types in the order of discourse, are of a diffuse nature. One

54

implication of this position is that enterprise discourse cannot be located in any text. The focus needs to be rather on processes across time and social space of text production, and the wider strategies that text production enters into.

But one also needs a complementary focus upon the reading of texts, and from this perspective the analyses I have offered in this chapter are too one-sided. Texts are open to multiple readings, and the ways in which they are read depend upon the purposes, commitments and strategies of readers – upon the reading positions the texts are exposed to. This, in turn, is a function of the distribution of a text – the set of contexts of reception it enters. The texts of face-to-face discourse have a relatively simple distribution, though even here there may be a context of overhearing as well as a context of address, and various contexts of reporting. Public discourse such as political speeches tends to have a complex distribution – perhaps an immediate audience of political supporters, but beyond that multiple audiences of political allies and opponents, multiple mass–media audiences, international audiences and so forth. Anticipation of the potential polyvalence of the texts that such complex distributions imply is a major factor in their design.

What the multiplicity of readings underscores is that strategies are inevitably pursued in circumstances of contestation and struggle. I have argued elsewhere (Fairclough 1989b), drawing upon Laclau 1977, that the Gramscian concept of hegemony is a rich one for conceptualizing such processes of struggle and their discoursal dimensions. Hegemony is a useful matrix and model for discourse. It is a matrix, in the sense that processes of discoursal change such as those around enterprise culture can be satisfactorily explicated if they are referred to wider hegemonic struggles to establish, maintain, undermine and restructure hegemonies on the part of alliances of social forces – the struggle of the Thatcherites for hegemony has been described, for instance, by Hall 1988. It is a model, in that there are homologies between hegemonies as unstable equilibria constantly open to contestation and restructuring, and linguistic and discoursal conventions. The view of meaning and meaning change I have outlined in terms of shifting salience hierarchies of senses invites such a comparison. So, too, do the shifting configurations of subject positions I have pointed to in the case of the DTI publicity.

A discourse type from this perspective is just a configuration of elements with greater or lesser durability – or rather a network of related (and perhaps quite loosely related) configurations across discoursal domains. What this implies in terms of the place of discourse in cultural change is a rather diffuse set of changes affecting orders of discourse that might be quite difficult to pin down, and might be overlooked if one is anticipating a well-defined code or formation triumphantly colonizing one bastion of cultural ascendancy after another. The investment of an order of discourse by a newly salient cultural dominant is perhaps a more subtle and even insidious process. If this is so, there are important political and ideological implications for those who wish to resist the achievement of cultural and discoursal hegemonies.

There are also implications for one's view of discourse analysis. 'Discourse' and 'discourse analysis' are fashionable in various disciplines and open to many interpretations. For some analysts, discourses are conceptual structures such as narratives, myths or schemata. Others are more oriented to language form, though with contrasting focuses on, for example, vocabulary and metaphor, or grammatical features of various sorts (e.g. pronouns, modality, voice, intersentential cohesion), or dialogical structures (e.g. turn-taking, formulating). Van Dijk 1987 shows some of the bewildering variety of analytical focuses, as well as the theoretical and disciplinary variations that cut across it.

A danger in this situation is that analysts will divide too quickly into separate camps. Of course this stifles intellectual exchange and is objectionable for that reason. But the unstable and diffuse character I have attributed to enterprise discourse in this chapter also suggests that it is objectionable on the grounds that a single type of discourse can 'show up' variously as aspects of either the content or the form of texts: as narratives, vocabularies, metaphors, particular selections in grammar, particular ways of conducting dialogue and so forth. It would, therefore, be unhelpful to see these various dimensions of content and form as alternatives that the discourse analyst has to choose between.

NOTES

1 The speeches referred to are listed at the end of Chapter Three, pp. 70–1, and the same abbreviations will be used here. We are grateful to Paul Morris for providing this material for analysis.

REFERENCES

Brown, P. and Levinson, S. (1978) 'Universals in language usage: politeness phenomena', in E.N. Goody (ed.) *Questions and Politeness*, Cambridge: Cambridge University Press.

Fairclough, N. (1989a) *Language and Power*, London: Longman.

—— (1989b) 'Language and ideology', *English Language Research Journal* 3: 9–27.

Frow, J. (1985) 'Discourse and power', *Economy and Society* 14: 23–43.

Hall, S. (1988) 'The toad in the garden: Thatcherism among the theorists', in C. Nelson and L. Grossberg (eds) *Marxism and the Interpretation of Culture*, London: Macmillan.

Hodge, R. (1984) 'Historical semantics and the meaning of "discourse" ', *Australian Journal of Cultural Studies* 2: 124–30.

Kristeva, J. (1986) 'Word, dialogue and novel', in T. Moi (ed.) *The Kristeva Reader*, Oxford: Blackwell.

Laclau, E. (1977) *Politics and Ideology in Marxist Theory*, London: NLB.

Leech, G.N. (1974) *Semantics*, Harmondsworth: Penguin.

Pecheux, M. (1982) *Language, Semantics and Ideology*, London: Macmillan.

van Dijk, T. (1987) *Handbook of Discourse Analysis*, 4 vols, New York: Academic Press.

Williams, R. (1976) *Keywords*, London: Fontana.

Chapter Three

THE RHETORIC
OF ENTERPRISE

RAMAN SELDEN

For use almost can change the stamp of nature.
(*Hamlet*, III.iv.170.
Hamlet is trying to persuade Gertrude to break the habit
of sleeping with Claudius)

The rhetoric of enterprise has dominated British culture at virtually every level during the 1980s. Its authority has been challenged from various directions to little effect. The discourse of the new market economics appears irresistible, as it washes over and overwhelms the languages of collectivism, humanism, egalitarian Christianity and the ethical discourses of the professions. There are two types of critical intervention: either one looks for diachronic incoherence in the rhetoric (U-turns, etc.), or one challenges the systematic (synchronic) order of the discourse. This chapter will take the second route in attempting to show the loose construction of the government's entire enterprise argument. The approach will not tackle the sequential logic of propositions but will explore their 'rhetoric'. The term rhetoric will be used in the sense employed by the exponents of deconstruction, who focus upon the ways in which the truth claims of particular discourses are underpinned by the silent endorsement and privileging of particular terms and concepts at the expense of their antitheses. Before I present deconstructive readings of government pronouncements on enterprise culture, it will be necessary to make some comments about the politics of post-structuralism in general and of deconstruction in particular.

THE POLITICS OF DECONSTRUCTION

Jonathan Arac has recently made a strong case for the political uses of contemporary post-structuralist literary criticism:

58

> Postmodern critics . . . can carry on a significant political activity
> by relating the concerns once enclosed within 'literature' to a
> broadly cultural sphere that is itself related to, although not iden-
> tical with, the larger concerns of the state and economy.
>
> (Arac 1986, xxx–xxxi)

Arac's view contrasts with the more usual notion – that post-structuralist
modes of reading are anarchic, hedonistic and quietist. And it is true
that post-structuralist critics have often encouraged textual signifiers
to slide sideways in an apolitical, ahistorical dance without end. What
Barthes called 'the pleasure of the text', that ecstatic *jouissance*, that
heady polysemic orgy of signification, refuses the closures of political
analysis or historical understanding. American deconstruction, in particular, has been castigated by Eagleton (Eagleton 1981: 53–65) and
others for its ahistorical subjectivism. The radicalism of Derrida's
epistemology, they argue, is tamed and incorporated into a native
formalism. The free play of reader and text suits admirably the notion
of free markets: interpretive pleasure is a sort of textual consumerism.
Nothing has encouraged this revivified formalism more than Derrida's
celebrated, but often one-sidedly interpreted, maxim – '*il n'y a pas de-
hors texte*' (there is nothing outside text). This essay adopts a less purely
textualist reading of Derrida's apothegm, interpreting it as saying that
there is nothing simply outside text; world and text interconnect.

While there is something in Derrida's work that condones a subjectivist and libertarian approach, it also instigates a contrary movement
towards radical cultural critique. As early as 1972 Derrida accepted that
his work could be compared with dialectical materialism in so far as
both come under the rubric 'critique of idealism' (Derrida 1981: 62).
He shares with neo-Marxist thought a strongly anti-teleological and
anti-essentialist epistemology. This is not to say, of course, that Marxist
thought has not also been deeply implicated in the metaphysics that
the deconstructors so avidly search out and destroy. Derrida himself
talks of investigating 'all the sediments deposited by the history of
metaphysics' (Derrida 1981: 74). Marxism often generates a 'realist'
counterpart of the idealist metaphysics it seeks to transcend. However,
we should also note that the Marxist thought that emerged from the
structuralist revolution was committed to a radical purging of
metaphysics from the body of Marxist texts. Michael Ryan sums up
what deconstruction and New Left philosophy have in common:

> an emphasis on plurality over authoritarian unity, a disposition to

criticize rather than to obey, a rejection of the logic of power and domination in all their forms, an advocation of difference against identity, and a questioning of state universalism.

(Ryan 1982: 213)

When used as an adjunct to materialist analysis, can deconstruction be regarded as a potent instrument of cultural critique? By way of answer I shall simply quote Christopher Norris's decisive interpretation of Derrida:

deconstruction is a rigorous attempt to *think the limits* of that principle of reason which has shaped the emergence of Western philosophy, science and technology at large. It is rigorous insofar as it acknowledges the need to engage with that principle in all its effects and discursive manifestations. Thus the activity of deconstruction is strictly inconceivable outside the tradition of enlightened rational critique whose classic formulations are still to be found in Kant. . . . deconstruction [is] a mode of thinking that can best exert its critical leverage at those points where rational discourse comes up against the limits of calculability.

(Norris 1987: 162)

Without rational critique there can be no effective resistance to the power of existing institutions. Norris proceeds to explore the logic of nuclear deterrence in which the limits of calculability are dramatically apparent. In turning to the entrepreneurial rhetoric of Thatcherism I shall be showing how an instrumental reason, dedicated to the radical transformation of British culture, comes up against the limits of its own rhetoric.

THE CONCEPT OF ENTERPRISE

The documents I shall be discussing are speeches and published papers by Lord Young and Nigel Lawson.* Authorship is not a privileged category from a post-structuralist viewpoint, because the text in question is not the embodiment of a personal style (though differences of that kind are discernible) but a type of discourse that exerts an effect within the actual power relations in play in contemporary Britain. There is nothing new to say about the themes that govern the discourse.

* The full list of speeches is given on pp. 70–1. They are referred to in the text by the codes given there.

I am interested in the fictional and rhetorical structures that underpin the discourse. Essentialism and teleology, not unexpectedly, provide the necessary metaphysics of the enterprise discourse. The very concept of 'enterprise culture' rests upon a foundational dichotomy between what is essential and what is contingent. Enterprise is seen as an essential human impulse, while culture is changeable. On the one hand, there is the synchronic perspective of the essentially human; on the other, the diachronic perspective of the historically contingent. I shall argue that deployment of this and related binary oppositions sets in motion a textual play that destabilizes the logic that the oppositions try to fix. Enterprise is both natural and cultural. The enterprise documents handle this familiar binary opposition (and others that stem from it) in ways that produce an effect of aporia (a logical undecidability): the logic of enterprise discourse comes up against its own limits. The name given by Derrida to what eludes and subverts the logocentric thrust of reason is not 'rhetoric' but 'writing'. We shall therefore be looking at the ways in which writing intervenes and prevents entrepreneurial reasoning from securing a logical grip upon itself.

Before I examine the textual play of terms, I would like to point out the larger historical context of the specific appropriation of enterprise values that we associate with the present government's policy statements. The *OED* reveals that the terms 'enterprise', 'enterprising' and 'entrepreneur' have chequered histories. Both the substantive 'enterprise' and the epithet 'enterprising' were ambivalent in their usage until the nineteenth century. Cotgrave (1621) says that 'an enterprising fool needs little wit', and Dr Wilcocks (1720) wrote that 'The King of Prussia . . . has a brisk enterprising look.' The modern positive connotation is there in J.H. Newman's: 'Marco Polo . . . was one of a company of enterprising Venetian merchants' (1876). The substantive 'enterprise' was ideologically contested at an early stage. E. Elton (1618) declares that: 'We must not be ignorant of Satan's enterprizes'. Shakespeare uses the word equally of bold and daring undertakings and of wicked and foolhardy ones. At the start of the Industrial Revolution the conservative Burke implies no full approval of the qualities of derring-do that the word connotes: 'In such [piratical] expeditions enterprize supplies the want of discipline.'

The earliest meanings of 'entrepreneur' relate to managing in general and particularly in relation to musical or military events. By the nineteenth century it could refer to any manager: at his hotel Paganini 'refused to receive any one but his *entrepreneur* and his dentist'.

The modern economic meaning appears in the later nineteenth century referring to a 'contractor (whether an individual or a corporation) acting as an intermediary between capital and labour'. This strictly technical meaning of entrepreneur, which has become the dominant usage, is no longer a site of ideological struggle. This is why it has little value for current enterprise discourse, which is almost exclusively focused on the other terms – 'enterprise' and 'enterprising', whose meanings are much less easily contained. For this reason the documents I shall discuss talk less of entrepreneurs than enterprise. The growing domination of enterprise discourse can be understood as the successful appropriation of 'enterprise' to the values of entrepreneurialism. The general human qualities the term 'enterprise' connotes are reinscribed within a specific and narrowly economistic discourse. It should be noted, however, that resistance to the dominant discourse of enterprise enters through the gaps and contradictions inherent in the terms of the discourse. Many universities and polytechnics, which have accepted money from the government's Enterprise in Higher Education scheme, are at present engaged in a dangerous bid to reinscribe the term 'enterprise' with non-entrepreneurial meanings. I am appealing here to a Gramscian notion of ideological struggle, according to which ideological formations achieve dominance through a complex process of articulation and disarticulation. Connotative links are forged between different discursive formations (other connotations are detached from their moorings), in order to secure a popular democratic ascendancy of a particular class interest.

NATURE AND THE ENTERPRISE INSTINCT

The path of least resistance for any ideological discourse is to appeal to natural instinct. If the 'subject' that the enterprise discourse interpellates can be viewed as a spontaneous subject (in effect, a subject pre-existing every discourse), the battle is won. Young argues that the Industrial Revolution, the first true moment of the enterprise culture, arose spontaneously and 'by consent'; that is, without state intervention (FR: 2). Lawson develops the philosophy of enterprise as follows: 'But capitalism is based on the idea of voluntary cooperation and voluntary exchange. Self-improvement is a basic human instinct. So is self-interest' (NB: 12). He adds 'The basic human instinct of self-interest encompasses the desire of a man to benefit his family as well as himself . . . without being told by the State that he should do so'

(NB: 13). Further on he confirms the central idea: 'It is the basic human – and essentially capitalist – instinct of self-improvement.' Capitalist development therefore goes 'with the grain of human nature'. The 'spread of personal ownership' is 'in harmony with the deepest instincts of the British people.' The changes since 1979 have not been imposed from above as an 'alien creed' but have 'emerged spontaneously on the ground' (NB: 14). Lord Young talks about 'the enterprising instincts of individuals' (FR: 11). According to a CPS conference paper, 'the natural desire for an individual is to be independent' (CPS: 4). The entrepreneurial instincts can, of course, be hampered or frustrated. The Barnett lecture declares that: 'The whole thrust of changes in our economy over more than a century has harmed enterprise and the enterprising instincts of individuals' (BL: 7). The boldest statement of this view comes in the Queen Elizabeth II Conference Centre speech:

> We are all born with enterprise. None of us would survive without enterprise. Every baby and toddler demonstrates every day . . . that early in life we all have an abundance of enterprise, initiative, the ability to spot an opportunity and take rapid advantage of it. So when we are young, we are all entrepreneurs. But along the way to adult life too many of us change.
>
> (PEJ: 2)

The binary opposition – instinct/culture (and its variants nature/ nurture, etc.) – takes on the form of a violent hierarchy (the superior, privileged term enforces a 'truth'). Culture (the inferior term) contaminates an unfallen condition: if we were left alone in a state of nature we would be enterprising. 'It's a question of the environment we've created.' A deconstructive reversal of the opposition is (ironically) provided by Lord Young in the Lords debate (24 February 1988) in which he supported social inequality with the argument that: 'Since Adam and Eve left Eden there have been differences in our society' (LD: 1). So, the entrepreneurial state of nature, like its Hobbesian precursor, turns out to be a fallen state of culture. Milton, an early advocate of the Protestant ethic, while lamenting the loss of paradise, puts into Adam's mouth an entrepreneurial consolation: 'with labour I must earn/ My bread; what harm? Idleness had been worse;/ My labour will sustain me' (*Paradise Lost*: X.1054–6). After the fall Milton imagines a period of social harmony and natural law under paternal rule,

> till one shall rise
> Of proud ambitious heart [Nimrod], who not content
> With fair equality, fraternal state,
> Will arrogate dominion undeserved
> Over his bretheren, and quite dispossess
> Concord and law of nature from the earth.
>
> (XII.24–9)

The problem of origins, as always, goes back even further for Milton, who cannot imagine even a prelapsarian existence without the need for labour and cultivation. So, in Milton's epic it is difficult to determine exactly when culture infected nature, or when the need for self-help, the law of the jungle, competition, difference and inequality became the new law of nature.

The origin of man's entrepreneurial nature is uncertain, because its contamination by culture seems to have occurred at an early and indeterminate date. Nevertheless, the documents interpret the Thatcherite revolution as a restoration of a natural and spontaneous form of social existence. At almost every stage in British history instinct has been suppressed, overlaid by anti-entrepreneurial thinking: 'The forgotten lesson that we had to earn our living has been gradually rediscovered along with the sense of entrepreneurship that was the well-spring of the Industrial Revolution' (FRE: 4). Lawson, too, desiderates the 'rediscovery of the enterprise culture' (BE: 34). The Oxford Speech on Government Economic Strategy talks about the need for 'a change in attitudes and a change in culture', which is also a 'rebirth of the enterprise culture' (OS: 1). It is evident that gradually from a synchronic view of natural human instincts we are moving towards a diachronic sequence – a narrative of change: the story of a revolution. We shall examine this narrative later.

First, we must note that the appeal to natural instinct is sustained alongside an appeal for cultural intervention. The British Institute of Management speech declares: 'But we have much more to do to ensure that the enterprise culture is given a chance to become part of the British way of life' (BIM: 4). The Oxford Speech on Government Economic Strategy states that: 'What we are looking for . . . is a change in attitudes and a change in culture' (OS: 1). The LSE seminar says: 'Our concern as a society should be to ignite the spark of individualism for all our citizens' (PE: 7). The interventionist tone is repeated in many speeches: 'In the past, there was an unfortunate and unnecessary bias against enterprise in British culture. In future, that bias must be overcome. People, especially young people, need positive encouragement' (MS: 2). None of this sounds like the language of spontaneity or instinct. The intractability of the nature/culture opposition is especially apparent in the Speech to the Chemical Industries Association, which concludes with an exhortation to support educational and economic action to 'set free the spirit of enterprise' (CIA: 7), but an earlier sentence in the speech completely reverses the rhetoric: 'Cut off from that competition [achieved by enforcing open markets] human nature tends to opt for the quieter life and inefficiency' (CIA: 3). Which is more natural – the quiet idyll of the Garden before the fall, or the enterprising spirit with which 'we are all born'? The loading of the dice against natural indolence tends to unsettle the rhetoric of naturalness, which underpins the enterprise case.

Other 'spontaneous' forms of consciousness also militate against enterprise. There are occasions when government speeches actually face the need to counter naïve, native empiricism. The Cobden lecture, for example, argues the case that the service sector is just as productive as the manufacturing sector. The argument goes against people's instinctive sense of reality: 'At the centre of many people's thinking there seems to lie a simple belief that only the tangible is real . . . the primeval belief that only something manufactured is real has prevented people from taking and exploiting new opportunities in service industries' (DM: 1–2). The new enterprise culture needs to replace the 'common sense' of an earlier industrial capitalism with a common sense more atuned to a highly mechanized and rationalized phase of (post-)industrial Britain.

To return to the narrative level of enterprise discourse, when did the original enterprise culture (whether post-lapsarian or bourgeois) receive its first setback? 1945? No! It turns out that the tide turned against enterprise a long time ago. 'The real culprits are bedded deep in our national history and culture. The whole thrust of changes in our economy since the late nineteenth century has been anti-enterprise' (SL: 16). 'The Empire elevated the administrator and downgraded the businessman' (FRE: 2). The prime culprit is education. 'Ivory tower blocks were a major industry in the late-nineteenth and early twentieth centuries' (FR: 11). In a period of empire, the country worshipped the professions, 'the gifted amateur and gentleman', but despised science, technology and business. We must add that this anti-technological bias did not, of course, originate in the late-nineteenth century, but runs back through Renaissance humanism to classical culture and perhaps back to the Garden.

FURTHER DECONSTRUCTIONS

A further dichotomy that is used to underpin the enterprise culture is 'myth' and 'reality'. The enterprising individual is a bedrock reality, while notions of society and collectivity are spurious, mythical concepts. Lawson, in 'This New Britain', traces the history of Britain's decline since 1945. Attlee was sustained by the myth that 'we were fighting for . . . a new Jerusalem' (NB: 5). In the Stockton Lecture, Young talks about the 'cherished myth that the unions are champions of the weak' (SL: 22). The myths were ultimately superseded by a new realism. Lawson's 'The New Britain' is subtitled 'The Tide of Ideas from Attlee to Thatcher'. The force that overcame Attlee was 'the tide of ideas'. After six years of 'economic failure and exhausted of ideas' (NB: 6) the 'tide of ideas began to turn'. He quotes Callaghan's mystification: perhaps once every thirty years there is a 'sea change' in politics; there is 'a shift in what the public wants and what it approves of' (NB: 9). However, by invoking the model of cyclical change, a Whiggish narrative about dissolving myths is threatened by a pattern of eternal recurrence: the myth of egalitarianism is replaced by the myth of enterprise ('Capitalism is based on the idea of voluntary cooperation and voluntary exchange' (NB: 12). By the conclusion, Lawson realizes that his metaphor has the effect of weakening the difference between myth and realism: 'how can we be sure that, at some point, the tide will not turn against us? The answer is that we cannot. Nothing is irreversible in politics' (NB: 17). This disarming recognition has to be cancelled immediately: 'But . . . whereas the tide at sea inevitably ebbs and flows, the same inevitability is not true of political tides.' After all, the tide is now flowing the right way: the 'New Britain . . . is in line with the deepest instincts of the British people' (NB: 17). The new ideas are not mythical because in them, human nature has prevailed; it should be possible, therefore, to stem the cultural tide in a successful Canutelike stand, and to keep it flowing one way. Rhetoric and logic here become entangled in a complex series of reversals. The final turn is a recognition that instinct, the guarantor of realism, cannot be relied upon. In order to secure 'the lasting transformation of a nation . . . you have to win the battles for hearts and minds as well as for wallets' (NB: 10). And as we know, battles for hearts and minds often come up against awkwardly obstructive countercultures.

A further movement of aporia flows from the arguments about government intervention. The rhetoric of Thatcherism privileges open markets and therefore non-interventionism. As Lord Young puts it in 'Britain Resurgent': 'We had learnt the lesson that intervention by previous governments prevented wealth creation more than encouraged it' (BR: 15). However, in the same paper he recognizes that the present government's policy actually requires intervention: 'Risktaking is at the heart of enterprise, but risks that can be calculated and these need stable foundations' (BR: 7). In order to guarantee the 'certainty and stability' that enterprise needs, government must intervene, but 'only where the interests of the decision makers in the market are likely to diverge from the public interest' (BR: 10). No doubt a government driven by socialist rather than enterprise values would be equally concerned to intervene where the interests of the decision makers in the market are likely to diverge from the public interest. The public interest is a notoriously tricky concept.

The rhetorical tangle of anti-interventionist interventionism is highlighted in Lawson's final argument in his Maise Lecture in 1984 when he praised the British Experiment for demonstrating that 'trade union power can be curbed within a free society' (BE: 37). Trade union freedoms are not consistent with a 'free society', and therefore intervention to limit those freedoms is consistent with non-interventionism. The Manchester speech puts it thus: 'Our role in government is to work with business as they find their own solutions. Our approach is not to preach, and not to meddle' (MS: 3).

One of the tasks the government has set itself is to claim the moral high ground. Lord Young looks to a time when 'creating businesses and creating jobs is regarded as a socially – perhaps even morally – acceptable occupation' (LD: 5). The government's rhetorical repertoire makes this difficult. The binary oppositions upon which it relies are unhelpful: the public sector is linked with 'caring', while private enterprise is associated with 'self-help' and even selfishness. Young laments the fact that the industrial revolution is 'popularly viewed as a period in which humanity was sacrificed for profits' and that 'feelings of guilt about the social evils of industrial capitalism have persisted' (FR: 9). 'Some people will attack us for encouraging the baser instincts in people – selfishness and general greed', but in view of the steady improvements in working conditions and pay 'we need not feel guilty that their [the generation of Victorian entrepreneurs] success was at the expense of the poor' (PE: 15–16) It is hardly surprising that the government has found itself constantly at odds with the more liberal minded bishops. Kenneth Baker's attack on the bishops in his speech to the General Synod includes the following revealingly awkward statement:

> It is one thing to affirm positively the value of community, and the central theological idea that human beings are all part of one another under the fatherhood of God, and that they should therefore love one another. It is quite another to use these ideas, valuable as they are, to advance, for example, a theological critique of the privatisation of state assets.
>
> (*Guardian*, 2 January 1989)

The language of morality and the language of economics are here alarmingly disengaged. One rhetorical response to this dilemma has been to use traditional non-capitalist rhetoric in the cause of enterprise. Images of inhumanity and disease are used to (dis-)colour economic arguments: inflation is a 'holocaust' and a 'disease' (NB: 8) and industrial confrontation is the 'virus of the British disease' (SL: 4).

The only way of dealing with the troublesome binary opposition between self-help and helping others is to suppress it by subordinating it to different and more manageable oppositions: voluntary versus compulsory, and individual versus state. However, as we shall see, no matter how smoothly this rhetorical slide is performed, the suppressed binary returns to disturb the controlling efforts of the discourse. A sentence from the Conservatives' 1979 manifesto takes a step towards breaking down the opposition between self-help and helping others: 'We want to work *with* the grain of human nature, helping people to help themselves – and others.' The elision of self-help and helping others is managed, of course, by the appeal to voluntary work and charity. Lawson manages this slide with dexterity: 'The basic human instinct encompasses the desire of a man to benefit his family as well as himself, and we see hundreds of examples in our daily lives of how man helps his neighbour – without being told by the State that he should do so' (NB: 13). The LSE Industrial Policy Seminar paper declares that 'private enterprise is directly related to public good' (PE: 1). Under the heading 'Community Responsibility' we read:

68

Some people may ask whether this spirit of individualism detracts
from the community.
Whether this pursuit of self-development leads to a lack of concern
for other people within our community.
I was interested to see the comments of the Director General of St
John's Ambulance. He said 'Voluntary work is not the antithesis
of popular capitalism; on the contrary the same spirit of individualism moves both.'

(PE: 8)

This is based on the fundamental premiss of the enterprise argument:
only by allowing the individual to act in an economically self-interested
manner can sufficient wealth be created to allow individuals to care
for others. The binary opposition 'self-help' versus 'caring for others'
turns out to be a violent hierarchy. Self-interest must take precedence
over helping others. As Young puts it, 'without creating the wealth
first we cannot invest in the kind of society that we all wish to see'
(BR: 15). That is why it is no use treating nationalized industries as
if they were social services. In the Stockton Lecture he concludes with
an echo of Disraeli's wet philosophy of 'one nation' Toryism:

If we are to evolve a society that values wealth creation as much
as wealth consumption, . . . that is concerned to achieve the
standard of living essential to a caring, civilised society, then we
will have to learn to work as one nation.

(SL: 25)

The entrepreneurial discourse is here in danger of undoing its binary
logic. The terms are clearly in uneasy relation:
Wealth creation versus wealth consumption.
Standard of living versus caring, civilized society.
We cannot have a caring, civilized society, we are told, unless we allow
individuals selfishly to reach the standard of living that makes helping
others possible. There is no way of knowing at what stage the creation of wealth overflows into the socially altruistic consumption of
wealth. It is necessary, it seems, to legitimize individual greed in order
to effect civilized ends. The priority of self-interest over helping others
remains.

The final sentence seems to strike a reconciliatory note, but conceals
a violent appropriation of the wet Tory slogan: we must learn to 'work
as one nation', not to *live* as one nation. We must all accept

the values of the enterprise culture. We must accept that helping ourselves comes before helping others. The enterprise discourse asks us to accept Hamlet's advice and to stop being the primarily social beings some of us feel we are. If we keep acting as though we *are* essentially entrepreneurial beings, we may actually start believing it; 'for', as Hamlet says, 'use almost can change the stamp of nature'. The genteel culture of empire and the socialist–liberal consensus of the mid-twentieth century both succeeded in almost changing the stamp of nature, and perhaps the proponents of Thatcherite enterprise culture may almost change it. That 'almost' reminds us that by deconstructing the rhetoric of the enterprise culture, we expose its precarious hold on discursive power. We create space for other discursive forces to redefine the terms of understanding and debate through which the prevailing common sense may be reconstructed. For example, enterprise concepts might be appropriated to a new collectivist discourse founded upon reworked traditional socialism, popular-democratic and other emergent cultural forms. The political and economic struggles against Thatcherism require discursive forms through which opposition and new positions can be articulated.

LIST OF SPEECHES
(given by Lord Young unless otherwise specified)

BCC: Birmingham Chamber of Commerce Speech (February 1988).
BE: 'The British Experiment'. The Fifth Mais Lecture, by Nigel Lawson, delivered 18 June 1984 (HM Treasury, Press Office).
BIM: British Institute of Management speech (16 November 1987).
BL: Barnett Lecture (11 March 1986).
BR: 'Britain Resurgent: Return to a Wealth Creating Economy.' CPS Autumn Address (Centre for Policy Studies, London, 1987).
CIA: Chemical Industries Association speech (12 November 1987).
CPS: CPS Conference speech (31 January 1986).
DM: 'The Debate on Manufacturing and Services.' The Cobden Lecture (1 November 1987).
EE: 'Enterprise and Employment', Bow Group speech (March 1985).
FR: 'The Fall and Rise of the Entrepreneur.' The Gresham Lecture (July 1984).
FRE: 'The Fall and Rise of Enterprise: New York Council on Foreign Relations' (n.d.).
LD: Lords' Debate, 24 February 1988. (Speech on motion by Lord Cledwyn of Penrhos.)

MS: Manchester Speech (14 January 1988).
NB: 'The New Britain: the Tide of Ideas from Attlee to Thatcher',
by Nigel Lawson (Centre for Policy Studies, London, 1988).
OS: 'Oxford Speech on Government Economic Policy' (28 July
1987).
PE: 'Private Enterprise for the Public Good.' LSE Industrial Policy
Seminar (2 March 1988).
PEJ: 'People, Enterprise and Jobs', NEDC 25th Anniversary (29
April 1987).
SL: Stockton Lecture (22 April 1986).

REFERENCES

Arac, J. (ed.) (1986) *Postmodernism and Politics*, Manchester: Manchester
University Press.
Eagleton, T. (1981) 'The Idealism of American Criticism', *New Left
Review* (127): 53–65.
Derrida, J. (1981) *Positions*, A. Bass (trans.) London: Athlone Press.
Norris, C. (1987) *Derrida*, London: Fontana.
Ryan, M. (1982) *Marxism and Deconstruction: A Critical Articulation*,
Baltimore and London: Johns Hopkins University Press.

Chapter Four

REFORMING THE SELF
Enterprise and the characters
of Thatcherism

PAUL HEELAS

Radical government must surely go to the heart of the matter – character reform. Political and institutional change *per se* counts for little unless it works, and this requires the commitment of those involved. So it comes as no surprise to find that reforming the self is high on the current political agenda. According to Margaret Thatcher, 'We can only build a responsible, independent community with responsible, independent people' (*Daily Telegraph*, 15 October 1988). More forcefully, it has been claimed that: 'The ultimate purpose of Thatcherism is nothing less than a revolution in British social attitudes . . . a modern capitalist society requires a climate that is vigorously competitive, not one that exudes the craven spirit of whining dependency' (Brian Walden, *Sunday Times*, 24 April 1988). And Nigel Lawson speaks of 'fighting and changing the culture and psychology of two generations . . . [which] cannot be achieved overnight . . . but let there be no doubt that this is our goal' (Lawson 1984).

The long-standing Thatcherite emphasis on institutional (market) reform to effect the rejuvenation of capitalism remains very much in force today. But as the 1980s have progressed, increasing attention has been paid to ensuring that the 'new' world of enterprise is populated by people whose self-understanding and psychological functioning is of the right kind. Arguably, a government intent on reforming attitudes, desires, values, expectations and goals must present a well-articulated, internally coherent, and psychologically plausible model to direct people to the desired end. But what we are, in fact, presented with is something rather different from this: a number of distinct 'characters', or models of the self, by no means obviously compatible with one another: the 'enterprising self' (displaying initiative and responsibility in economic production); the 'sovereign

72

consumer' (exercising freedom to satisfy its wishes); the 'active citizen' (concerned to contribute to the wellbeing of the community) and what I shall call the 'conservative self' (the bearer of traditional or Victorian values).[1]

These four characters will first be portrayed and analysed, with particular reference to their relations with one another. Do they represent different aspects of a unitary self (or coherent set of selves), or are they instead bound up with incompatible moralities? More specifically, are the enterprising self and the sovereign consumer (the pivotal modes of self-understanding of the enterprise culture) located in a different moral geography from that inhabited by the active citizen and the conservative self? This analysis of 'the characters of Thatcherism' will then provide a platform from which to reflect on their suitability as vehicles for the implementation of character reform in everyday life. Several vistas are sketched, each exploring some of the psychological and moral implications of these four models of selfhood. Their psychological plausibility, and thus effectiveness, arguably owes much to how they relate to one another, not just to their *sui generis* properties. Matters to do with their conceptual coherence are brought to bear on the psychological 'fit' between them. Is it reasonable to suppose that they add up to a scheme that can readily be adopted as a legitimate and effective form of existence, or instead that they operate in a more fragmented fashion, perhaps even helping to set in train 'habits of the heart' that deviate from what is intended?

THE CAST OF CHARACTERS

A sketch of these characters, as portrayed by their advocates, is now provided, together with brief comments on their roles. First, a picture of the 'enterprising self', provided by Norman Fowler at the launch of the Enterprise in Higher Education Initiative. The student is envisaged as 'generating and taking ideas and putting them to work; taking decisions and taking responsibility; taking considered risks; welcoming change and helping to shape it; and creating wealth . . . [all should acquire] key managerial and business competencies' (THES, 1 July 1988). In similar vein, a Manpower Services Commission document states that the student should be:

> a person who has belief in his own destiny . . . welcomes change and is not frightened of the unknown . . . sets out to influence events

. . . has powers of persuasion . . . is of good health, robust, with energy and willing to work beyond that which is specified . . . is competitive, moderated by concern for others . . . is rigorous in self-evaluation.

(TI, 28 January 1988)

More generally, presentations of this figure largely dwell on the self as the producer of goods or profit, specifying those attributes required to effect the resurgence of capitalism. It is no coincidence that the term (more exactly 'enterprise man') is closely associated with Lord Young and the Department of Trade and Industry (see Chapters One, Two and Three, this volume). A related observation is that the enterprising self is primarily spoken of in terms of opposition to modes of self-understanding (bound up with welfare institutions and bureaucratic/collectivist corporations) where the self is assumed to be dependent on others and 'weak' (in the sense of abnegating individual responsibility and initiative).

Second, the figure of the 'sovereign consumer', primarily defined in terms of a particular view of freedom. As Brian Walden puts it: 'The right supports freedom from state control which, providing everybody behaves according to conventionally established patterns, permits individuals to do as they please' (ST, 26 February 1989). The consumer is portrayed as 'sovereign', someone whose wishes and demands cannot properly be challenged; and much emphasis is placed here upon 'extending individual choice' (Michael Heseltine, DT, 7 July 1987). Accordingly, this figure is generally spoken of as opposed to that ('passive') consumer who simply accepts or receives whatever happens to be offered or provided. This is apparent in government policy concerning the main home of the so-called 'culture of dependency', welfare provision: 'The conservatives had to put greater consumer choice [and 'opportunity'] for those dependent on health, education and other welfare services at the centre of their political agenda for the 1990s, Sir Geoffrey Howe . . . said in . . . a speech outlining Tory priorities for the next decade' (reported by George Jones, DT, 28 April 1989).

Third, there is the 'active citizen', coming to the fore in Thatcher's address to the 10th Conservative Party conference and directed at 'selfish' and 'loadsamoney' accusations:

Does someone's natural desire to do well for himself, to build a better life for his family and provide opportunities for his children, does all this make him a materialist? Of course it doesn't. It makes him a decent human being, committed to his family and his community. . . . As prosperity has increased, so the fundamental generosity of our people has prompted far more personal giving. Of course, there will always be a minority whose sole concern is themselves. But those who care, and they are the great majority of us, now have the means to give. . . . The fact is that prosperity has created not the selfish society but the generous society.

(DT, 15 October 1989)

On a more personal note, an interview runs:

Mrs Thatcher wants grandson Michael to grow up in a world 'where people accept their responsibilities to others. After all you are here to use your talents and abilities, and you really only use them as part of a community'. . . . Mrs Thatcher says people cannot flower as individuals except in relation to others: 'I want my grandchildren to grow up in a world in which people recognise that they are born free, and that that is an immense privilege, and that freedom incurs responsibility to others.'

(reported by Ben Fenton, DT, 11 April 1989)

And that leading advocate of this figure, Douglas Hurd, affirms: 'We've got to say to those people doing quite well, look, there's a community to which you also belong – be an active citizen within it' (ST, 16 October 1989). Presentations of the active citizen, it should be apparent, are basically aimed at criticizing selfish individualism.

Finally, the 'conservative self', defined in terms of those 'traditional' virtues that specify how people should understand and lead their lives. This mode is often spoken of in connection with education, in the family and at school. In a relatively recent interview, it is reported,

Mrs Margaret Thatcher put herself at the head of a crusade to clean up the country, both morally and spiritually, yesterday as she became the longest-serving Prime Minister this century. . . . Thatcher said . . . that she yearned for the return of traditional values of fairness, integrity, honesty and courtesy. She was particularly worried about young people, who were 'crying out' for a code of behaviour by which they could live their lives.

(Nicholas Wood, ST, 4 January 1988)

75

Likewise, Thatcher has spoken of the 'born-again prophets of the permissive society', claiming that 'these people are the ones who blurred the distinction between right and wrong' (NOTW, 19 March 1989). As for what is 'right', pronouncements have been made concerning thrift (hence Lawson on the importance of exercising self-discipline (DT, 14 October 1989), hard work ('She stressed that restoring a "work ethic" would be a central feature of her third term in Power' writes George Jones (DT, 9 April 1988), patriotism (Thatcher affirming that: 'She would use her power to stop Europe going wrong because she could not bear to see Europe undermining and reversing the great values of freedom and democracy that it had given to the world' (DM 18 May 1989), civic responsibility (Thatcher stating that 'she saw it as her Government's business to bring a new sense of civic responsibility to daily life' (Nicholas Wood, ST, 4 January 1988) and family life ('A move to change sex education in State schools was announced by the Government . . . with the aim of "encouraging pupils to have due regard to moral considerations and the value of family life" ', reports James Wightman (DT, 3 June 1986). Here, it is clearly the permissive self that is seen as the main threat.

TENSIONS AND RESOLUTIONS

There seem to be considerable tensions between these various characters, not least between the freedom of the sovereign consumer and the disciplined (that is, anti-permissive or anti-hedonistic) morality of the conservative self; and one may begin to suspect the presence of some considerable degree of 'moral chaos'. To arrive at a more determinate picture of these tensions, the analytical scheme developed by Robert Bellah and elaborated by Steven Tipton is now employed.[2] It suggests that the Thatcherite cast of characters is informed by two distinct kinds of morality: on the one hand, what Tipton (1982: 7) calls the 'moral culture' of 'utilitarian individualism', and on the other, an 'authoritative style of ethical evaluation' (ibid: 3).

The first of these is characterized as follows:

> utilitarianism begins with the individual person as an agent seeking to satisfy his own wants or interests. Utilitarianism is quite clear about which acts are right: those that produce the greatest amount of good consequences. It is less clear about what consequences are good, usually taking wants or interests as given or self-evident in

a way that suggests notions like happiness, pleasure, or self-preservation to define what is good in itself.

Because self-interest determines right action, freedom for the utilitarian is freedom *from* restraint, freedom to pursue his own unspecified ends, whatever they might be. . . . Because the right act is one that *maximizes* good consequences, choosing the right act becomes an empirical question of accurately calculating consequences, not an evaluative question of conscientiously judging acts themselves.

(Tipton 1982: 7)

By contrast, the second kind of morality is:

oriented mainly to an authoritative moral source (God or Marx, for example). Its will is revealed to us directly or via some scripture or institution (Bible or *Kapital*, Papacy or Party), discerned by literal exegesis and by faith. An act is right because it is commanded by this authoritative source and to do it, therefore, is an act of obedience, the cardinal virtue of this ethic.

(ibid: 3)

Unlike utilitarian morality, the authoritative form identifies acts that are right or wrong independently of their good or bad consequences as judged in terms of the wishes or interests of individual agents. Further, whereas the utilitarian ethic is essentially individualistic, the authoritative is not, and is instead well able to support values of a more relational or collective nature.

It can now be suggested, as an initial hypothesis, that whereas the morality of the enterprising self and the sovereign consumer is of a broadly 'utilitarian individualistic' kind, that of the active citizen and the conservative self is by contrast 'authoritative'. Consider first the enterprising self. Tuned for production, this figure is portrayed as highly motivated and energized, competitive, ambitious, goal-setting and strongly oriented towards free market rewards; and underlying all these are the ideals of individual autonomy and independence. As Heseltine puts it: 'Wherever possible we want individuals to control, influence and determine their own destiny', and as he continues, 'the psychology of independence' is to the fore (DT, 7 July 1987). People should exercise their abilities (serving as authors of their own decisions, seizing opportunities, and so on) in order to 'help themselves' (see Thatcher (ST, 15 January 1989)). There is much talk of what should 'derive' from the individual: 'self-motivation', 'personal drive and vitality', 'self-assertion', 'self-reliance' and engaging in 'self-help' to become 'self-made'.

And the enterprising self would appear to be radically utilitarian in its individualism. Talk of freedom and the autonomous self means that 'authority' lies with the wants of the agent, who is to be allowed as much scope as possible to define what is good by reference to these (cf. Walden's '. . . the ultimate authority lies within ourselves' (ST, 11 September 1988)). And 'authority' also lies with the agent in that he or she should be responsible for working out which actions are right by calculating which of them produce the greatest amount of good consequences (cf. Walden's 'each individual must order his or her life by the guidance of his or her own intellect' (ibid)). Similar points can be made about the portrayal of the consumer, whose 'sovereignty' is couched in terms of an individualistic ethic, which endorses the open-ended satisfaction of autonomous desires.

However, in contrast to both the enterprising self and the consumer, the conservative self seems firmly set in the authoritative style of ethical evaluation, where one's own wants or interests have no 'authority'. One might be tempted to be permissive or hedonistic, but this does not mean that selfish or indulgent behaviour is justified. Such is apparent in the following summary of Kenneth Baker's speech to a fringe meeting of the General Synod of the Church of England:

> Education was one area where Church and State could agree. . . .
> There was a general belief that moral values, which had been 'undermined by those whose views became fashionable in the 1960s', could be imparted in a much better way in schools. . . .
> Even those parents who do not themselves hold religious belief know that their children need a framework of good behaviour based on a clear sense of right and wrong.
>
> (John Clare, DT, 2 February 1987)

A similar moral 'location' is indicated for the active citizen, a figure often talked about in terms of a Tory tradition, reaching back into the social reforms of the last century, and which teaches support for those who cannot help themselves. Appeal is made to traditional conservative values that are simply 'right', and which take their place alongside the other authoritative 'ultimates' of Thatcherism. Thus, during her speech to the 10th Conservative Party conference: 'The Prime Minister outlined her own vision of "social Thatcherism" in which personal effort by the individual citizen benefited the community. Freedom, she said, entailed responsibilities, first to the family then to neighbours and then to the nation' (George Jones, DT, 15 October 1988). These responsibilities (said to be 'entailed' by freedom) essentially involve duties and obligations to others, Thatcher elsewhere stating that 'When you have finished as a taxpayer, you have not finished your duty as a citizen' (cited by Peter Pallot, DT, 28 April 1989). Cf. Pallot's report of a speech made by Kenneth Baker to the Tory Bow group:

> Mrs Thatcher had given birth to the age of 'acquisitive individualism', but those who had been enriched had a strong moral duty to help the wider community, he said. 'There is another side to the coin of economic individualism. Those who succeed have obligations over and beyond that of celebrating their own success'.
>
> (ibid)

It should also be noted that the citizen's duty to others is often envisaged in terms of a more relational, less individualistic view of selfhood: recall Thatcher's 'people cannot flower as individuals except in relation to others', and Hurd's 'look, there is a community to which you also belong'.

Such portrayals, then, seem to suggest that the enterprising self and the consumer are variants of the ethic of utilitarian individualism, whilst the conservative self and the active citizen belong to the authoritative (and on occasion collectivist) mode; and clearly there are tensions between the two 'camps'. For example, the independence and authority of the individual clashes with the relational ethic of the duties of the active citizen; and whilst scorn is cast on that paradigm case of radically free consumerism, the permissive self, because it transgresses the canons embodied in the conservative figure, the freedom of the consumer is at the same time accorded sovereignty. But before such tensions can be explored further, this initial 'mapping' of the characters on to the two moralities needs to be significantly modified. The situation is more complicated than so far presented, since, as will now be shown, the portrayals of these characters often incorporate elements drawn from *both* ethics.

Thus the utilitarianism of the enterprising individual is itself couched in terms of authoritative values, including those of the market ethic. The 'ideal' enterprising self acts to obtain that highly esteemed *sui generis* 'good', namely material wealth. The freedom of the radical utilitarian is curtailed by the duty to be productive in market terms. Goals such as the desire to be an artist, an 'ivory tower' academic or a self-actualized human being are much less highly valued and are often criticized: their activities are deemed not to provide 'real' success. Indeed, the value attached to wealth creation authorizes the systematic commodification of the figure. Thus profit is the main yardstick of success as a human being; and success depends on the person functioning as a 'business', treating psychological life – 'initiative', 'personal drive', 'vitality', 'using our own loaf, using our nous' (as Thatcher sometimes puts it) – as the means for obtaining these financially measurable rewards.

But as well as being defined in terms of the market ethic, the ideal enterprising self also incorporates many of the virtues of the conservative self, such as hard work and thrift (saving to invest), thus differing from the strictly utilitarian figures, found, for example, in the film *Wall Street*.[3] And Christianity is often enlisted to sanctify this ideal version of the enterprising self, lending authority to its 'traditional' virtues as well as to the market ethic. The following illustration of the 'gospel' of prosperity is taken from Thatcher's address to the General Assembly of the Church of Scotland:

> I believe that by taking together these key elements from the Old and New Testaments, we gain: a view of the universe, a proper attitude to work, and principles to shape economic and social life.
>
> We are told we must work and use our talents to create wealth. 'If a man will not work he shall not eat', wrote St Paul to the Thessalonians. Indeed, abundance rather than poverty has a legitimacy which derives from the very nature of Creation.
>
> (quoted by Jonathan Raban 1989: 12)

An authoritative ethic also informs the ideal consumer, who must not be purely hedonistic or indulge in immoral purchases (drugs, video nasties), or in other ways transgress the duties of the conservative self and active citizen. Furthermore, the consumer is often depicted as having to acquire many of the characteristics of the ideal enterprising self. What can be called the 'responsible' (or even 'enterprising') consumer provides the key for explicating this. In contrast to the strictly sovereign consumer, whose freedom of choice means that the agent can decide to engage in forms of consumption that do not have appropriate 'pay-offs', the responsible consumer should never lose sight of his or her role as a successfully enterprising producer (or, for that matter, as an active citizen, a role that often requires giving to others rather than spending entirely on oneself).

Many portrayals of the responsible consumer suggest that such people thrive when they are given the opportunity to buy goods and services that had previously been supplied by the state (health provision and council houses, for example). Although these opportunities enhance consumer sovereignty, they also involve weighty responsibilities. The consumer has to choose carefully, for the financial (etc.) penalties for making the wrong choice are considerable. The consumer's freedom is curtailed by having to make carefully calculated decisions, exercising discipline and self-restraint, in order to maximize the benefits provided by ownership of council houses or similar new options (cf. Walden's article 'A moral road, built of bricks and mortar', and his view that 'capitalism is not going to be entrenched by lectures on morality, but by the diffusion of home ownership' (ST, 29 May 1988)). And the consumer also becomes more enterprising because he or she has been freed from the dependency culture. Thus, writing of 'A new sense of responsibility', Mick Brown refers to 'the individual taking responsibility for himself, or herself, in all areas of life – health, education, housing – rather than relying on the offices of the state' (ST, 27 December 1987); and Thatcher, in her 10th Conservative Party conference speech, having made her 'We can only build a responsible, independent community with responsible, independent people' point, continues: 'That is why Conservative policies have given more of them the chance to buy homes, build up capital and acquire shares in their companies' (DT, 15 October 1988).

Having seen how the authoritative mode 'enters into' the two otherwise most obviously utilitarian characters, what of the converse possibility? In most respects, the authoritative ethic of the conservative self remains 'uncontaminated' by the utilitarian. However, the active citizen is sometimes portrayed in ways that suggest a utilitarian rationale. It is seen as displaying the 'natural' tendency of individuals to want to benefit others, so that the authoritative appeal to duty prescribes something consonant with, indeed generated by, utilitarian individualism. Referring again to Thatcher's speech to the 10th Party Conference, her observations on 'social Thatcherism' include the claim, 'The truth is that what we are actually encouraging is the best in human nature' (as reported by William Weekes et al., DT, 15 October 1988). Generosity and the sense of having responsibilities for others naturally flow from the person freed from the shackles of the state. Her claim, in the same speech, that 'as prosperity has increased, so the fundamental generosity of our people has prompted far more personal giving', has already been noted; and one can also think of the assertion in the 1979 Government Manifesto that: 'We want to work with the grain of human nature, helping people to help themselves – and others'. This is an (optimistic) version of the utilitarian ethic: the wants and interests that agents seek to satisfy remain their 'own', but include the wants and interests of the (deserving) other.[4] Individualistic virtues do not clash with wanting to help others, Thatcher speaking of both in the same breath as when she talks of the 'virtues of self-reliance, personal responsibility, good neighbourliness, and generosity' (cited by Simon Jenkins, ST, 15 January 1985).

The overall picture that emerges, then, is one in which there is a marked tendency for the two, seemingly contradictory, moral cultures to be fused (or at least combined) in each of the characters, and in such a way that each of them 'takes on' some of the features of the others. There is thus some measure of conceptual rhyme and reason about the corpus; and this is especially so in what is arguably its central figure, the (ideal) enterprising self – a synthesis of the enterprising producer and the (responsible) consumer, incorporating much of what it is to be an active citizen, and informed by many of the values of the conservative self. The authoritative market ethic means that other, potentially antithetical utilitarian tendencies are held in check, but without eliminating the individualism of this ethic; or again, the active citizen is sometimes presented as the natural outcome of the ideal enterprising self, thus providing further support for a character that already has authoritative status.

However, these kinds of 'tension-resolution' themselves pave the way for tensions *within* the characters. Attention was drawn earlier to differences *between* the figures, deriving from Thatcherite emphasis on both the utilitarian and the authoritative. But none of the resolutions can incorporate the more radical 'poles' of the two ethics, and the outcome of this inability is that presentations of the various figures themselves are divided. Thus the enterprising self and the consumer are presented either in the language of that radical individualism so important to Thatcherite discourse, or in the language of an authoritative market ethic and conservative values; portrayals of the enterprising self as autonomous run alongside others that stress the discipline of enterprise and other authoritative virtues; the consumer is informed by two sets of values, one emphasizing its sovereignty, the other attaching importance to the exercise of responsibility and moral constraint; and the active citizen is portrayed sometimes in the terms of an (optimistic) utilitarian individualism, at other times in the non-individualistic mode of an authoritative relational ethic. 'Look, there is a community to which you belong' is at some remove from talk of the 'generosity' and 'responsibility' that flow naturally from the free self.

IMPLICATIONS FOR EVERYDAY LIFE

Turning now from conceptual representations to the 'realities' of every-day life, we need to consider whether and how far the kinds of tensions that have emerged from the preceding analysis are likely to hinder the Thatcherite goal of character reform. It might, of course, be argued that there is no great problem here: the cast of characters is 'effective' precisely because different figures can be called into play when the need for them arises. Thus the role of the enterprising self is to 'turn the self around', to help do the same for the economy; but when it becomes apparent that a counterweight is required to handle the excesses of the radical individualism thereby generated, the active citizen and the corpus of sanctified authoritative virtues come into prominence (witness Thatcher's recent speech at the City of London's Guildhall during which she asserted, in Calvinistic fashion, that 'Our job is to find constraints' to handle 'the real problems of human nature', problems that are blamed for the fact that increased prosperity has failed to eradicate social evils (DT, 27 September 1989)).[5]

Yet, the adoption in practice of any particular element in this variegated and tension-laden corpus seems likely to contribute to the erosion of others. It certainly appears to be the case that the more effective the authoritative mode is in holding permissiveness and consumer indulgence in check, the less plausible will the idea of individual sovereignty seem to people. Indeed, it might well be argued that 'freedom from state control' actually involves a kind of 'freedom' that is itself to be nurtured or engineered by the state. The agenda is thus for a form of 'sovereignty' that is heavily qualified by the authoritative ethic of a government that is not happy with populism until it is of the right kind. Hence the exercise of centralized authority, in any number of 'control mode' attempts at social and cultural engineering-cum-character reform, to create the kind of person who can be trusted to be 'free'. Talk of 'cutting back the state's involve-ment in everyday life' clearly loses much of its force.

This problem of 'erosion' is one that arises especially for the ideal enterprising self. To appreciate the point, it is important to bear in mind that this figure should serve to combat the excesses of radical utilitarian individualism. Left to its own devices, the utilitarian mode of being is fraught with danger. Anarchical desires are only too likely to be unleashed if valued ends and means are determined by reference to desire satisfaction alone.[6] People should not exercise their consumer sovereignty to engage in grossly hedonistic or permissive activities, for among other things rampant consumerism would threaten the viability of 'enterprise Britain', the wrong ('born to shop') kind of person fuelling the credit card boom, which contributes to imports and so to the balance-of-payments problem. Likewise, people should not take advantage of their freedom by diverting their productive energies towards activities that do not have commodifiable outcomes. By its fusion of the utilitarian with the authoritative, the ideal enterprising self is intended to ensure that people are duty-bound to perform on the right (economically productive) lines and are responsible, disciplined consumers. However, it is likely that 'cracks' that are 'masked' in public representations of the figure are exposed (indeed highlighted) and exploited in everyday life. Rhetorical attempts to handle incoherence founder in the face of psychological and sociocultural realities; and the goal of cathecting enterprising selves to authoritative values involves an implausible psychomoral dynamic.

The appeal exercised by the more individualistic aspects of Thatcherite rhetoric, together with a wide range of sociocultural factors, means that people are likely to become 'enterprising' in the wrong sort of way, acquiring a hedonistic outlook. Thus few are likely to be happy living in the ethos of enterprise whilst holding 'Protestant ethic' attitudes in their roles as producers and consumers. People are told that enterprise must be rewarded, but also that pay demands should be kept to a minimum. Talk of personal drive and ambition, of personal success, of 'enriching the individual', of the 'self-made' person, and of the freedom of the consumer – in general, talk of the agent as someone who should function in individualistic fashion to compete in the market – can readily encourage people to take advantage of their 'freedom' to indulge in self-obsessed ambition and greed. Here lies the self consumed with materialistic aspirations, and happy to build up debts instead of saving and investing. Authoritative values thereby lose their credibility, with the exception, that is, of those (specifically the status accorded wealth creation) that have contributed to this erosion.

Further, many sociocultural factors could be operating to 'discredit' the ideal enterprising self. The desire-stimulating effects of advertisements and indeed the whole ideology of progress ('always wanting more') fuel utilitarian aspirations; institutional (enterprise) reforms result in an emphasis on the bait of profit, which undermines, for example, the value attached to thrift; the demolition of 'civil society', designed to encourage enterprise, is contributing to a narrow form of self-interest; and so on. In short, factors deriving from the nature of life primarily defined in terms of enterprise capitalism do not help to sustain the ideal character of enterprise itself. And there may well be many like the entrepreneur who, we are told, believes that 'Margaret Thatcher is simply the deliverer, the woman who has enabled a Welsh miner's son to make it big, the woman who has saved Coventry from slump', but who 'doesn't go along with Margaret Thatcher's taste for Victorian morality' (TG, 24 May 1989).

Enterprising individuals of this kind are unlikely to make good active citizens. Active citizenship is presented in the rhetoric as generated by the increased prosperity of the person who has the 'natural desire to do well for himself'. But what is much more likely is that enterprise capitalism undermines active citizenship. Why should those who live their lives as 'businesses', who have taken on board the doctrine of the sovereign consumer, who are intent on seizing the 'chance of bettering themselves' (Thatcher, DT, 15 October 1989) and who have adopted what is likely to be a utilitarian work ethic be motivated to contribute to the public good? It is implausible to believe, for example, that many of those who have been 'rewarded' for their enterprise by the 1988 budget will sacrifice their reward to help those in need; or that someone who has been operating in the 'self-driven' mode of possessive or 'acquisitive individualism' (a term sometimes used by government ministers) should suddenly shift gear and start giving, in largely non-competitive spirit, to others – especially as this will diminish the resources required for successful competition.[7] Furthermore, enterprise-minded people might well be expected to suppose that charitable donations are themselves counterproductive, encouraging the addiction of dependency. Finally, practice of an individualistic self-ethic is likely to undermine the psychological valiancy of the relational, 'other directed', moral fabric that is sometimes employed to ground the active citizen. A self primarily defined in terms of market standards does not easily accept the influence of values that transcend the marketplace – especially when the institutions of 'civil society' which, it may be claimed, have traditionally served to commit people to public life, have themselves been eroded in the name of freedom (cf. Nicholas Boyle 1988).

It is sometimes claimed that capitalism generates permissiveness but requires discipline (both to be economically effective and socially beneficial): more exactly, that individualistic and intensified capitalism tends to generate problematic (selfish and so forth) personal qualities, which need to be handled by authoritative virtues, but that these virtues are themselves undermined by the value attached to self-gratification.[8] If this is so, then the 'vehicle' provided by the ideal enterprising self is unlikely to be making a significant contribution to the resolution of the 'cultural contradiction' between the paths provided by utilitarian and authoritative moralities. What suits the Prime Minister, brought up in the milieu of enterprising Methodism, and that Protestant ethic that blesses those who work hard at wealth creation whilst demanding responsibility and self-discipline, might well not suit the values and expectations of the majority.

However, the scenarios that have been presented here, including the claims embedded in Thatcherite rhetoric, have ultimately to be assessed in terms of how the character models are actually faring in the everyday world. It is not yet possible to do this in a satisfactory fashion: the available evidence is fragmentary and inconclusive. Thus on the one hand, there are indications that many people are becoming the 'wrong' kind of (simply utilitarian) enterprising selves and consumers (credit runs at a record level, and personal savings at the lowest for forty years; pay requests run ahead of inflation; the increasingly prosperous 24–45 age bracket is giving considerably less to charity than ten years ago); whilst on the other hand there are indications of a shift from permissiveness to traditional values (Stephen Harding 1988). Research is thus required to address a wide range of issues. We need to establish the extent to which the ideal enterprising self has taken root, and assaults on rival modes of selfhood have been successful. We need to explore the role played by sociocultural factors in encouraging or hindering character reform. We need to know whether and in what ways the cast of characters is reinterpreted, distorted, transformed or exploited when put to work in particular settings (e.g. the 'Enterprise in Higher Education Initiative'). Thus, one priority is research on the 'lived' or 'practical' moralities of life in Thatcher's Britain, if we are to understand, for example, what happens when enterprise reforms are introduced in institutions where rival modes of selfhood are entrenched, or how particular figures actually operate in every-day life (for example, the enterprising self in relation to active citizenship).[9]

Looking to the future, assessments of the effects of enterprise-oriented character reform will have to attend to the possibility that 'crudely' utilitarian selfhood may come increasingly to erode itself. For although the functional, utility-laden design of this mode of identity may appear to exalt the individual, it actually places severe limits on what it is to be human. Those who constitute themselves in terms of their consumer activities (the self defined by its accessories) and their productive endeavours (the self defined by working life) may thus be prompted to seek other modes of being. In contrast to the central Thatcherite assumption that people essentially seek self-fulfilment and enrichment through materialistic consumption and production, it may increasingly be felt that 'life is too rich to be conducted as a business'. The historical record (the Romantic movement, the 1960s sensibility) of similar reactions to 'the reduction of being to efficient functioning' (Boyle 1988: 321), together with indications that values are already changing (the Green movement, the decline of the 'value' of the City) suggest that the crudely utilitarian enterprising self may not fare so well in the decade to come.

If this were so, then the authoritative virtues incorporated by the ideal enterprising self might well be less threatened by hedonistic individualism. Yet for this figure to flourish, wealth creation and the Protestant ethic have to be given an authoritative backing. It remains to be seen whether evolving configurations of cultural values will actually lend support to the dynamic implied by Thatcher's assertion that 'it is not the creation of wealth that is wrong but love of money for its own sake' (see Raban 1989: 13). But I doubt it: so long as wealth creation retains its hold, and in the absence of suitably fashioned commitments, 'love of money' and self-aggrandizement are more likely outcomes. And to the extent that wealth creation loses its hold, so too will the ideal enterprising self.

NOTES

1 The term 'character' is employed in Alasdair MacIntyre's sense:

> A *character* is an object of regard by the members of the culture generally or by some significant segment of them. He furnishes them with a cultural and moral ideal. Hence the demand is that

. . . role and personality be fused. Social type and psychological type are required to coincide. The *character* morally legitimates a mode of social existence.

(MacIntyre 1985: 28); cf. Bellah *et al.*'s usage (1985)

The majority of the character portrayals used in this paper are taken from newspapers broadly sympathetic to Thatcherism. Newspapers are referred to as follows: DM (*Daily Mail*); DT (*Daily Telegraph*); NOTW (*News of the World*); ST (*Sunday Times*); THES (*Times Higher Educational Supplement*); TG (The *Guardian*); TI (The *Independent*).

2 Drawing on moral philosophy, the scheme addresses cultural values or moral configurations, and modes of selfhood. In particular, it provides a way of identifying the moral dynamics embedded in language and practice, including tensions between moralities and attempts to resolve them. Emile Durkheim (especially 1973) is an important precursor of this approach; see also Talcott Parsons, including his analysis of the utilitarian system (Parsons 1968: 51–60; 87–125).

3 The 'classic' speech of this film runs:

It's all about results kid, and the rest is simply conversation. . . . Greed, for lack of a better word, is good; greed is right; greed works; greed evolved cuts through and captures the essence of the evolutionary spirit. Greed in all of its forms, greed for life, money, for love, knowledge, has marked the upward surge of mankind and greed, you mark my words, will not only save the paper but that other malfunctioning corporation, the USA.

For more portrayals of the 'wrong' enterprising self, see Lewis Lapham (1989).

4 Another theme, related to this, is that active citizenship is generated by what Lord Young has called 'enterprise in the community'. This means that people acquire a vested interest to be socially responsible. As Heseltine puts it:

The Government's commitment to the stress areas is to push the frontiers of personal responsibility ever further into the fabric of society. . . . In extending individual choice . . . council tenants are to be encouraged to take responsibility for the management of their own estates directly or through housing associations, building societies, or similar bodies.

(DT, 7 July 1987)

5 Paddy Ashdown's claim that:

It is the weaknesses of the Thatcherite position that lie at the root of the renewed interest in citizenship. Conservative interest arose out of the charge that the new right had ushered in a selfish and divisive society concerned only with personal success. Douglas Hurd's 'active citizen' was an acknowledgement of a human deficiency in the logic of where his leader was taking him.

(DT, 6 January 1989)

6 In terms of sociological theory, the functional plausibility of locating
   enterprise in an authoritative setting is supported by those who argue
   that radical utilitarian individualism does not provide a basis for social
   life. As Durkheim puts it:

   It is not hard, in effect, to denounce as an ideal without grandeur
   that narrow commercialism which reduces society to nothing more
   than a vast apparatus of production and exchange, and it is only
   too clear that all social life would be impossible if there did not
   exist interests superior to the interests of individuals.

   (Durkheim, 1973: 2)

   Cf. Parsons on the 'problem of order', which arises when ends are
   'random' because 'the good is simply that which any man desires'
   (Parsons 1968: 60, 89).
7 Here is someone who has bought a council house and seems far from
   being a responsible consumer or active citizen:

   'It's no use sitting on your backside, is it? Everyone's selfish,
   aren't they? No one needs to be out of work, do they? An
   Englishman's home is his castle!' The former council house, now
   the property of Trevor and Jackie Harvey, is a virtuous microcosm
   of Thatcherism.

   (ST, 30 April 1989)

8 Cf. Weber's argument that capitalism has undermined the
   authoritative ethic and associated mode of selfhood to which it owed
   so much (Weber 1985: see especially p. 175 for a vivid illustration
   concerning John Wesley). The thesis has more recently been advanced
   by Daniel Bell (1979).
9 Robert Jackall's *Moral Mazes* (1988) provides one of the best examples
   of the study of practical moralities, attending to the (decidedly non-
   enterprising) 'occupational ethics' of managers in three large USA
   companies.

REFERENCES

Bell, D. (1979) *The Cultural Contradictions of Capitalism*, London:
   Heinemann.
Bellah, R., Madsen, R., Sullivan, W., Swidler, A. and Tipton, S.
   (1985) *Habits of the Heart*, London: University of California Press.
Boyle, N. (1988) 'Understanding Thatcherism', *New Blackfriars*,
   July/August, pp. 307–24.
Durkheim, E. (1973) 'Individualism and the intellectuals' in R. Bellah
   (ed.) *Emile Durkheim on Morality and Society*, London: University of
   Chicago Press.
Harding, S. (1988) 'Trends in permissiveness' in R. Jowell, S.
   Witherspoon and L. Booth (eds) *British Social Attitudes, the 5th Report*,
   Aldershot: Gower.

Jackall, R. (1988) *Moral Mazes*, Oxford: Oxford University Press.

Lapham, L. (1989) *Money & Class in America*, London: Picador.

Lawson, N. (1984) 'The British Experiment', *The Fifth Mais Lecture*, London: H M Treasury.

MacIntyre, A. (1985) *After Virtue*, London: Duckworth.

Parsons, T. (1968) *The Structure of Social Action*, London: Collier-Macmillan.

Raban, J. (1989) *God, Man and Mrs Thatcher*, London: Chatto & Windus.

Tipton, S. (1982) *Getting Saved from the Sixties*, London: University of California Press.

Weber, M. (1985) *The Protestant Ethic and the Spirit of Capitalism*, London: Unwin.

Part Two

ENTERPRISE CULTURE IN DIFFERENT CONTEXTS

The chapters in this section take the discussion of enterprise culture beyond its specifically British political context. They examine the similarities and differences between the British case and analogous phenomena in other countries, and explore some of the broader developments now affecting many societies which may provide a basis for the emergence of 'enterprise cultures'.

Crawshaw discusses France in the 1980s, arguing that one can find there a form of enterprise culture whose characteristics are related both to the socialist politics of the Mitterrand Government, and to other aspects of its political history and culture. He focuses especially on French management schools, and outlines a sociolinguistic analysis of the representations of enterprise in some of their promotional literature.

Ray considers the very different situation of Hungary where, amidst the current political ferment, a radical programme of 'marketization' of the economy is beginning to take shape. He examines critically the tendency of Hungarian intellectuals to associate this programme with the development of 'civil society' and political freedom, and also points to the likely consequences of the economy's exposure to international capital.

Schwengel analyses the similarities and differences between British 'enterprise culture' and West German *Kulturgesellschaft* – literally 'culture-society', but more specifically a vision of (post-industrial) society in which a pluralistic cultural sphere becomes increasingly significant as the basis for expressing and resolving the choices and uncertainties presented by contemporary forms of modernization. He argues that enterprise culture and *Kulturgesellschaft* can be seen as alternative responses to a number of common problems faced by western societies.

Finally, Bagguley examines the theoretical literature on 'post-Fordism', addressing the question of how far the kinds of changes in the organization of production depicted there give credibility to the idea of an enterprise culture. He identifies several distinct theoretical schools, and argues that they provide different answers to this question, and suggest politically divergent conceptions of enterprise culture.

Chapter Five

ENTERPRISE CULTURE AND MANAGEMENT EDUCATION IN FRANCE

Sociolinguistic perspectives

ROBERT CRAWSHAW

In 1985, a visitor to the Ecole Supérieure de Commerce de Lyon would have been assailed by stickers featuring the simple statement '*J'aime réussir*' (I love success), the word '*aime*' being replaced by the universal red heart. A centre page spread of the magazine *L'Etudiant* of the same date features the slogan: '*En 1985, adoptez le look grenoblois de la réussite.* In a slightly different vein, Diana Pinto cites the example of metro advertisements: 'that show young men saying, "*J'abandonne les boîtes pour créer la mienne*", a play on words meaning: "I'm giving up nightclubs to start my own business"' (Pinto 1987: 226). The key words that abound in the French commercial and educational journals of the mid-80s carry the same simple and endlessly reiterated messages: passion, energy, success, innovation, competition, ambition and willpower. These direct invocations testify to a flourishing enterprise culture that many academic and journalistic commentators see as one of the most striking and paradoxical features of the Socialist government of France between 1981 and 1986. Indeed, in many respects, the outspokenness of the language and images associated with enterprise in the France of the 1980s goes far beyond that of their equivalents in Britain, and while that effect may partly be dismissed as strident symbolism, the outlook it expresses is underpinned by institutions whose entrepreneurial focus has, in certain cases, been much sharper than in this country.

This reality would appear to belie the assertion that the ideology of enterprise is necessarily a product of right-wing governments and perhaps to diminish the argument that the growth of enterprise culture in the UK is wholly the product of Thatcherism. It is not inconceivable that a cultural shift similar to the one which took place in Britain in the 1980s would have made itself felt just as strongly if a centre-left party had been in power. In this chapter, I would like first, to review in broad outline some of the political and economic factors underlying the French paradox; next, to consider the distinctive and committed way in which the higher education system in France both anticipated and promoted the growth of enterprise culture; finally, to analyse a limited sample of the language of educational promotion through which the beliefs and myths of entrepreneurship have been propounded. In so doing, my aim is to evoke a climate and illustrate a process.[1]

THE SOCIOECONOMIC BACKGROUND[2]

The Socialist government that was elected in 1981 came to power on a 'pink tide'. Despite the relatively limited success of the left in the first ballot of the presidential election, the extensive transfer of votes to François Mitterrand in the second round gave the new president a majority that was consolidated by the parliamentary elections in which the left gained 54 per cent of the vote. In the euphoria of the next few months, the new government embarked on a substantial programme of nationalization, and introduced, over the following two years, a system of wage increases combined with taxation and company regulations designed to redistribute income and stimulate consumer demand. Investment derived from tax revenue was directed primarily towards large public enterprises and government research projects. The ethos that accompanied these rapidly implemented reforms was one based on 'citizenship' and 'participation' in a collective project. It was marked by radical idealism and carried through by a strong *volontariste* government. The ideology that underpinned the government's policies was based on a tradition of hostility towards the *patronat*, and, in its more extreme manifestations, questioned the very legitimacy of private enterprise: 'that long-standing and unresolved malady in French life' (Berger 1987: 191) for which nationalization was presented as the only cure.

This enthusiastic experiment in reflation was accompanied by a state-centred programme of cultural redefinition and ideological 'triumphalism', whose certainties ran counter to the pluralism and individuality associated with enterprise. It was not long before an intelligentsia wary of universal panaceas and suspicious of Soviet-style cultural totalitarianism began to protest against the 'fusion of culture with national grandeur' (Pinto 1987: 221), which was accompanied by state intervention in publishing and the media. This opposition was expressed even more strongly in the economic sphere (e.g. Massenet 1983). Finally, after two refreshing but increasingly uneasy years, the growing number of bankruptcies, the rise in unemployment, the substantial trade deficit and the depletion of foreign reserves leading to three successive devaluations of the franc, forced Mitterrand in 1983 to opt for a policy of deflation more in line with those of other western industrial societies, notably Britain and the USA.

It would be simplistic to view the development of an 'enterprise culture' in France as a product only of the 'post-1983 phase' of the Socialist government's term of office. It was during this latter period, under the prime ministership of Laurent Fabius, that the French government sought to inject new life into the flagging French economy by promoting the values and aspirations of individual initiative and entrepreneurial opportunity. However, there had been strong lines of development in French society during the previous decade that did not materialize to the same extent in Britain and had already encouraged the growth of a 'management class'. The values of many of the younger members of this group, the products of late 1960s and early 1970s, were far from opposed to the ideals of the socialist experiment. Indeed, it was partly their votes that formed the basis of the 1981 majority. Many embraced the left's challenge to traditional corporatism, privilege and educational elitism and were ready to welcome a change from the patronizing liberalism of Giscard d'Estaing.

The image of Giscard d'Estaing as a reformer had largely become tarnished by 1981, and his presidency was ultimately viewed as one in which the power of the administrative elite became reinforced rather than diminished in favour of a more 'enterprise driven' economy. None the less, the sentiments expressed in his book *Démocratie Française* (Giscard d'Estaing 1976) had been those of a 'new liberalism' in which the values of the free economy would be preserved by stimulating individuals' 'right to take initiative' and by educational measures designed to counteract endemic French 'scepticism' towards the market. This was not enterprise '*à la* Thatcher', although Giscard emphasized a belief in the family as a core social unit; the then President was at pains to disassociate his 'modern' philosophy of government based on participation and loyalty to society from the 'traditional' free market values with which post-1979 Conservative Britain has since been identified.

As an instrument of Giscard d'Estaing's political philosophy, the pugnacious minister, Alice Saunier-Seité, pushed through a number of educational reforms after 1974 that obliged universities to be more accountable to the demands of business. Courses should be 'professionalized', university education should be more responsive to the needs of the outside world. At a time when little was being done in a Britain riven by the trauma of the miners' strike and the reversion to Wilson-style socialism, a significant effort was made by the French government to infuse the post-1968 generation of university students with a spirit of enterprise founded on realism and a sense of social responsibility. Unfortunately, as far as the universities were concerned, these political initiatives met with only limited success. Despite the existence since the late 1950s of the university-based *Instituts d'Administration des Entreprises* (IAE), which in 1977 produced as many as 1,500 graduates (Menissez 1979), and the creation in 1974 of specialist postgraduate programmes in management related disciplines (DESS), the '*jeune cadre dynamique et joyeux*' (the dynamic, carefree young executive) represented more an object of satire than a model to be emulated. The structures and attitudes prevalent in universities remained essentially unchanged: the growth of enterprise culture continued to be subordinated to the intellectual quest for personal and political autonomy that had been inherited from the 1960s.

The same was not true, however, of the burgeoning private sector of French higher education. This expanded rapidly during the 1970s as a consequence of dissatisfaction with the sluggishness and over-crowding of the university system. Established mainly during the 1960s (in some cases much earlier) and generally run by regional Chambers of Commerce, the provincial *Ecoles Supérieures de Commerce et d'Administration des Entreprises* (ESCAE) limited the entry of growing numbers of applicants by means of increasingly competitive examinations. At the same time, a small number of schools recognized as having the status of *Grandes Ecoles de Commerce* maintained their distinctiveness from the ESCAE by forming a consortium (*Chapitre*) with common entrance examinations and certain prescribed features of the curriculum. Led by an 'inner circle' composed of the three leading Parisian schools (HEC, ESSEC, ESCP) and the Ecole Supérieure de Commerce de Lyon, the *Grandes Ecoles de Commerce* sought to rival in status and academic excellence the elite state-run schools of engineering, electronic science, mining, agriculture, political administration, arts and letters. Thus the 1970s saw the reinforcement of an inherently hierarchical, highly selective system of management education that, by

96

1977, was producing more than 2,000 graduates annually and promoting an ethos founded on professionalism, competitiveness, ambition and the desire for material prosperity.

Despite the increasing pressure on admission, the private schools still only catered for a limited group of students consisting mainly of the sons and daughters of the *haute bourgeoisie*, or, in the case of the ESCAE, of the regional 'managerial class'. However, since 1966, the state-run *Instituts Universitaires de Technologie* (IUT) had also offered training in general and specialist management skills . . . but to a wider public. After a hesitant start, the increasing competition in the 1970s for places at the IUTs due to the career opportunities in middle management to which they gave access, created a paradoxical cultural climate. In these vocationally oriented schools, students from working- and lower middle-class families found themselves unconsciously mixing socialist idioms with the metaphors of a capitalist culture, which held the key to their own futures. Moreover, by the mid-1970s, the social composition of IUT students was changing. Rather than simply providing access to the universities, or otherwise to a professional training regarded as practical and therefore inferior, IUTs were fast becoming the universities' rivals. Their selective entry enhanced their prestige to such an extent that for students who, 10 years previously, would have regarded university as their natural educational avenue after the *baccalauréat*, the IUTs came to represent a respectable alternative to a *Grande Ecole* or ESCAE. In 1977 alone, graduates from the IUT numbered more than 6,000 (Menissez 1979). It was in the atmosphere of '*embourgeoisement*', fostered by these intensive two-year programmes, that many of the managers of the 1980s formed their beliefs and attitudes. For young people living in the shadow of the *crise*, socialist beliefs and entrepreneurial values were far from irreconcilable.

The Socialist government of 1981 therefore came to power against an educational background that was in part already attuned to the needs of an enterprise–driven economy. Indeed, despite its commitment to a radical programme of central planning, nationalization and reflation, the new administration made a number of statements that demonstrated its support for entrepreneurship. Private enterprise, it was argued, should flourish under an umbrella of state ownership. In a letter of exhortation written in February 1982 to the newly appointed chief executives of the nationalized industries (cited in Béaud 1985), the then Minister for Research and Industry, Jean-Pierre

Chévénement, reminded them that their 'entrepreneurial capacity would be a major element in enabling the state to achieve its principal objectives'. Above all, they should pursue 'economic efficiency' and 'competitiveness'. While creating more jobs, they should focus on modernization and export. Human relations (*relations sociales*) are of course referred to in the document, but only in the penultimate paragraph. Alain Gomez, the president of Thomson, expressed the point more bluntly in an interview in May 1982 with *L'Expansion*:

> To be a supporter of left-wing policies means having a particular view as to how national wealth should be shared out. But this has no bearing on the steps which have to be taken in order to produce that wealth.
>
> (Béaud 1985)

Already, in May 1981, President Mitterrand himself had been careful to emphasize the complementary relationship that should exist between the state and the business community. As he told an audience of 4,000 senior managers, France needed 'firms which were strong and vital'; the only way out of the economic crisis would be to infuse the nation as a whole with a 'formidable spirit of enterprise' (ibid).

Such verbal palliatives did not, of course, stifle the bitter recriminations of industrialists and right-wing academics against what they saw as the undermining of the French economy (e.g. Massenet 1983). The measures to which they were particularly opposed were price controls, increased social security costs for companies and the state's monitoring of redundancies (*Autorisations de Licenciement*). As they saw it, these policies placed industry in a straitjacket and could only encourage what Bertrand Jacquillat called 'the profound and insidious erosion produced by the combined effects of inflation and taxation' (Jacquillat 1983: 183). To rigorous critics such as these, the Socialists' appeal to collective enterprise was no consolation. It was merely confused rhetoric that demonstrated the inherent contradictions and incoherence of the government's policies.

But however well-founded and carefully researched these criticisms might have been, they could not overlook the fact that the Socialists had taken a number of substantive steps to stimulate industrial regeneration during the period 1981–83. By 1983, financial aid to industry was double what it had been in 1980. Particular emphasis had been given to export and research and development (mainly in the form of low-interest loans and tax relief linked to improved efficiency, energy conservation and waste disposal). Further support was provided for technological innovation, and, last but not least, enterprise creation schemes, which formed part of regional develop-ment plans. Such macro-economic initiatives did not in themselves represent the inculcation of cultural values. However, they allowed entrepreneurs, particularly the owners of small and medium enter-prises (PMEs) who had an instinctive belief in the moral legitimacy of the Socialists' political objectives, to survive the economic pressures of the early 1980s and to buttress themselves against the mounting tide of anti-government opinion.

Whatever contradictions may have predominated in the first two and a half years of the Socialists' period in office, these were largely swept aside in 1983 by the government's wholesale commitment to a policy of austerity. This commitment was combined with a shift away from state intervention in business. The government of Laurent Fabius (1983–6) sought actively to promote the role of the individual as the mainspring of economic development. In France, as in the United Kingdom, the cult of the entrepreneur very quickly gained ground as an identifiable social phenomenon. According to Suzanne Berger: 'The notion of entrepreneurship as creative invention and romantic adventure is at the heart of much media treatment of [French] firms in the eighties and becomes an important component in the Socialist discourse on enterprises after 1983' (Berger 1987: 191).

In order to minimize the loss of credibility that this U-turn neces-sarily entailed for the government, ministers attempted to differen-tiate between their own definition of 'enterprise culture' (*La culture d'entreprise*) and traditional *libéralisme* – that is the essentially right-wing, free market policies of *laissez-faire*. For the Socialists, enterprise culture meant respect for the individual's freedom to innovate, compete, take risks. Turning right-wing rhetoric on its head, individual enterprise was presented almost as a 'human right' that the Socialist government was seeking to protect against the simultaneous threats of multinational corporations and state bureaucracy.

This exercise in political conjuring was well illustrated in Pierre Bérégovoy's December 1984 interview with *Le Nouvel Economiste*. As Socialist Minister of Finance, he was replying to the criticism that he was 'provoking the left' by using the word *libéralisme* to describe his policies:

I did not say *libéralisme*, I said *liberté*! Economic liberalism has acted primarily as a screen to protect monopolies and has caused the public good to be subordinated to private interest. In practice, the pseudo-liberals have introduced more and more regulations and controls which have stifled economic growth. Today, their only objective is to safeguard or re-establish the privileges of a bygone age. I believe in competition, innovation and initiative; less paperwork and more freedom, more authority and less bureaucracy. What matters today is the will to win. To be successful you have to be bold. That's the state of mind which I want to encourage, even though the taste for risk-taking may not be to everyone's liking.

(*Le Nouvel Economiste* no. 470, 24 December 1984: 64–5)

By May 1986, in a special number celebrating 12 months of existence, the magazine *L'Entreprise*, typical of a whole range of similar weekly or monthly journals that sprang up about this period, describes France as being in the grip of enterprise mania (*entreprenomanie*). There had been 3,000 applications to appear on the television programme 'Ambitions'; 100,000 founders of new firms had been identified in 1985; and in response to a questionnaire, 86 per cent of the readership had cited '*l'esprit d'entreprise*' as their principal personal attribute (*L'Entreprise* no. 12, May 1986; 110). Freed of its political overtones, French enterprise culture had evidently become a collective psychological phenomenon, a question of attitude in which economic survival was the potential product of individual initiative. As Yvon Gattaz, President of the *Confédération Nationale du Patronat Français* (CNPF) and Socialist sympathizer, had written in 1983:

> The owner of a company is a citizen and so is the firm, even though it does not vote. It participates directly in economic and social life, indeed it is the principal actor in it. Our private companies support most of the French population and this activity gives them civic rights and duties.

(cit, Berger 1987: 191–2)

This was as much an incitement to the individual citizen to engage in enterprise as it was to the company to develop a sense of moral commitment to the welfare of its employees and that of society as a whole. For Gattaz, risk-taking and competition were not just individual attributes, they were social responsibilities. By the time the right regained power in the legislative elections in 1986, self-interest and the interest of the state had become symbiotic.

LANGUAGE AND CULTURAL CHANGE

Clearly, language is not merely a reflection of cultural change. It also promotes it. In so far as linguistic messages have a communicative function, they may be expected to a greater or lesser extent to affect the outlook, attitude or state of knowledge of the person or group to whom they are addressed. The relationship between culture and language is therefore interdependent, dynamic and constantly changing. The context in which an act of communication takes place may be describable in terms of the behavioural norms of a given community. Indeed, such reiterated behavioural patterns are at one level the criteria according to which a culture is most readily identifiable; yet despite these superficial indicators, it is hardly surprising that it has not yet proved possible to produce a model, taxonomy or 'situational matrix' capable of representing the culture of a particular social group, let alone the aggregation of disparate communities that make up a nation.[3]

It remains, none the less, one of the principal tasks of sociolinguists to select and analyse samples of language that both illustrate and contribute to the process of social and cultural change. For the language sample or 'text' to be revealing, it is important, for the reasons just described, that it typify a communicative 'act' that is recurrent and therefore 'significant' as a cultural 'fragment'. It should also be definable in terms of its producer, its intended audience, its marked stylistic features and the properties of the external environment in which it is created. Texts of this kind may simply exemplify behaviour, for instance, exploiting a business letter as a model of 'good practice' for teaching purposes. On the other hand, they may serve as evidence to support or disprove a particular sociolinguistic theory. Alternatively, and this is the case here, they may illustrate a specific aspect of the relationship between language and society.

One sociopsychological effect of enterprise culture is a phenomenon that can be called 'exteriorization'. Exteriorization is little more than the intensification in the 1980s of collective participation in the process of myth creation. Originally analysed by Roland Barthes in 1957, but described by the French social philosopher Montesquieu as long ago as 1721, 'mythologising', a term coined by Montesquieu himself (Vernière 1960: 305), has since become recognized as one of the clichés of modern capitalist society. The concept can be associated with anomie, the state of insecurity induced by a period of social change linked to a desire for the immediately unattainable. It implies a pre-occupation with appearance bred of uncertainty, a readiness to accept status symbols at face value and correspondingly to believe in the individual's or organization's ability to translate myth into reality. Indeed, in one sense, the individual's conviction of his or her capacity to transcend reality and in so doing to achieve self-fulfilment could be said to be a central feature of 'enterprise' and a key element in the popular image of the entrepreneur.

At times when the stability of established institutions is threatened and when traditional codes of practice within existing organizations are no longer generally recognized as valid, public performance – presentational skills – inevitably gains greater significance. The same applies in a social environment where quick-wittedness, the ability to think on one's feet (street wisdom) has become essential to survival. To apply the speculative principles of the financial market to wider spheres of human interchange is necessarily destabilizing. In an unpredictable world, subject to the vagaries of supply and demand, short-term benefit becomes a priority. The ephemeral and the substantial become confused and so distort society's perception of the relationship between appearance and reality. The importance of superficial credibility as a feature of 'enterprise culture', which is reflected in the growth of communication itself as a commodity, affects the character and role of language in promoting exchange. In terms of the marketplace, it becomes increasingly essential for language to 'create an impression' as much to inform in a literal sense. The nature of meaning thereby shifts from the conceptual to the affective and the metaphorical. The form of the linguistic message tends to predominate over its content, the associative or connotational meaning of words over their referential value. Thus, the exploitation of grammatical patterns and the interplay of verbal images generally associated with poetry can be seen as one outcome of an active culture in which risk, impact and rapid exchange are the main driving forces. In certain respects, as Malcolm Bradbury wittily illustrates in his novel *Rates of Exchange* (1983), the relationship of words and structures to each other is analagous to the variable exchange rates of currencies. Both can alter their values without direct reference to the real world.

It is not the task of this chapter to say whether the exteriorization associated with fashion, design, advertising, salesmanship or the spread of the in-house jargon of the 'golden boys' is a good or bad thing – in England or in France. Suffice to say that Montesquieu was one of the first to launch a bitter attack on the pernicious moral consequences of what he saw as the transient, self-seeking and predatory society that financial speculation had created in the France of the Regency (Vernière 1960: 322). In its turn, even the Thatcher government has been careful to distance itself from the cupidity associated with financial trading, insisting instead on the productive aspects of enterprise – a 'disengagement' of which Montesquieu, like Pierre Bérégovoy, would undoubtedly have approved!

As far as language is concerned, however, there is a sense in which the separation between an advertisement's internal coherence and the function of the product or service it is promoting could be said to have a liberating and hence a positive effect on the art of message creation. The 1988 award-winning television advertisement for British Rail is an intriguing case in point.[4] The knowledge that it has no bearing whatsoever on the reality of rail travel in Britain in no way diminishes our appreciation of its aesthetic quality. We are happy to accept it as a cultural artefact. It is a paradox that despite the potentially perverse moral implications of confusing appearance and reality, enterprise promotes culture, not simply economically, but also aesthetically in that the everyday process of myth creation, which is the by-product of entrepreneurial activity, itself becomes an art form.

PROMOTING FRENCH MANAGEMENT EDUCATION

The principal difference between educational promotion in France and England is that created by the cleavage already discussed between the French state and private sectors. The obvious consequence is that while few French university prospectuses make any concessions to their readers, the opposite appears to be true of the documentation produced by all but the most complacent business schools. Appearances, however, can be deceptive. The primary objective of the texts analysed in the following section is less to inform their future recruits than to project an image of distinctiveness and exclusivity. By focusing on a restricted 'clientèle' and gauging their style accordingly, they succeed in appealing to the consumer while at the same time 'protecting [their product] from the adulterating effect of the market' (Fairclough 1988: 122).

ESSEC

Se préparer aux fonctions de gestion et de direction des entreprises exige la connaissance et la pratique des techniques les plus avancées dans ces domaines. Et aussi une pédagogie qui développe le sens des responsabilités, le souci de la communication, la passion d'entreprendre. La renommée de l'ESSEC se fonde sur ces deux exigences.

L'excellence dans la formation

La passion d'entreprendre

GROUPE
ESSEC

École Supérieure des Sciences Économiques et Commerciales, Établissement Supérieur Privé reconnu par l'État Avenue de la Grande École – B.P. 105 – 95021 CERGY-PONTOISE CEDEX – Tél. : (1) 30.38.38.00

Figure 5.1 ESSEC
Source: Guide des Métiers 1986–7

Text One: 'ESSEC: *L'excellence dans la formation. La passion d'entreprendre'*

This example of prestige advertising is taken from a journal addressed to the student population exploring job outlets or educational opportunities. The magazine includes suggestions as to the appropriate procedures to follow when applying for jobs (draft letters of application, model CVs etc.) and has a wide circulation in France. *Le Guide des Métiers* is a middle-of-the-market rather than a prestige publication. It is therefore surprising to find a promotional text of extremely high quality advertising a private business school (*L'Ecole Supérieure des Sciences Economiques et Commerciales*) reputed to be ranked amongst the top four in France. The text's very inclusion in *Le Guide des Métiers* is a clear indication of the acute competition between schools in 1986. It reflects ESSEC's readiness to spread its promotional net as widely as possible whilst at the same time safeguarding its position in the educational hierarchy. Uniform in tone, the text is above all marked by discretion, conciseness, clarity and poetic harmony. It is not informative in a referential sense, but the image of quality that it projects is powerful and finely drawn. As such, it is a good example of a text whose strongest feature is its internal coherence, a product of enterprise culture whose distinctiveness in a publication of this kind would have been more-or-less guaranteed.

The text can be translated literally as follows:

ESSEC . . . To prepare oneself for the twin tasks of financially managing and directing companies demands knowledge and practical experience of the most advanced techniques available in the fields concerned. It also calls for an educational approach, which develops a sense of responsibility, a concern for communication and a passion for enterprise. ESSEC's reputation is based on these two requirements:

Excellence in training
Passion for enterprise.

The translation does not do credit to the complex meanings of the text. Given the deliberately ambivalent structures, the exploitation of phonic relationships and the lack of adequate verbal equivalents for certain key expressions, this would not be possible. In the first line, the use of the reflexive '*se*' is both transitive and passive. It means both to prepare 'yourself' or, impersonally, 'oneself' in an active sense, and also 'to become prepared' from an intransitive or objective point of view. The same dual connotation applies to the use of the reflexive

105

passive '*se fonde*' in the last line of the main body of the text, which is enhanced in this instance by the use of the present tense: ESSEC's reputation is not static. The 'foundation' on which it is based is being actively and constantly renewed. The presence of the two structures at the beginning and the end of the text reinforced by the phonic link between '*fonction*' and '*fonde*' makes the tension between institutional action and the stasis of an established reputation one of the text's main cohesive features.

Another major structural element that does not lend itself to translation is the artificial division into two parts of the first long sentence of the main paragraph. This separation allows a clear distinction to be made between technical knowledge and skills and the personal qualities that the future manager must develop if he or she is to be successful. These two areas of development are not simply features of an educational programme. They are the essential prerequisites of an adequate training for senior management, a fact that is clearly drummed in by the repetition of the word *exige . . . exigence* (demands . . . demand [requirement]). It follows that the programme itself will be demanding. Not everyone will be up to it. Certain clearly defined qualities will be needed. Once again, the different character of these qualifications is reflected in the opposition between the 'hard' consonants, which evoke the character of the technical and practical aspects of the knowledge required, and the alliterated 's' sounds, which link the more human qualities.

The balance between the text's two overriding themes is emphasized by the semantic, phonic and grammatical structures of the noun phrases that form the main subheadings, the four key words being 'excellence' and 'passion' on the one hand, 'training' and 'enterprise' on the other. The first two (excellence and passion) are the qualities (in linguistic terminology, the 'comment') which are applied to the substance of experience ('topic'): 'training' and 'enterprise' respectively. The difference in the relationship between topic and comment in each noun phrase is perfectly defined by the phonic identity of the syllables '*dans*' and '*d'en . . .*'. In the first case, the quality of excellence is *intrinsic* to the experience of the training programme. The two concepts are totally bound up with each other. In the second, the relationship between 'comment' and 'topic' is one of *intention*: passion is required *in order to* undertake bold and innovatory initiatives! At the same time all four key elements are linked semantically by the subtle interplay of sound and syllable: '*formation*' . . . *passion*', '*excellence . . .*

106

d'entreprendre', etc. . . . whilst the formal symmetry of the subheadings is completed by the chiasmic arrangement of article and abbreviation: *'L'* . . . *la* . . . */La* . . . *d'* . . .'.

The predominant feature of this text is therefore its classical control of form that implies a balance of responsibility between the consumer – the future student – and the institution. The school will provide the potential recruit with the opportunity to acquire and develop the necessary technical knowledge and human qualities in a culture in which competence, distinctiveness, risk-taking and commitment are essential ingredients of success. However, those qualities can only be actualized *collectively*. *'La passion d'entreprendre'*, an expression for which, interestingly, there is no satisfactory English equivalent, is not portrayed here as a purely personal or instinctive property, it is something that can only be realized through the properly controlled interaction between the individual and an appropriate educational environment. The compound structure and message of this text is one small indication of the degree to which, by 1986, enterprise culture in France had already become institutionalized.

AU FAIT, POURQUOI SUP DE CO GRENOBLE?

Sup de Co Grenoble est née d'une volonté grenobloise. Les entreprises de la région commençaient à s'inquiéter: elles se développaient, s'internationalisaient, se restructuraient, se modernisaient, mais qui allait gérer tout cela dans les années à venir? On n'est jamais aussi bien servi que par soi-même, aussi la CCI de Grenoble décida de créer une grande Ecole de Commerce. A Grenoble à l'origine, Sup de Co Grenoble existe donc pour répondre aux besoins des entreprises grenobloises. Pour les élèves, cela tombe plutôt bien; car non seulement les débouchés régionaux en sortie d'école sont multiples, mais le dynamisme du tissu industriel grenoblois, la variété de ses activités ont porté les exigences pédagogiques au plus haut. L'Ecole de Commerce de Grenoble est Supérieure par ses différences. Elle les revendique.

Figure 5.2 Au fait, pourquoi Sup de Co Grenoble?
Source: The 1988 prospectus/brochure of the Ecole Supérieure de Commerce de Grenoble

Text two *'Au fait, pourquoi Sup de Co Grenoble?'*

The text can be translated literally as follows:

So, why *Sup de Co Grenoble?*

Sup de Co Grenoble was born out of the collective will of the town and region of Grenoble. The firms in the area were beginning to get worried: they were developing, becoming international, restructuring, modernizing, but who was going to run things in the future? It is said that if you want a job done well, the best thing is to do it yourself, so the Grenoble Chamber of Commerce decided to create a *'grande Ecole de Commerce'*. In virtue of having its roots in Grenoble, *Sup de Co Grenoble* exists in order to respond to the needs of the firms in the Grenoble region. Which is good news for the students: as well as providing multiple opportunities for graduates, the dynamism of the area's industrial infrastructure combined with the range of companies' activities have called for education and training of the highest order. What makes Grenoble Business School *'supérieure'* is its distinctiveness, of which it is justly proud.

This text is clearly different from Text one in that it addresses itself directly to intending students. Hence, it appeals more overtly to the linguistic propensities of future recruits by exploiting the techniques of stylistic variation or 'register-mixing' (cf. Fairclough 1988). An informal tone is deliberately created by presenting the text as a dialogue, begun *in medias res ('Au fait . . . ')*. The conversational style is developed through the use of rhetorical questions including the casual *'tout cela'*, the popular aphorism introduced by the familiar *'on'* (*'On n'est jamais aussi bien servi que par soi-même'*), and the manipulation of word order; *'Pour les élèves cela tombe plutôt bien'*.

At the same time however, a more serious message is being conveyed. Admission to the *Ecole Supérieure de Commerce de Grenoble* will involve participation in the entrepreneurial dynamism of a region whose reputation for technological innovation is known throughout France. The region's vitality is expressed in strikingly anthropomorphic terms. The town and its surroundings have 'will power' (*volonté*) out of which *'Sup de Co Grenoble'* 'was born'. The firms of the region had entertained 'anxieties', which could only be resolved by the creation of the school. These needs were not only of the past. The imperfect tense emphasizes earlier processes of change in which companies in the area 'were participating', whilst the aorist 'decided' (*décida*) marks the school's foundation as a turning point in the region's fortunes. The tense then switches to the present in which the text describes the current diversity of opportunity and the high quality of training that the local context now 'demands' (*exigences pédagogiques*). The grammatical representation of Grenoble's early involvement in a continuing process of economic and cultural evolution is further developed by the accumulation of verbs ('. . . *se développaient, s'internationalisaient, se restructuraient, se modernisaient* . . .'). In this, the region was not simply responding to external pressures; the companies had been progressively introducing changes 'by themselves' and 'on themselves' ('*se* . . . *s'* . . . *se* . . . *se* . . .'. Hence, of course, the pressure ('*mais* . . .') for an educational centre that would cater for their future needs.

Whilst clearly a product of enterprise culture and therefore the proponent of a deliberately self-generating myth, this text is also an illustration of the growth of collective enterprise in a prosperous region of France. Furthermore, from a more general point of view, it can be interpreted as a portrayal of the way in which active promoters of enterprise in the France of the late 1980s see themselves and the individuals that they hope will become the entrepreneurs of the future. As a text, it demonstrates a self-conscious concern with style that undoubtedly achieves its objective; the attractive reputation of the Grenoble area is one of the strongest selling points of the school. However, the text does not present a view of enterprise in which individual initiative for its own sake is a priority. Its message is rather that the surest route to personal entrepreneurial success will depend on the individual's contribution to the collective enterprise of the region and thereby indirectly to the school of which it is the sponsor. This focus emphasizes the importance of the close relationship between regional identity and educational provision, a distinctive feature of French enterprise culture that has no real equivalent in the United Kingdom.

CONCLUDING REMARKS

These two texts and others like them do not project an image of the young French 'enterprise person' as a superficial, self-seeking materialist. This is a distorted view reflected by other cultures, impressed or repelled by what they see as the elitist character of French, private-sector management education. It is certainly true, however, that the growth of *Ecoles de Commerce* encouraged by successive government since the war, together with the parallel development of the IUTs, laid the basis for a sudden efflorescence of 'enterprise culture' that has not yet died down; further, that the popular belief in the value of achieving self-fulfilment through independent commercial enterprise was fostered as strongly by the French Socialist government between 1983 and 1986 as it ever was in the Britain of Margaret Thatcher and Lord Young.

The essential distinctions between the enterprise cultures of France and Britain in the 1980s lie partly in the rhetoric that has been used to promote them, and partly in more deep-seated economic and cultural differences. The relative achievement of the Socialist government in France was to combine its support for individual enterprise with measures that sought to demonstrate its continuing commitment to Socialist principles. Despite its political reversals, the success of its rhetoric and that of the educational media in France lay in its ability to infuse 'the spirit of enterprise' with a sense of social purpose and personal idealism that has been so markedly lacking in Britain. It could even be said that under a Socialist President and successive governments of the centre-left and centre-right, France has succeeded both rhetorically and institutionally in creating an authentic 'culture' of enterprise of which the language of educational promotion is one manifestation. In Britain, the cultural enrichment promoted by enterprise is perhaps most strongly evident in design and in the integrated messages of television advertising, so frequently infused with a spirit of ironic humour and detached social comment. As such, many of these brilliant cultural artefacts are at odds with the forceful, moralistic and utilitarian discourse of the Thatcher government.

In contrast, the French *'esprit d'entreprise'* has been characterized by what an Anglo-Saxon might see as a startling yet sincere combination of euphoric commitment and stylistic sophistication. Its garish preoccupation with excellence and technological innovation, passion and personal realization is allied to wider social concerns. This strictly utopian synthesis of individualism and communal solidarity, which has always been one of the hallmarks of French political and cultural tradition, finds perfect expression in the introduction to the 1988 promotional brochure published by the *Ecole Supérieure de Commerce de Lyon*: an invocation of which Kipling himself would not have been ashamed.

*"*A *voir une vision claire de son entreprise*
et de sa vocation.

Savoir la communiquer simplement,
à l'intérieur comme à l'extérieur de l'entreprise.

Etre capable de l'incarner
en dépassant sans cesse ses propres préoccupations.

Savoir formuler clairement ses objectifs et ses projets,
écouter ceux qui vous entourent, les mobiliser
pour mettre en œuvre, avec eux, ces projets.

Garder son sang-froid en face des difficultés,
se replier avec méthode,
réduire les risques et repartir avec élan
dès que l'environnement le permet.

Etre enthousiaste et rigoureux,
flexible et déterminé, créatif et tenace.

Avoir l'esprit d'entreprise, le cœur en plus.

Ce sont des hommes et des femmes de cette trempe
que l'ESC Lyon veut former
pour l'entreprise et le monde de demain. **" "**

Figure 5.3 Avoir une vision claire . . .
Source: Ecole Supérieure de Commerce de Lyon

Text three: '*Avoir une vision claire . . .*'

The text can be translated literally as follows:

To have a clear vision of your enterprise and of its vocation.

To know how to communicate your vision with simplicity, inside and outside the enterprise.

To be capable of embodying your vision and in so doing to be capable at all times of rising above your personal concerns.

To know how to formulate your goals and your projects with clarity; To know how to listen to those around you and to engage their support so as to realize your projects together.

To remain calm when confronted by difficulties, to withdraw with circumspection, to reduce the risks and, boldly, to begin again as soon as the context is right.

To be enthusiastic and rigorous, flexible and determined, creative and tenacious.

To have the spirit of enterprise; courage and feeling, too. Such is the temper of the men and women that ESC Lyon wishes to prepare for the enterprise and the world of tomorrow.

NOTES

1 I am grateful to my colleague Naaman Kessous for his comments and bibliographical recommendations.

2 The anthology of articles entitled *The Mitterrand Experiment* (Ross *et al.* 1987), provides an excellent overview of the economic and cultural climate that prevailed in France between 1980 and 1986.

3 This is not to suggest that the formal models explored by Halliday (1973, 1978, 1988) do not represent a workable paradigm. On the contrary, it is only because of Halliday's illuminating functional analyses of the relationship between language and culture that it is credible to hazard the kind of generalizations made in this and the following paragraph.

4 This brief but celebrated film features a slow-motion, silent train journey in which inanimate objects (a pair of slippers, a chess piece, the logo on the cover of a Penguin book) come to life and casually adopt soporific poses to the languid, nasal tones of the song 'So Relax' by Leon Redbone.

REFERENCES

Barthes, R. (1957) *Mythologies*, Paris: Du Seuil.

Béaud, M. (1985) *La Politique Economique de la Gauche*, Paris: Syros.

Berger, S. (1987) 'French Business: from transition to transition', in G. Ross, S. Hoffman and S. Malsacher (eds) *The Mitterrand Experiment*, Oxford: Blackwell.

Birch, D. and O'Toole, M. (eds) (1987) *Functions of Style*, London: Pinter.

Bradbury, M. (1983) *Rates of Exchange*, London: Secker & Warburg.
Fairclough, N. (1988) 'Register, power and socio-semantic change', in
   D. Birch and M. O'Toole (eds) *Functions of Style*, London: Pinter.
Giscard d'Estaing, V. (1976) *Démocratie Française*, Paris: Favard.
Halliday, M.A.K. (1973) *Explorations in the Functions of Language*, London:
   Edward Arnold.
—— (1978) *Language as Social Semiotic: The Social Interpretation of Language
   and Meaning*, London: Edward Arnold.
—— (1988) 'Foreword' in D. Birch and M. O'Toole (eds) *Functions of
   Style*, London: Pinter.
Jacquillat, B. (1983) 'L'Entreprise et l'Etat prédateur' in M. Massenet
   (ed.) *La France Socialiste*, Paris: Hachette.
Massenet, M. (ed.) (1983) *La France Socialiste*, Paris: Hachette.
Menissez, Y. (1979) *L'Enseignement de la Gestion en France*, Paris:
   Documentation Francaise.
Montesquieu, C. (1721) *Lettres Persanes*, in P. Vernière (ed.) (1960) *Lettres
   Persanes*, Paris: Garnier.
Pinto, D. (1987) 'The Left, intellectuals, and culture' in G. Ross, S.
   Hoffman and S. Malsacher (eds) *The Mitterrand Experiment*, Oxford:
   Blackwell.
Ross, G., Hoffman, S. and Malsacher, S. (eds) (1987) *The Mitterrand
   Experiment*, Oxford: Blackwell.
Vernière, P. (ed.) (1960) *Lettres Persanes*, Paris: Garnier.

Chapter Six

A THATCHER EXPORT PHENOMENON?

The enterprise culture in Eastern Europe

LARRY RAY

This chapter is concerned with the development of the economic principles associated with the 'enterprise culture' in what might be regarded as their least fertile ground – the state socialist societies of Eastern Europe. This is particularly important at a time when the possibility of an end to the Cold War coincides with what is a profound crisis of the communist systems. In China a gerontocracy retains power only through terror. In the Soviet Union the process of de-Stalinization reveals not only the full barbarity of the crimes committed in the name of the proletariat, but also the extent to which the system has failed in its own terms to deliver the goods. None other than the Soviet Prime Minister Nikolai Ryzhkov announces that 40m. people live below the poverty line, that Soviet factories emit 100m. tonnes of pollution each year, or that 40 per cent of the country's industrial plant is obsolete. Never in the past forty years have the possibilities been so ripe for a fundamental shift in the social organization of Soviet societies, and hence in the social relations in Europe in general, something that Gorbachev's July 1989 speech in Paris places on the agenda: ' . . . we must build a common European home'. Yet this is a process, as events in China indicate, with enormous dangers: after Tiananmen Square, no-one can rule out the possibility of a Stalinist reversion elsewhere. None the less, *glasnost* and *perestroika* remain the best chance for Eastern European reformers to develop new models and initiatives in social organization, at least in some parts of the Soviet bloc. At the same time, it can hardly escape anyone's attention that one strong contender in this reform process is the programme of radical marketization of social relations, which can appear similar to the enterprise culture in the UK. Some assessment is therefore needed of the origin of these ideas in Eastern Europe, and their likely consequences.

This analysis will focus on Hungary, where almost every political grouping from the reform wing of the Socialist Workers' Party (MSZMP – renamed the Hungarian Socialist Party in October 1989) to the diverse groups represented in the Democratic Round Table, announces the project of marketizaton as inseparable from the 'transition to democracy'. It is here, more so far than in the Soviet Union, or elsewhere in Eastern Europe, that extensive marketization of socialized relations is taking place. The analysis has potential relevance to the Soviet Union though, in that Hungary is frequently viewed by Soviet economists as a kind of testing ground in which to assess the consequences of both economic and political pluralism (e.g. Aganbegyan 1988). Of course, the origins of the economic restructuring taking place in Hungary do not lie specifically in an application of the policies of Thatcherism, which as Neal Ascherson says, is not as influential internationally as is often supposed.[1] The origins of marketization in Hungary and in other Soviet societies are diverse, and have antecedents in, for example, the Liberman Reforms in the Soviet Union in the 1960s, the Yugoslavian model of self-management and the New Economic Mechanism in Hungary in the 1970s. Indeed, it is necessary to situate current Hungarian developments in the context of a process that has been unfolding since the 1960s. None the less, the emergence of programmes in Hungary to create a de-centralized, market-driven economy, open to more-or-less unlimited foreign capital, as concomitant to a multiparty political pluralism, go beyond previously established notions of 'market socialism' and signal what could potentially constitute a full restoration of capitalist social relations. In this sense, one can pose the question of how close an association exists between the Hungarian reforms and the spirit of the enterprise culture as this is understood in the west, especially since the object of both movements is similar, namely the destruction of what is viewed as an outmoded, failed, *étatist* socialism. When Minister of State Imre Pozsgay announced in May 1989 that the communist system that had been imposed on Central Europe in the 1940s had failed, and could be reformed no further, he articulated a profound sense of crisis that had existed for a long time among dissident intellectuals, but had finally reached the Hungarian leadership itself. At the same time, one should bear in mind that the most ardent advocates of the enterprise culture in Hungary remain largely within the relatively narrowly defined circles of intellectuals, especially in the Alliance of Free Democrats.

This crisis has its origins in the objective systemic problems of state socialism, in the perceived failures of Hungary's experiment in 'market socialism', and in the political and intellectual frames of meaning through which socialism and the history of Stalinism are understood. In order to appreciate both the attraction of market relations to Hungarian reformers as well as whatever differences or similarities there might be with the western (and particularly British) experience of 'enterprise culture', it is necessary briefly to outline the frames of meaning through which the systemic problems of state socialism are broadly understood. Objective systemic problems most often cited are those of economic irrationality (chronic shortages, for example, of consumer goods, medical care, housing and imports, combined with overproduction of capital goods), which necessitate political repression to prevent the articulation of needs that a command economy cannot deliver. Thus Feher *et al.*, in their systematic theorization of this phenomenon as 'dictatorship over needs' refer to the ' . . . impotent rage [of the consumer] when confronted with the sheer irrationality of this acclaimed logic of planning' (Feher *et al* 1984: 14). Further, amongst many dissident writers, the command economy dominated by the bureaucratic planner is often challenged by an almost Burkean conservativism, in which the free market and private property are seen as essential guarantors of political liberty. It is in this context, too, that the (ambiguously used) notion of 'civil society' has become a buzz word amongst reformers throughout Eastern Europe. This chapter then, first examines the background to the reform movement in Hungary, stressing that what is being proposed now, in the economy, in social welfare, and in terms of Hungary's relations with western capital, goes so far beyond the 'market socialism' of the Kádár period as to constitute a qualitative break with the past. Second, it considers the social implications of the proposed changes, and their relationship with the general programme of the 'enterprise culture'.[2]

REFORM AND PLURALITY

The political and economic framework for contemporary developments in Hungary was established through the 'social contract' offered by János Kádár following the 1956 uprising and the Stalinist terror 1956-8.[3] Explicitly stated, this involved offering an exchange of limited political freedoms and a degree of economic plurality in return for popular legitimacy, or, at any rate, acquiescence. From the late 1960s, the New Economic Mechanism involved opening up the

116

'second economy', a limited marketization of services and consumer goods, whilst most agricultural production, capital goods and national distribution remained in the state socialist sector, or 'first economy'. According to Kornai (1986) the theoretical justification for this distinction was that 'simple reproduction' (predominantly small-scale household production and its distribution) would be governed by the market, whilst 'extended reproduction' (large-scale capital investment) would remain governed by the plan, which would also co-ordinate the two sectors. The first economy would be subject to 'soft' budgetary constraint in that prices and investment decisions were to reflect market criteria, along with other social considerations, in particular, the maintenance of full employment and social welfare (see, for example, Ferge 1979).

This dual system gave rise to a multilayered economy of state-owned firms, agricultural co-operatives, non-agricultural co-operatives and a formal and informal private sector (as well as forms of mixed ownership and leasing of state property to private entrepreneurship). But two processes in particular have been crucial for recent developments. First, has been the growth of an 'informal' sector alongside the second economy, of partly legal but unregulated, partly illegal but increasingly tolerated enterprise. The extent of this activity is difficult to estimate and economists disagree as to its parameters, but the evidence suggests that it is considerable. Kornai, for example, suggests that whilst only 4.2 per cent of the working population were engaged in the formal private sector (i.e. were registered as full-time engaged in private enterprise) in 1984, a micro-survey of time spent in the second economy indicated that overall, only 67 per cent of time was spent in the state sector, as opposed to 33 per cent in the informal economy. In 'repair and maintenance' informal sector activity was as high as 87 per cent, and in 'residential construction' 55 per cent (Kornai 1986; there are similar findings in Haraszi (1977), and it is unlikely that self-reported informal entrepreneurship will be fully reported). The second crucial development has been the growth of rural entrepreneurship, of independent smallholders producing primarily for the market and running specialized enterprises. Szelenyi (1988: 58) describes this as 'The most striking change in rural Hungary during the last decade', and emphasizes that this is no survival of an 'archaic' form of production, but rather 'a new social form in the making'. Rural entrepreneurs cultivate over 12 per cent of arable land, and produce 34 per cent of gross farm product, which makes up for the inefficiency of the collective farms and thus has 'kept the political system legitimate and society content' (Szelenyi 1988: 41).

During the Kádár period, it was the search for legitimacy that guided the economic strategies of opening up the system to entrepreneurship. Indeed, the current situation needs to be understood as the outcome of a complex balancing act, in which increased economic and political freedoms are responses to systemic problems of stagnation and inefficiency. Yet they are also attempts to harness these 'free initiatives' within a framework of legality, whilst at the same time coping with the unintended consequences of allowing an entrepreneurial culture to co-exist within state socialism. The guiding philosophy of 'market socialism' of the Kádár years involved the gradual reduction of state repression (described by Anderson and Lovas (1982), as 'friendly repression'), combined with a consumer boom in the 1970s, which itself prompted the further development of an entrepreneurial culture. Yet, this could only be given political impetus after Kádár's removal from office in May 1988, and the strengthening of the reform wing of the MSZMP under Pozsgay, Miklos Nemeth and Reszo Nyers. Whereas the 1970s and 1980s had seen cycles of repression and tolerance, Kádár's removal allowed the redrafted constitution permitting the free formation of opposition political parties, the intention to hold free elections and the 1988 Company Act, which prepares the way for widespread marketization of the economy and attraction of foreign capital. Let us examine the ways in which the Kádár period set the conditions for this.

Kádár's post-1958 policy of legitimating the regime meant that economic liberalization and greater use of incentives gradually replaced compulsion in economic relations. Thus by mid-1957 even, only 6.1 per cent of agricultural labourers were organized into the *Termelöszövetkezet*, the collective farms (Heinrich, 1986: 35). Alongside the state economy the second economy produced greater opportunities for initiative, which meant that Hungary (along with Poland, which has a private economy in agriculture), was unusual in the Soviet bloc in allowing private entrepreneurship extensive room for development. However, this programme of legitimation (often referred to in the 1970s as Hungary's 'economic miracle') had unintended consequences. In particular, those of greater social differentiation, the delegitimating consequences of which were well-known to MSZMP social scientists, and of foreign indebtedness. Inequalities re-emerged during the 1970s, such that wealth and conspicuous consumption were openly displayed alongside poverty, especially in rural areas. By 1984, the average income (in the first economy) was Fl.4,800 per month (about £480 sterling), whilst the poverty line was drawn at Fl.2,500 per month. Five per cent of the population earned 10 per cent above the average, whilst 28 per cent earned less than the subsistence minimum. The better-off sections included professionals, party *nomenclatura*, private artisans, collective farmers with private plots and business contractors. Many entrepreneurs grew through earnings in the second economy, but especially through the informal market, which increasingly permeated most aspects of everyday life. The poorest group included pensioners (many of whom have to work to supplement their pension), single mothers, unskilled female white collar workers and people living in sublet rooms. Poverty became concentrated in rural areas, which by the 1980s began to suffer from unemployment, which was marked especially amongst gypsies (between 2.4 and 5 per cent of the population), who found that with the depopulation of villages, and the increased use of mechanization and manufactured goods, there was little demand for their traditional skills (e.g. horse trading or handmade building materials).

The trend between 1950–80 was towards an increasingly consumer society, as sales of consumer goods rose by 1,600 per cent. By 1980, 99 per cent of households earning a regular income owned a TV, compared with 66 per cent in 1970; 91 per cent owned a washing machine, compared with 70 per cent in 1970; 87 per cent owned a refrigerator, compared with 35 per cent; and 26 per cent owned a car compared with only 6 per cent in 1970 (*Statistical Abstract*, 1989). However, this was made possible through extensive international borrowing in the 1970s, such that Hungary's foreign debt stood at $18 billion (US dollars) in 1988, costing over $500m p.a. to service. This makes it more difficult for Hungary to sustain welfare and social benefits, and has prompted consumer price increases of over 100 per cent (Krasso 1989). Further, for the consumers, higher living standards were financed not only through first economy income, but for many people, necessitated work in the second economy (e.g. an evening job as a taxi driver, private tuition or various forms of moonlighting, such as factory workers using state economy time or materials to make 'foreigners', as described by Haraszi, 1977). Moreover, the adoption of second economy work as a means of survival, or at any rate as a means of increasing consumption patterns, involved more than just economic activity. It also established networks of mutual assistance and dependency, informal networks of non-monetary exchanges that are common throughout Eastern Europe.

This has led some writers, such as Hankiss (1989), to suggest that in these informal networks of exchange there can be found a new 'civil society', independent not only from the state, but from the official organs of the socialist system. This point of view is important for understanding the argument of many Hungarian social scientists that society can be reconstituted through networks of voluntary associations, without state provision of welfare. Yet it also uses 'civil society' in an ambiguous way – to refer not only to a public sphere of political action and initiative, but also to private relations of exchange and interdependence. Since the notion of 'civil society' is assuming such importance in Eastern Europe, it is useful to distinguish its different possible meanings and bases. As well as existing in these informal networks, 'civil society' is also attributed to the extension of market relations, and to the growth of a realm of intellectual activity – a public domain in the traditional sense. The reason these meanings become blurred is that, until recently in Hungary, the DDR, Czechoslovakia, Bulgaria or Romania, a critical intellectual public could exist only 'underground', i.e. in informal networks of colleagues and friends.

By the later 1970s, amongst intellectuals, the publication and dissemination of political literature was taking place through similar networks of free association. Facing by then generally mild police attention, there was a growth in *Samizdat* journals (e.g. *Beszélö* 'The Talker', *Tájékoztaló* 'The Signpost', or *Hirmondò* 'The Messenger'). These were sold most of the time relatively openly and circulated widely amongst informal networks of friends and colleagues. Indeed, it was said that intellectuals could make their careers through 'illicit' publication in *Samizdat*. Thus there was the irony, as Janos Kis, the editor of *Beszélö* pointed out (Gorlice 1986) that whereas in the west civil society had dissolved into a kind of apolitical privatism (or 'lifeworld'), in state socialist societies repression had forced actors into a new type of civil society based on the only apparently 'private' realm of family and friends, out of which new social movements could develop. Indeed, marketization is understood not just in economic terms, but as a redefining of the boundaries of the public and private, less in terms of opposition, and more in terms of mutuality.

At the same time, and in the atmosphere of dialogue between the ruling party and intellectuals, economists and sociologists began during the later 1970s and 1980s to propose new models for a dynamic but increasingly marketized society. Reform proposals in general strive towards two objectives: both to accommodate and legalize the already existing informal economic and social networks, and to create the conditions for new enterprise initiatives. In this sense, it might be possible to suggest that whereas Thatcherism represents 'enterprise culture from above' the initial reform movements amongst intellectuals and party reformers represented 'enterprise culture from below' – the attempt to provide institutional space for the networks that had already come into existence. Examples of these would include proposals to increase the scope of the second economy relative to the state sector, which amounted to an extension of the concept of a mixed economy. Thus Márton Tardos, Tibor Liska an Tamas Bauer, for example, proposed the restriction of national plans to macro-economic tasks, allowing enterprises more independence from the state, which might involve transforming state enterprises into stockholding corporations, an expanded role for the market and a capital market independent of state administration. In the area of health policy, reform proposals both articulated the interests of doctors in greater control over practice, and strove to institutionalize the already established practices of tipping for service. Reformers proposed decentralization, increased patient choice, the use of voucher or coupon systems for the 'purchase' of medical services and the further liberalization of private practice (Csaszi and Kullberg 1985). In the field of welfare in general, churches and charitable organizations are encouraged to take an increasingly active role, whilst some crucial aspects of the social contract such as food subsidies, nominal health care charges, cheap and efficient public transport or nominal rents in the public housing sector, are being eroded.

All this took a great leap forward at the Party Congress in May 1988, where the reform wing consolidated their position. Kádár was shunted first into a ceremonial position, and a year later removed from the Central Committee altogether. Following this realignment, many of the reform proposals, for extensive marketization and political pluralism, began to take concrete form.

One of the most dramatic has been the 1988 Company Act, followed by the Transformation Act in 1989, which aim to give a legal frame to private enterprise and to attract foreign capital into the state sector. In January 1989, a form of stock market opened in Budapest, through which state banks buy shares equivalent to 60 per cent of the stock of state enterprises, and which effectively creates a market in capital. State enterprises are to join with foreign capital, the state no longer insisting on 51 per cent ownership in joint ventures. Private individuals can set up companies with a maximum of 500 employees, and minimum flotation capital of Fl.1 million ($US 18,500). The new banking system aims to mobilize private, dormant capital presently in the form of savings, through cross-investment in state and private enterprises. State enterprises become autonomous and must operate according to market accounting practices, and prices will be determined by costs of production plus the amount of investment surplus held back. Investment decisions will be determined by interest rates, and the security of production. Subsidies to inefficient enterprises will be cut and loss-making enterprises eventually liquidated. 'Anyone with the will and strength', said Deputy Prime Minister József Marjai, 'should be able to join market activities.' Again, Mihály Laki argues for a full programme of marketization, recognizing that 'sophisticated markets exist already', but that they are at present 'only partial'. Thus obstacles such as artificial barriers, monopolistic submarkets, shortages, lack of infrastructure and 'the anti-market attitudes of society' should be removed (Laki 1989). Such thinking is in tune with the attitude of the reform wing of the Party. In May 1989, under pressure from the IMF, a package of cuts in state expenditure amounting to Fl.2 billion ($US 218m) was announced. Pozsgay suggested that those who become unemployed as a result of this contraction should become self-employed!

POLITICS AND ENTERPRISE

An extremely widely held view, amongst intellectuals, reform circles in the Party and across virtually all oppositional groups, is that the programme for decreasing political control of the economy is inseparable from that of political pluralism and the transition to democracy (a similar view is expressed by many Polish social scientists, e.g. Kolarska-Bobinska and Rychard, 1989). It is true that following the reform coup within the Party in May 1988, the process of political liberalization that was already under way received huge additional impetus. The upshot of this is that there now exists a range of legally constituted opposition parties and proto-parties, and free elections are planned for 1990 (the earlier they are held of course, the better for the MZSMP).[4] Two aspects of this process are particularly relevant for the emergence of an 'enterprise culture'. First is the anti-*étatist* programme of the opposition. The second is the relationship between political pluralism and the informal civil society referred to p.120.

Following the 1988 Law on Associations, which permitted the formation of legally constituted social and political groups, there has emerged an at-present loose coalition of social forces represented in the 'Democratic Round Table', with slightly differing programmes and social bases, which are summarized in Table 6.1. The 'Democratic Round Table' includes the Social Democrats (MSZDP), the Bajcsy-Zsilinszky Society (BZSBT), the Hungarian Democratic Forum (MDF), the Young Democrats' Alliance (FIDESZ), the Council of Free Trades Unions and the Free Democrats (SZDSZ). There are other political groupings, such as the Smallholders Party (FKGP), the (Stalinist) Ferenc Munnich Society, or the socialist BAL, which are not part of the forum. The groups in the round table share a common programme of democratization, but membership of each group is not mutually exclusive (MSZMP members can also join); so the situation is at present very fluid, and it would be premature to speak yet of parties in the western sense having crystallized. Apart from sharing a programme of democratization, some concept of marketization is shared by each of the groups in the round table, as is the intention to open the Hungarian economy further to international capital. Disagreements extend only to the question of how far this should go The MSZMP reform wing has adopted a social democratic programme of a mixed economy, which will involve the privatization of large sections of state property, (though to whom they will be sold off remains a crucial and as yet unresolved issue). The Social Democrats agree (though their leadership has deep personal differences with the ruling party), whilst the Free Democrats propose a more radical programme of marketization of all social relations, and the 'entire eradication of the state from the economic sphere'.[5]

At the same time, the new climate of freedom of speech and publication has allowed the emergence of vigorous publishing in the private sector. Between May 1988 and May 1989 nearly 300 private publishing houses have opened, producing Hungarian literature, western social science, Soviet literature, that had not previously been available, as well as new work that is being generated to meet the new markets. At almost every metro station there are private bookstands selling previously unavailable literature (e.g. Koestler, Solzhenitsyn, Trotsky)

Table 6.1 Main political groups and parties in Hungary, 1989

Group	Issues	Social bases
Hungarian Socialist Workers' Party (MSZMP):		
Ferenc Munnich Society (MFT)	Stalinist. Centralized planned economy. One-party system	Older party *nomenclatura*
Centre	Stability. Party unity. Democratic centralism	Bureaucracy. Cadre-elite.
Reformers: Union for Leftist Alternative (BAL); Democratic Youth Alliance (DEMISZ); Hungarian Socialist Party.	Multiparty system. Socialist mixed economy. Local self-government. Privatization and marketization	Younger MSZMP members. Party leadership. Some intellectuals
Hungarian Social Democratic Party (MSZDP) Young Social Democrats (SZIK), FIDESZ-SZDSZ left wing	Multiparty system. Mixed economy. Social Policy. Foreign investment. Marketization	Urban middle-class. Some workers
Free Democrats (SZDSZ) Young Democrats' Alliance FIDESZ)	Civil liberties. Multiparty system. Free initiatives. Social minorities. Social policy	Urban intellectuals. Students. Private entrepreneurs
Smallholders' Party (FKGP)	Multiparty system. Mixed economy. Local communities. Minorities. Direct democracy. Rural issues	Countryside. Intellectuals. Private entrepreneurs
Hungarian Democratic Forum (MDF)	Democratization. Individualism. Markets. Populism	Urban intellectuals
Bajcsy-Zsilinszky Society (BZSBT)	Nationalist. Populist. Community and nation. Society as a moral organism	Rural *petite bourgeoisie*
Christian Democratic People's Party	Tradition. Collective rights. 'God and Father land'	
MDF right-wing Party for Independence (MFP)		

Source: From a table compiled by András Bozóki, Institute of Sociology, Budapest

and opposition papers and journals. Amongst the intelligentsia many are finding new occupations, or supplementary occupations in the private publishing sector. There is also a growing popular culture, especially in electronic media. All this has implications for the state publishing house, which might find itself faced with a declining market for unprofitable tracts, especially political works, and in future publishing is likely to be increasingly consumer (and profit) driven. This could well indicate the kind of shift described elsewhere in this volume by Abercrombie (see Chapter Nine), from producer to consumer culture – although this is by no means an unmixed blessing, since there is at present considerable state sponsorship of cultural activity, which provides cheap theatre, opera, concert and film tickets etc. and which is threatened by the commercialization of culture.

On the one hand, this illustrates, with its advantages and disadvantages, the creation of an institutionalized space for entrepreneurial activity that had existed anyway through the informal culture of *Samizdat*. On the other hand, though, in the context of the increasing internationalization of the Hungarian economy, it also signals the openings that will exist for increased western investment in publishing. The Party recently approved a new press law that will revolutionize the media, and allow western publishing companies a foothold in the Hungarian market. The law allows anyone to found a paper, a local or commercial radio and television station and to own or use printing equipment. Foreign capital will also be able to participate in Hungarian media ventures (though at present there will be a ceiling on the percentage of foreign ownership, and the Party will continue to run the main TV networks). Since 1988, hundreds of thousands of households watch satellite and cable TV, and Hungarian language copies of Murdoch papers will be only a short way off.

Against the background of forty years of state socialism, the emerging ethic of competition in the realms of both political and economic society leads to close identification in the minds of many people between marketization and political freedom. A polarity is often posed between the state and unfreedom on the one hand, and markets and self-actualization on the other. This is occurring to a degree that many on the western left would no doubt find disconcerting. This is partly because the ideology of the supremacy of consumer choice as the foundation of political freedoms has resonance with classical liberalism and the western new right – it also begs the questions of who are the consumers, and whether a consumer society allows for the articulation of genuine as opposed to manipulated needs. The concept of a non-statist society of free initiatives, invokes a number of ideas. First, there is the notion of an informal network of mutual support that has existed outside the state, in private or 'underground' life. One manifestation of this has been the survival of intellectual activity in *Samizdat*. Second, there is the idea that political freedoms are premised upon the creation of a market economy, that will not only be more efficient than the command economy, but will guarantee a critical public. It should be said, though, that not all commentators are so confident on the last point. Szelenyi (1988), for example, suggests that the expansion of private entrepreneurship, whilst attesting to the ability of people to resist the statist project of collectivization, could be a mixed blessing. He does not see in the new entrepreneurial class the dual status of *citoyen* and *bourgeois* (implied in the notion of *Bürger*; or *polgár* in Hungarian). Rather, he sees 'little civic consciousness' in the new *petite bourgeoisie*, since 'they may be forced to rip off the system (and their customers) as often and quickly as possible' (Szelenyi 1988: 215). In the remainder of this discussion, some attempt is made to place these dramatic changes in the broader contexts of the more familiar enterprise culture in Britain, and also in the context of the internationalization of the global economy.

MARKETS AND INTERNATIONAL CAPITAL

Although there is a consensus across the Hungarian political spectrum in favour of a market economy, the meanings of the concept 'market' are diverse, and can reflect the experiences of entrepreneurship of different social groups. In particular, whilst the actual growth of entrepreneurship has occurred as a result of rural and urban producers' efforts to resist proletarianization, the enthusiasm for marketization, and the idea of a free initiatives society, has been largely an intellectuals' affair. Despite the involvement of some workers, such as bus drivers and building maintenance workers, in the new trades unions, the process of social mobilization around the new civil society has been concentrated amongst the intelligentsia (e.g. the Democratic Trade Union of Scientific Workers – TDDSZ). Thus, it is not surprising that the notion of entrepreneurship favoured by intellectuals relates to their sense of civil society as activity independent of the state, that is, as something positive, self-affirming and empowering. For Szelenyi (1980) as for Feher *et al.* (1984), marketization of commodity production would liberate the direct producer from the control of the New Class of planners and *nomenclatura*, in that producers could respond to a market, and would keep the profits of commodity exchange, rather than produce as directed by bureaucrats, who themselves rake off the surplus product in the form of privileges, access to better housing, schools, etc.[6] In some ways, this seems to be precisely what is being proposed by the reform movements, both within and outside the MSZMP. Yet radical marketization will have highly differentiated consequences for different social groups.

Thus it is necessary to delineate different notions of the market, 'free initiatives' (or enterprise), and the social transformations that are under way in Hungary. First, the market can be understood in different ways, and these are generally not differentiated in reform discussions. There is the romantic notion of the market, which seems to underlie a great deal of the enterprise culture enthusiasm in both east and west. This view corresponds in some ways to Marx's concept of simple commodity circulation: C-M-C, in which commodities are converted into money, which in turn is converted into new commodities. In this form of circulation, money remains essentially a use-value, since its purpose is to exchange one commodity for another. This idea of the market as simple commodity circulation fits in well, say, with the notion of the collective farmer who sells the surplus product from a private plot of land. It also fits in well with the marketization of the service economy – the small boutiques, restaurants, etc.; and with the notion of a free trade in intellectual work evidenced in the burgeoning small publishing houses referred to on pp. 123-4. It is a *petit bourgeois* notion of the market, which no doubt does provide expanded opportunities for initiative and self-determination. Even if a limited degree of accumulation is taking place amongst these small entrepreneurs, it does not yet begin to look like expanded reproduction, and affects only 2-3 per cent of producers. Further Szelenyi himself says that ' . . . in a market system proper, most of them would go bankrupt immediately: the rest would starve in their one-acre farms' (Szelenyi 1988: 14). In the context of an industrial society that aims to become integrated into the global capitalist economy, it is a romantic idea to imagine that this is the principal aspect of marketization, and the reform economists know this themselves.[7]

Second, expanded reproduction in a market economy involves the circuit of capital M-C-M, in which money is converted into capital accumulation through the commodification of labour. Elemer Hankiss (1989) argues that what is actually occurring in Hungary is not *petit bourgeoisification* but precisely the formation of a new *grande-bourgeoisie*, a new ruling class that will comprise the *nomenclatura*, managers, state administrators and entrepreneurs. This is at present, he suggests, only a trend rather than a completed process, but can be identified in the Company Act and Transformation Act, which will create a group of interlocking and independent owners of state enterprise. It can also be identified in the Land Reform Bill that will liberalize land purchase, to allow managers of collective farms to become owners. It further bears upon the unresolved question of who should own state enterprises if the first economy is to be privatized, since the most likely outcome for Hankiss is that the existing managers and bureaucrats will become owners. An analogy is drawn between this process and the transition from feudalism to capitalism, in which sovereign property was parcelled out amongst the barons. This thesis would explain, in a somewhat instrumental and functionalist way, how easily the ruling group has embraced the principles of an enterprise culture, and of political democracy, since the emergent process of capital accumulation will be more successful if it is legitimated through a democratic system.[8]

Whether or not Hankiss (1989) is correct, it is the case that in the current enthusiasm for marketization little consideration is given to the needs or interests of the workers in state enterprises who (unlike collective farmers) have few possibilities for entrepreneurial activity. Further, the programme of releasing initiatives through radical marketization runs up against a more general set of issues to do first, with the relative strength of national *vis-à-vis* international capital, and second, with the effects of the desocialization of non-profitable services, such as welfare. Both of these have some bearing on the general theme of the political economy of enterprise culture. Let us look briefly at each.

First, whether or not one accepts Hankiss's (1989) essentially conspirational view of the interests of the ruling elite in the reform process, or whether one views this as a genuine attempt to solve problems of inefficiency and shortage, the reformers like any other social actors operate in a world of global relations, in which actions have unintended consequences. Any attempt to revitalize Hungarian industry and agriculture through privatization inevitably encounters the problem of foreign investment, with which Hungarian capital (whether privately owned, state owned or under workers' self-management) will have little competitive advantage. This is accepted by the government. A recent recommendation from the government's 'reform committee' under

Nyers proposed a three-year recovery plan involving $US 1.5 billion foreign investment, trade with the Soviet Union to be conducted in foreign currency (which would mean Hungary competing for trade with western suppliers) and the creation of the infrastructure of a domestic market by 1992(!). This will involve factory closures, privatization and budget cuts. The danger involved here is that rather than revitalizing the economy, exposure to EC competition and investment will create conditions of uneven development, a low wage area on the periphery of the EC – in fact 'Third Worldization'. The most serious casualties of this will of course be the Hungarian working class and the marginal underclass of rural poor.[9]

There is some parallel here with the ideology of the enterprise culture in Britain. Despite all the rhetoric of national interest and revival, Thatcherism is actually a response to the internationalization of British capital, which no longer needs any national base for the valorization *and* realization of capital. This is because the global company has evolved integrated production and marketing strategies to enhance its share of profits not in any one market, but globally. In this context, the post-war object of Keynesian interventionism, to secure domestic demand, has become redundant. The Thatcherite project of dismantling the welfare state is justified ideologically in terms of locality-based self-organization as an alternative to state dependency, and in particular in terms of the 'active citizen'. Notions of self-reliance, drawn from a model of marketized exchange, are applied to the weak, the powerless, the socially disadvantaged. Thus an idea that might be attractive to intellectuals, especially in the sphere of the communication of academic work, or to managers of enterprises seeking more autonomy, might have disastrous consequences when applied to social relations in general. As Peter Kellner says: 'Active citizens are those who contribute to the success of the free market economy by picking up the pieces that the free market drops: helping charities, clearing litter, helping inner city reconstruction' (The *Independent*, October 1988).

This analysis bears on the second point, namely that the restructuring of the Hungarian economy through privatization, the dismantling of welfare services and the introduction of wage incentives is proceeding without consultation with those who will be most adversely affected. Namely, those for whom entrepreneurial activity was less a matter of self-actualization, and more a strategy of survival, but whose condition of life was also dependent upon the provision of welfare services in the form of cheap housing, subsidised food, cheap energy, guaranteed employment, medical facilities, universal crèche and maternity rights. Mandel comments in relation to the Soviet Union, though the same point could be made in relation to Hungary, that amidst the enthusiasm for marketization:

> almost no serious attention is being paid in the press or scientific literature or in practice, to the development of the social measures necessary to soften the economic and social blows that would inevitably be the immediate experience of a very large part of the population.

(Mandel 1988: 142)

The likely consequence of this aspect of marketization, and the gearing of Hungarian domestic capital to compete with global corporations, is not only a serious worsening of the conditions of life of a large section of the population (Mihály Vajda suggests 25 per cent), but in particular, the reprivatization of welfare. More important here than commodification is the increased dependence on domestic labour, specifically, on the role of women as carers. The public realm of activity and entrepreneurship, in both political and economic senses, is a male realm, and in the absence of the socialization of private domestic relations is expanded only through the more intense exploitation of women. This is as much the case in an enterprise culture in the east or the west, except that paradoxically in socialist countries the near complete participation of women in the labour market means that the burden of double exploitation of women in the latter is all the more intense. One looks in vain for any programme for women's emancipation amongst the array of oppositional proto-parties, except for a broad statement from the Social Democrats that they intend to give the issue attention.

In general, though, the prospect of declining living standards for the working stratum carries for the reformers a more serious danger perhaps than do privatization programmes in the west, namely that it conflicts with what the Soviet economist Lisichkin disparagingly calls the 'archaic levelling consciousness' of the working class. To put it another way, its effects conflict with the central principle of legitimation of the socialist system: the substantive equalization of social relations. Already the Party talks not of substantive equality, but of 'equality of opportunity'; yet as a principle of legitimation, this might not be successful. The hardliners in the Party, in the Ferenc Munnich Society,[10] are organizing on the platform that conditions were better when socialism was defended by an authoritarian state. It is not impossible that this could, especially in an immature democracy, be the focus for backlash of the dispossessed.

CONCLUSIONS

The programme for marketization of social relations in Hungary is not in a literal sense an 'export' of Thatcherism, notwithstanding Károly Grósz's admiration for Thatcher. Yet Thatcherism offers a language in which to give the process at a national level meaning and legitimacy, and sure enough the language is present in the Hungarian reform movements, in terms such as 'privatization', 'self-reliance', 'initiatives', etc. and the frequent citations of the British example in the Hungarian press. Certainly, we should be cautious about imposing our experience of Thatcherism on to the understandings of Central and East Europeans,[11] for whom concepts like enterprise have different meanings, in particular the freedom from repression and from an economy of shortages. Hungarian reforms respond to a different set of historical experiences, partly those following 1956, but also the perceived failure of the Kádár regime ultimately to resolve the systemic crisis through market socialism. The sense of crisis that they address, that the old way of doing things can continue no longer, is basically more profound than that in Britain in 1979. Further, a crucial difference should be noted. Thatcherism has attempted to create what some on the right approvingly call 'authoritarian individualism', a strong central state that 'protects' the emancipated individual from intermediate layers in society, such as trades unions, local authorities, welfare agencies, the professions, etc. In Hungary the reverse has occurred, in that the erosion of state power has been matched by the *creation* of intermediate layers, as a defence against totalitarianism. In this sense, 'civil society' in state socialism, in its various manifestations, is defined as *the other* of the state – everything outside of the state and its agencies.

Yet when Pozsgay says in an inteview with Radio Free Europe that the existing system in Central and Eastern Europe and the Soviet Union cannot be reformed, but must be liquidated, there is also a sense of urgency that does not admit of any alternative. If the alternative in Eastern Europe is a social democracy, as Pozsgay suggests, then the outcome of the reform process will indeed be closer to the historical examples of Central Europe than to Thatcher's Britain. Yet it is too early to say whether the current reforms are moving ultimately in the direction of Thatcherism or of welfare capitalism. Further, it is important to disentangle the models of enterprising or 'free initiative' activity that are in use, and the forms of economic exchange they invoke. The *petit bourgeois* model of simple circulation actually has little relevance to an economy that is both opening up to foreign capital and restructuring to compete in international markets, except in so far as it devalorizes labour inputs. Aside from the rhetoric, and the intellectuals' justifiable enthusiasm about new opportunities for the free circulation of ideas, radical privatization might have objectively determined consequences that are not only unintended, but act to frustrate the formation of a democratic and plural public.

Underlying much of this debate is the question of the viability of a 'third way' that is neither state socialist nor capitalist. This has several variants. Szelenyi (1988) suggests that a third way has the potential to emerge from the renewed process of *'petit embourgeoise-ment'*, that in his view would have been the trajectory for Central Europe, had the Stalinist system not been imposed in 1948. Yet as we have seen, he, too, has reservations as to the viability of a third way based on petty-commodity production, and insists that the *petite bourgeoisie* is anyway only a class *in situ nascendi*. Others such as the Democratic Forum look to resurrect a pre-war notion of anti-capitalist populism. Again, the Movement for a Left Alternative (BAL) seeks a third way in the combination of state socialism and participatory democracy, which is the idea most familiar to the western left. But the crucial point is that the leading figures in the reform movement argue against any idea of a 'third way'. Their thesis is that Hungary needs the first way namely liberal democracy, a welfare state and mixed economy.

Placing Hungary in the context of the general crisis of the socialist systems finally, the current situation is fraught with problems and possibilities. Problems in that dangers lurk either of a Stalinist reversion, especially in response to the Soviet nationalities question, or on the other extreme of an abandonment of the collectivist project altogether, in favour of an entrepreneurial individualism. Possibilities, in that for the first time in this half of the twentieth century, dynamic and radical forces are emerging that promise a new democratic Europe emancipated from the Cold War and the threat of mutual destruction. Let us hope that the radical individualism represented by Thatcherism turns out to have been a transitory phenomenon on the

European scene, and that Europe, east and west, grasps the opportunities for forms of self-realization that are both genuinely democratic and emancipatory.

ACKNOWLEDGEMENTS

I am indebted to Dr Péter Somlai, Department of Sociology, Loránd Eötvös University, Budapest, for his helpful comments on an earlier draft of this chapter.

NOTES

1 In the *Observer* (30 April 1989) he says: 'Thatcherism as an international movement is a myth. Other countries borrow details: privatisation practice, or reform of the bureaucracy. . . . No other European country would dare to incur the degree of social division and inequality which is accepted here as the price of change.' He is writing primarily, though, of western Europe. It is ironic that Hungary might be prepared to go much further along this road than, say, Italy, or West Germany.

2 As a matter of historical context, it is worth noting that until 1945 Hungary was a feudal-bourgeois society with an authoritarian state. The majority of entrepreneurs were regarded as being of 'non-Hungarian origin', i.e. Jewish or German families. The national ideology was hostile to entrepreneurship, stressing romantic populist nationalism. After the Second World War, this fitted well with the state socialist version of anti-entrepreneurship.

3 In 1957 around 20,000 people were arrested and 2,000 executed. Imre Nagy was arrested in November 1956 and executed in June 1958. These events are part of the immediate life and family histories of many who are currently in the reform or opposition democratic movements. It inevitably colours Hungarian thinking about the role of the state and the necessity for an independent civil society.

4 There is clearly a sense in which these developments are being viewed by some in Moscow as a test case in the consequences of radical reform. Oleg Bogomolov has said to the Hungarian press more than once that 'Hungary would not pose a threat to Moscow even if it adopted a Swedish or Austrian system', and Boris Yeltsin said on Austrian television that 'there is no need to fear a multiparty system in Hungary'.

5 This was said by a SZDSZ spokesperson at a round-table meeting of the 'democratic opposition', Budapest May 1989.

6 This is part of a more complex argument in Szelenyi (1979), in which he claims that social inequalities in the provision of basic needs, in particular housing, actually increase in 'state redistributive

societies', and that this is part of their essential nature. Flakierschi (1988), however, claims that in Hungary and Poland the spread of markets has produced greater inequalities; and Pickvance (1988) challenges Szelenyi's interpretation of the social implications of Hungarian housing policies.

7 For Szelenyi (1988), though, the resurgence of '*petit bourgeoisification*' (a remarkably more ugly term than the Hungarian *polgárosodás*) holds out the possibility that the region might resume its 'own organic evolutionary path' towards a 'third way' that was 'interrupted' in 1948. This envisages an economy of small independent producers (not unlike the notion of an 'enterprising society'). But the crucial question, for Hungary or the UK, is how these small producers exchange with international capital.

8 Hankiss, it should be said, believes that this process is all to the good, since finally, Hungary will have a capitalist class and pluralistic system. Hankiss, paper to 'Citizenship in Europe', May 1989.

9 However, reformers (inside and outside the MSZMP) argue that Hungary is now in a process of 'Third-Worldization', and that this can be arrested only through development of a market economy. South Korea is sometimes cited as the possible model for this.

10 Ferenc Munnich was a Hungarian Bolshevik who in later life became associated with the repressions after 1956, as the head of the security service.

11 With the diminution of the Cold War, the post-Second World War division of Europe into east/west is challenged by Hungarian politicians such as Pozsgay, and by many intellectuals, who insist on the separate cultural and historical identity of 'Central Europe', which includes Germany, Austria, Hungary, Switzerland and probably Czechoslovakia.

REFERENCES

Aganbegyan, A. (1988) *The Challenge – The Economics of Perestroika*, London: Hutchinson.

Anderson, K. and Lovas, I. (1982) 'State terrorism in Hungary, the case of friendly repression', *Telos* 54.

Csaszi, L. and Kullberg, P. (1985) 'Reforming health care in Hungary', *Social Science and Medicine*, 21: 8.

Feher, F., Heller, A. and Markus, G. (1984) *Dictatorship Over Needs – An Analysis of Soviet Societies*, Oxford: Blackwell.

Ferge, Z. (1979) *A Society in the Making – Hungarian Social and Societal Policy 1945–75*, London: Penguin.

Flakierschi, H. (1988) *Economic Reform and Income Distribution – a Study of Hungary and Poland*, New York: Sharp.

Gorlice, J. (1986) 'Introduction to the Hungarian Democratic Opposition', *Berkeley Journal of Sociology* 31.

Hankiss, E. (1989) 'East European alternatives – are there any?' paper to 'Citizenship in Europe' Conference, Budapest, May 24-26.

Haraszi, M. (1977) *Piece Worker*, London: Penguin.

Heinrich, H.G. (1986) *Hungary – Politics, Economics, and Society*, London: Frances Pinter.

Kolarska-Bobinska, L. and Rychard, A. (1989) 'Economy and politics: an evaluation of interrelations', paper to 'Citizenship in Europe' Conference, Budapest, 24-26 May.

Kornai, J. (1986) 'The Hungarian reform process – visions, hopes and reality', *Journal of Economic Literature* 24: 1687-37.

Krasso, G. (1989) 'Hungary at the Crossroads', *The Bloc*, nos 149-151.

Laki, M. (1989) 'The traps of marketization in Hungary', paper to 'Citizenship in Europe' Conference, Budapest, 24-26 May.

Mandel, D. (1988) 'Economic Reform and Democracy in the Soviet Union', *Socialist Register*.

Pickvance, G. (1988) 'Employers, labour markets and redistribution', *Sociology*, 22, 2.

Statistical Abstract (1989) Central Statistical Office, Budapest.

Szelenyi, I. (1980) 'Whose alternative?', *New German Critique* 20 Spring.

—— (1988) *Socialist Entrepreneurs – Embourgeoisement in Rural Hungary*, London: Polity Press.

ADDITIONAL SOURCE

Szelenyi, I. (1979) 'Social inequalities in state socialist redistributive economies', *International Journal of Comparative Sociology*, XIX 1-2.

Chapter Seven

BRITISH ENTERPRISE CULTURE AND GERMAN *KULTURGESELLSCHAFT*

HERMANN SCHWENGEL

There are three ways of underestimating the significance of the discourse of enterprise culture. If you link it culturally to Thatcherism, you miss the long-term changes that are in a way articulated in the ideas of enterprise culture. If you think of enterprise culture only in economic terms, or as a business ideology, then although everything does indeed 'begin with the economy', you miss the changes in political leadership that enterprise culture implies. And if you merely accuse enterprise culture of inconsistency or the like, you do not recognize it as a process that will still be important even when many British people may have forgotten that once there was a seemingly irresistible blue tide of conservatism. Indeed, it is quite possible that the future social historian will begin his or her work on the 1980s by echoing a famous sentence: 'There was no such thing as Thatcherism – only the take-off of a new wave of modernization and its specific antagonism to the British institutions of political modernity.'

By distinguishing three basic levels of political argument since the middle of the 1970s, we can understand to which structural problems the ideas of enterprise culture were trying to give an answer. First, what are the right economic policies against the process of stagflation that began to characterize western capitalist societies from the early 1970s, and were emphasized dramatically by the oil-price crises of 1973? Second, what are the institutional resources for efficient and legitimate government action, if it has to compete with the intermediate powers of business, trade unions, local authorities and transnational organizations? What, third, are the right attitudes, habits and motivations for both individuals and the public to cope with the speed and complexity of modernization, ready for decision where the open process of self-regulation needs competent definition, deliberation and responsible choice? Besides all its ideological defending of popular capitalism, its 'remembrance' of certain entrepreneurial Victorian values, and even besides the defence of the class interests of privately employed professionals, the discourse of enterprise culture is primarily an answer to this third question, and the key to both the other two.

For these reasons it would be insufficient merely to look for parallel symptoms of a narrowly defined enterprise culture in West Germany, although it would not be difficult to find some. The appropriate counterpart of enterprise culture is not, I would suggest, the moral–spiritual turn in German politics back to the virtues before 1968, suggested by a normative German right since the 1970s, nor the demand for institutional deregulation suggested by enlightened conservatives as well as neo-liberals; and certainly it is not the eclectic ideology of Bonn's current governing coalition. Rather, it is the image of a *Kulturgesellschaft*, which is present in the discourses of modernizers in the Christian Democratic Party as well as in the Social Democratic Party – for example, around the former general secretaries Geibler and Gotz, and the modernist urban wings of the Green Party, all opposing the mainstream. It is also present in professional discussions about the change from *Arbeitgesellschaft* (work society) to *Kulturgesellschaft* since the early 1980s, as well as in controversies about the culture boom in German cities and its costs, and in the new interest in culture as compensating for the risks of high-speed technology and social change.[1]

Although *Kulturgesellschaft* is not an ideological focus in the way that enterprise culture is, and some participants in the discussion use more general observations about the critical role of culture for further economic and social development, the image is none the less powerful. *Kulturgesellschaft* means a future society whose qualities are already beginning to shape the present, coexisting and competing with former stages of social development. Rapid technological change and the structural dominance of the service sector are not only linked to growing technical and organizational knowledge, but are also creating free space for general knowledge, reflexive attitudes and critical self-observation. Thus a culture of choice is no longer a class privilege but could become a necessity, civilizing both supply and demand.

In the concept of *Kulturgesellschaft* there is a utopian element, but also an empirical hypothesis that, in the choices between different sets of goods and services, culture as the permanent examination of preferences will become the key factor. The cultural policies of a city,

137

for example, are more important than the budget alone – although investment is already rising sharply. *Kulturgesellschaft* also means that the axis between hierarchy and work is less determining of lifestyles and careers. Command over other people's work as well as identification with a certain kind of work or with compensatory leisure, becomes less important in comparison to independence, options for change and flexible engagement. Again there is a utopian sense as well as an empirical expectation that these attitudes are in many respects typical for young entrepreneurs as well as for a growing number of young qualified workers. The discussion about the 35-hour work week is linked to this discussion on time sovereignty as well as to traditional trade union demands. As green issues raise the question of appropriate behaviour towards the environment, and as the necessary changes of behaviour can only be stabilized in a new cultural setting, the world of *Kulturgesellschaft* also becomes an extension of the green debate. Even for its protagonists, *Kulturgesellschaft* is not only a rosy project but a risky one, too, opening up space for a new elitism and aestheticism. But *Kulturgesellschaft* is clearly separated from the former German defence of *Kultur* against English, American and French 'civilization'. *Kulturgesellschaft* is a multicultural concept, however ambivalent other aspects of it may be.

ENTERPRISE CULTURE AND *KULTURGESELLSCHAFT:* SIMILARITIES AND DIFFERENCES[2]

At a first glance the different stress on culture only seems to reflect the different economic progress of Britain and West Germany, in the same way as observers explain the late rise of a green movement in Britain as due to a lack of modernization.[3]

The speed and depth of technological economic development needs a counterbalance in the world of *Kulturgesellschaft* to avoid the risks of disintegrated growth. The future of a country is the more dependent on this type of reflection, which gives interpretation and sense to the new forms of production and consumption, the more complex its goods and services are. Future production has to be simulated in cultural experimentation if there is to be long-term perspective and political control of the objective process. Knowledge, creativity and innovative abilities lose their growth milieux if they are linked only to a narrowly defined scientific and technological progress. All the growing leisure opportunities, the risks and chances for an ageing population, the new technological chances of linking work and creativity within the labour process itself, can only be taken seriously if there is an accepted climate of cultural experimentalism. The interdependency of export and imports and the growing complexity of exported goods and services imply a cultural understanding of different countries, their habits and institutions; and the more ambitious export projects, an understanding of cultural evolution. In the mid 1980s in Germany there have been workshops and meetings on the theme 'high tech-high culture?'[4]

The discourse of *Kulturgesellschaft* is on the agenda of city politics. Culture has been recognized as an important business, as an accelerator for further investment, as an attractive environment for growth industries and the workforce. In the medium of *Kulturgesellschaft* the weakened enterprise of industrialism seems to have found a gradual path to transcend itself, and to regulate the social conflicts of this transition. *Kulturgesellschaft* seems to mark a middle way between the 'soft' debate on aesthetic modernism and post-modernism, and the 'hard' debate on internationalist post-Fordist competition in the world market, ecological crisis and the dramatic risks of a class war between the north and the south.

In this respect, enterprise culture could be seen as working at the same project, but from a different side: regaining competitiveness not by restructuring industrialism, but by prosperous post-industrial firms and economic activities; linking small-size business to competitive strategic behaviour, which has been unusual in British economical history; encouraging new business in the areas of elaborated consumption, fashionable, high-quality manufacturing and knowledge-based services. Enterprise culture would thus be the more conservative strategy, giving priority to the middle classes and their 'private sector', whilst *Kulturgesellschaft* would be the more liberal one, giving more space to the public sector and to the liberal establishment. Under the pressure of competition, *Kulturgesellschaft* might have to return to enterprise culture; and conversely, the reward for success by enterprise culture might involve its coming closer to *Kulturgesellschaft*.

But the structural similarities as well as the differences between both concepts go beyond a 'stages' theory of modernization. First, both concepts no longer want to rely on the middle ground of classic corporatist consensus society. This is obvious in the case of British enterprise culture, breaking even with Churchill's wartime consensus; but even in leftist versions of the *Kulturgesellschaft* in Germany there is a deep disenchantment with traditional corporatist politics. The answer to the challenges and complexities of the world market and to the differentiated needs of the people can no longer primarily be public investment, planning and corporate agreement, as it was in the 1950s and 1960s. Instead what is necessary is a long-term change of attitudes, motives and habits, embedded in a culture interacting directly with economic incentives.

But the causal forces are very different in the worlds of enterprise culture and *Kulturgesellschaft*. In enterprise culture it is the observation of the world market, the experience of decline and losing competitiveness, as well as the expected chances of the new flexible differentiated character of internationalized production, which seem no longer to favour the counterstrategy of a 'national plan'. The discourse of *Kulturgesellschaft* reflects the pressure of the world market, too, but it is interpreted in images of the internal market: the disintegrating effect of one-sided technological interests and idle consumerism might end in stable patterns of consumption, where preferences are intensified and then unfulfilled – which would threaten not only the work ethic and social solidarities, but also future demand.

Second, in enterprise culture as well as in *Kulturgesellschaft* these new attitudes are founded in a direct exchange between economy and culture. The competition between, and mutual acceptance of, different lifestyles, career and consumption patterns, and the changing meanings of sex and age, are directly transferred into supply and demand without intervention by the state. This is obvious in the case of *Kulturgesellschaft*. But enterprise culture is likewise opening free space between the monetary framework and the activities of individuals, and not in order to recreate the old blocks of industrial labour, class-divided milieux and established life cycles. The means, however, are very different. In a strange realization of a motif of the French revolution, enterprise culture is suspicious of all intermediate powers, which could challenge the relations between the institutions of the market and individuals. Money is the ruler of macro-economics, whereas the micro-economy is the field of permanent interaction between different forces, whose relations must be unstable and flexible to keep the process going on. Persistent intermediate powers are inflexible obstacles in this exchange. Trade unions have to be turned again into friendly societies if necessary, and local authorities into the simple business of service, in order to open free space for the direct interaction between money and culture. Between individuals and the financial state there is only space for procedures, not for institutions.

In a way, enterprise culture realizes and legitimates the nervous activism and hedonism of the 1960s criticized so often by the Prime Minister. As long as hedonism can pay or better still invest, it is part of consumerist hedonism by moral reason; money is the preferred institutional framework for a better interaction between culture and economy than a moralistic corporatist state. The new meritocracy guaranteeing this free space is itself defined by competitiveness. Nobody should be forever 'one of us'.

In the discourse of *Kulturgesellschaft*, however, the exchange between economy and culture is opening up new chances for the creation of new intermediate powers. In so far as strategic groups of the new middle classes are accepted as engineers of social change, and are able to transform and translate minority experience into the life of majorities, they gain real power, counterbalancing the power of economic and administrative elites. Their lifestyle may relate them to the liberal conservatism of the wealthy and educated middle classes, but in their strategic position their highly tuned sensibility and the desire for sophisticated consumption can change very soon into progressive political options for representation and identification, and vice versa. The conflict between different groups – sometimes the same groups in different life-cycle situations – participating in *Kulturgesellschaft* may thus indeed create innovative cultural areas beyond traditional political elites and the market. If opening up space for an extended market is the principle of enterprise culture, the creation of free space for intermediate powers between economy and culture is the principle of *Kulturgesellschaft*. Both reject the idea of classic elitist modernism – that cultural experimentalism can only be experienced by a minority.

Third, in enterprise culture as well as in *Kulturgesellschaft*, appropriate and unlimited communication is necessary to cope with the speed of modernization and change. Both agree that the institutions of corporatist society had insufficient sensitivity to the signals coming from the market, as well as from the libertarian and populist social movements at the grass roots. In the discourse of enterprise culture, however, there is more than enough appropriate communication provided that there is free space between economic institutions and individuals and their families. Here, classic British conservatism makes its entry. The richness of heritage and the British way of life, freed from corporatist institutions, will automatically provide the necessary means for communication. In the discourse of *Kulturgesellschaft*, by contrast, there is recognition of a basic scarcity of appropriate communication in modernized societies.

Kulturgesellschaft is thus using a quite different motif from the 1960s: the criticism of materialistic society as a mistaken compromise between labourism and monopolized capital that expels the question of what is produced, how and why. One should not confuse this criticism with the older radical or conservative criticism, that prosperity and consumption might destroy the values of family and community or undermine the long-term interests of the working class. Rather, there is principally a scarcity of appropriate communication because complex societies do not spontaneously build up capacities to observe and control themselves. More than this they become blind just because of their own success. This is obvious today in the ecological crises, but may be even more decisively in the illusion that new cultural structures of supply and demand would occur in the same manner as they did in the decades before, and that either the market or the state would provide a correct mirror image of what will be happening. But the future character and speed of cultural change, the fragile composition of families, neighbourhoods and communities once they have lost their traditional slow mode of change, cannot be seen in this mirror: you have, instead, to listen to minority experience, to the arts, and to the undertones in the talk of ordinary people. For very different reasons, *Kulturgesellschaft* is thus promoting direct and early interaction between economy and culture, and is keen to develop appropriate communication.

WHICH SHALL GOVERN MODERNIZATION – THE PRIVATE OR THE PUBLIC SECTOR?

The discourses of enterprise culture and *Kulturgesellschaft* are both answers to structural problems of democratic capitalist societies since the 1970s, but they are located in two different strategic positions. Enterprise culture is in a way developing an agenda for private sector leadership in society beyond the narrow scope of neo-liberal economics, but without a theory of culture reflecting the real change in work patterns, family, community and social habits and so on. *Kulturgesellschaft*, on the other hand, is anticipating public sector leadership as a framework for cultural change beyond corporatist state regulation, but without a sound economic theory reflecting the opportunities as well as the risks of the new world economy, which is both too global and too local for the corporatist national state.

At a first analytical level they are answers to the challenge of stagflation, which indicated that since the early 1970s the long wave of modernization, which began in the 1930s (or in Europe at least since the end of the Second World War) was basically exhausted. Stagflation was not the result of socialist, Keynesian spending policies, which were already more of a reaction to the slowdown of growth and productivity. A much more complex set of economic, political and cultural arrangements changed, which form a wave of modernization reflecting the decline of the resources for American leadership as well as the changing technological patterns of production and service. But this consensus was conservative in so far as it had no sense of the overall change in the type of modernization that was already beginning, no 'General Theory' for the lack of growth and productivity.

This wave of modernization came under pressure from two quite different sides: from the internationalization of money and capital; and from the cultural revolution of the 1960s, which simultaneously emphasized sophisticated consumption, and also dramatized the criticism of the reasons for this sophistication. An important part of the elite could no longer live their way of life; influential minorities wanted no longer to live it the same way; and a lot of people in between no longer found good reasons to defend it.

Facing these antagonisms, the 1970s became one of the most ambiguous decades. On the one hand, and early on, social democratic corporatism had its best time in Sweden and Austria as well as in the Federal Republic of Germany and the UK – although in the last case the institutional weakness of British corporatism limited the chances for success. Successfully matching the first oil-price crisis, and substituting for the declining American leadership an embryonic international, social–liberal consensus, including massive credits for the Third World, this model seemed irresistible. There were three basic reasons for this: first, the decisively growing powerful internationalization of capital and of money markets; second, an American government not interested in giving a corporatist coalition of labour and state any national framework; and third because of the ability of money and markets to lead open-ended change, where political institutions were less competent to govern. But on the other hand, social democracy began to lose its cultural plausibility and intellectual leadership: both against the libertarian populism of the right, which emphasized the freedom of consumption and choosing one's own way in insurance, housing and career building; and also against the left-libertarian populism, which emphasized the freedom to create new relations between the sexes and the ages, and the need to protect the environment and to develop a new responsibility for the basic problems of the Third World.[5]

The solution to this double-bind situation, which had its ideal type in the Germany of the late 1970s, did not come from within this constellation but instead from developments at the level of the international economy and politics. Since the beginning of the 1980s the 'terms of trade' between capital, labour and the state changed. National monetary policies got more and more dependent on international markets, where higher American interest rates and deficits, a rising dollar and financial opportunities as alternatives to industrial investment, allowed capital to 'expect' a redistribution towards capital. Under these conditions, social democratic politics was caught in a trap: the only politics that was possible, namely redistribution towards capital, was of course not legitimate, whilst the only politics that was legitimate, namely increasing the role of the state sector, was not possible.

This was the situation for recreating the political leadership of the private sector in the whole society. Internationalization of the economy; opening up markets and urging national capital to compete on international markets, linking all institutional reforms to the basic need for competitiveness; using the centralized power of the national state against trade unions and local authorities to introduce only one type of decentralization, the fragmented open space between money and consumption – all this fitted very well into the new international scenario. But it gave, of course, no answer to the other half of the corporatist heritage, namely the cultural criticism of the 1960s. Strengthening only the desire for differentiated consumption and, paradoxically, the hedonism so often criticized by the Prime Minister, would, in fact, weaken political leadership, as it was not compatible with other conservative values.

At this second level of argument we can introduce the systematic location of enterprise culture: extending the political leadership of the private sector into the key areas of cultural change – into future growth areas as well as the 'homeland' of the enemy, the cultural criticism of the 1960s.

At the end of the 1980s this project of extended leadership of the private sector seems to be fragile and limited in three characteristic ways, which will also determine the future relevance of the discourse of enterprise culture. First, for a long time the tensions between monetarism and nationalism – between an internationalistic strategy towards competitiveness and a mercantilistic defence of interests especially against some European partners, between the acceptance of world leadership by the United States and the capital markets and the defence of a certain British role in political leadership – all these tensions seemed to be manageable. More than this, they seemed actually to provide the resources for British recovery.

The ideological conflict on 'Europeanization' is not primarily based on the growing interests of the British in Europe, but more on the fact that in this image of 'Europeanization' the decreasing productivity of the strategy of the 1980s is symbolized. There are hard choices: combating inflation by joining the European monetary system or by national monetary politics; neo-liberal partnership with the United States against the threat of a 'social Europe', or participation in European modernization compromises; conquering the massive regional disparities in the UK by introducing the southern model into the whole country, or the European regional and industrial policies.

Second, there are rising doubts that the private sector will ever be able to create sufficient infrastructure because of financial squeezes, different working cultures in the private and public sectors and the different complexities of public services. Third, the private-led recreation of the inner cities is strengthening the class barriers between the wealthy majority and the poor one-third of society, instead of opening free space for the development of all.

In sum, the more that arguments and strategies have to move from the conditions of international competitiveness to the necessity of finding an answer to social and cultural change since the 1960s, the more the political leadership of the private sector becomes difficult. A culture of choice promoted by the ideas of enterprise culture cannot be reduced to a culture of consumption, but needs a new framework for choice, one that, indeed, the old corporatist state was not able to provide, but which the private sector is not able to provide either.

Kulturgesellschaft may thus be seen as beginning where enterprise culture leaves off, offering the possibility of political leadership by the public sector. The two have also found some common ground, where conflicts about the moral limits of differentiated lifestyles and the social limits of moral criticism become fruitful. The long gestation period of the Green Party and green issues is proving this, as is the counter-

145

reaction in the rise of the right-wing 'Republicans', who are defending their authoritarian values against the threat of just this new common ground, based on differentiation and multicultural heterogeneity. If the discourse of enterprise culture is in a way the epilogue of neo-liberal economics, the discourse of *Kulturgesellschaft* could be a prologue to the political leadership of the public sector beyond the old state corporatism. The discourse is, of course, not unchallenged: it has to compete with the stubborn defence of corporatist strategies and privileged positions, especially in the public service, as well as with the neo-liberal attacks on the welfare state. But the changing cultural expectations since the 1960s have indeed found here an alternative focus, perhaps preparing the way for a change in power too. For elaborated consumption, as well as the demand for a more responsible lifestyle, have, to a certain extent, trickled down to the mentalities of everyday life, from the cities to the countryside, from the educated middle classes to younger decisive parts of the working class.

The libertarian progressive mentality of many founders of new business and services in the cities is, of course, different from the normative populism of the ecological movement, and from the moral demands for democratic reform of the welfare state made by various groups. And all three differ deeply from the traditional structures of industrial society. But the conflict between these 'yellow', 'green' and 'red' expectations and desires, which seemed to neutralize German politics in the first half of the 1980s, was in the long run, perhaps, a process of learning and civilization, offering German society some valuable means for cultural and institutional change. Until now one must admit there are more expectations and hopes than decisions.

If the first comparative view of the German neo-conservative 1980s tells us that the German version is a 'softer' one than the American and British, the second tells us that under the manifest contradictions between advanced technological society and protest, there is the possibility of a hidden learning effect providing the means for future development. But we must add a third story.

Enterprise culture does not try to transform a traditional society into a modern one, but rather to force already modern political institutions, e.g. the British welfare state, under the command of the private sector. Even if you admit that these institutions as they were no longer fitted into the needs of modernization, it makes a difference whether modernization is directed towards a traditional society or towards already modern political institutions. British industrial

146

parliamentarism had developed an early model of political modernity, which did not cultivate the French illusion of the abstract identity of free individuals in the nation. Instead of this, it accepted the material and cultural evidence of different classes, but forced them to express themselves in a network of intermediate institutions, such as clubs, societies, neighbourhoods and pubs, giving a visitor this special sense of the separation and density of British class society. This structure both favoured the expression of class interests and civilized their antagonisms.

These early structures of political modernity were building effective barriers against a certain modern authoritarianism, providing the ground for the British welfare state and professional society after the Second World War. These structures always limited the abstract principles of modernization, such as differentiation and mobility, individualistic participation and conflict regulation. So different institutions, like the National Health Service and the elitist cultural establishment, had, in common, the attempt to limit modernization by non-traditional means. Losing the comparative privileges of leadership in the world market and in world society, these structural advantages turned into disadvantages, combining in the end the worst of both worlds.

By contrast, in the vacuum of political modernity in Germany after the Second World War the abstract process of modernization found a fertile ground. Differentiation, mobility, individualistic participation and conflict regulation could be established, so that it seems sometimes that there is nothing but modernization in Germany. The discourse of *Kulturgesellschaft* would, then, indicate that the real test for the promises of political modernity in Germany is still to come. If the discourse of *Kulturgesellschaft* is only expressing a more comfortable and prosperous version of enterprise culture, then its risks are greater than those of the discourse of enterprise culture, because it has not the insurance of the British experience. But if the discourse of *Kulturgesellschaft* is really transcending the limits of enterprise culture, then it has to develop an idea of political modernity to challenge the uncontrolled speed and diffusion of modernization.

A NEW CLASSICAL CONFLICT: SOCIAL MODERNIZATION OR POLITICAL MODERNITY[6]

In spite of the renaissance of modernization theory, our image of modernization is still formed by the ideas of the 1950s and 1960s.

Modernization seemed to be a general evolutionary process in world society, linking differentiation, mobility, participation and institutionalized conflict to a mode of social reproduction, which guaranteed political modernity without any additional institutional framework. The bitter historical antagonisms that accompanied the development of the British welfare state as well as the pluralism of the American way of life, seemed to have cooled down, allowing modernization to be a neutral instrument.

The radical awakening period of the 1990s and the neo-conservative mood of the 1980s had, in common, the destruction of this fiction of identity. But at the end of the 1980s, we miss a self-evident idea of modernization that naturally leads to modernity. We may have a post-Fordist theory of production, technology and consumption; we may understand the change from organized capitalism to disorganized institutions of regulation; we may understand the transformation of modernist texture into post-modernist figuration. But we have no alternative, political symbolic centre as a necessary fiction. A new theory of modernization, which will be one of the most decisive intellectual battlefields between the right and the left in the 1990s, has explicitly to conceptualize the difference between social modernization and political modernity. The discourses of enterprise culture and *Kulturgesellschaft* are already providing arguments for both sides.

The classical idea of modernization is founded on three institutions: organized market economy, competitive democracy and a prosperous society. But only the first two have been defined to a sufficient degree. The cultural definition of prosperity is either a by-product of the two other institutions, or the natural free space of individuals where they define what is good for them, and in which politics could not and should not intervene. If we admit the historical evidence that this 'natural' definition of prosperity no longer meets the ecological and political problems of world society, that this 'barbarian' definition of prosperity we share to a high degree has to be civilized, then the dialectical antagonism between social modernization and political modernity becomes visible: within the logic of modernization a social definition of prosperity is working in the same way as the self-regulation of markets and democratic institutions.

Within the context of market and political competition the actual choice between commodities and political preferences does not only mean a decision between present alternatives, but participation in decisions about future structures of supply and demand as well as in political decision-making. Consumer markets transform the signals of the consumers by several steps into the markets of investment and money. The competition between parties and issues transforms the signals of the electorate at one election to the creation of future issues, social movements and parties. The definition of prosperity would thus be established in a 'third sector' in society, where competing lifestyles, attitudes, fashions and biographies would not only regulate present interaction within a pluralist society, but also develop the incentives for future cultural change.

If complex modernization needs decisions about new ecological limits, about new forms of interaction between the sexes and ages, then the decision-making process about these issues can only be organized in the same indirect way as markets and competitive democracy organize their own long-term changes. In many respects, this radical view of modernization is based on the American experience built into the structure of American society since the populist and progressive period in the decades around 1900.

No doubt, this is still a civilizing achievement, for no modern society can live without these radicalized modernizations. But there is also the question whether radical modernization guarantees permanent modernity. In a way, Leon Trotsky's demand for permanent revolution to destroy the constantly reappearing structures of the old regimes has been used by capitalist modernization only to accept its own permanence.

It is exactly the success of modernization that is creating the necessity to differentiate the process of modernization from the process of defining political modernity, to protect modernization against itself without squeezing its productivity. The ironic consequence of the taming of permanent revolution into modernization is the need for values and political institutions of permanent modernity. Concerning the definition of prosperity, political modernity cannot rely on the indirect communication of lifestyles, attitudes and cultural markets, but needs direct political interaction and organized conflict between different definitions of collective ways of life. Political compromise between the representatives of cultural interest groups will come to different results than will the indirect communication of lifestyle enclaves. Differentiation, mobility, individualistic participation and conflict regulation – the abstract principles of modernization – prove no longer the self-evidence of modernity, but have to compete with the organized defence of immobility, the preference for collective ways

149

of participation and conflict regulation, as well as with lower degrees of differentiation, because all these alternative ideas are no less 'modern' than the principles of modernization.

With the rise of the private sector in the 1980s to political leadership, the political control of modernization will be dependent on a changing 'management of scale'. Despite all its rhetoric of change, the leadership of the private sector is embedded in the axis of world-market, national state and private consumer household. Strengthening the process of Europeanization, the anatomy of cities and regions, and a responsible individualism, will have to be a part of political modernity, or else a one-dimensional modernization will go on.

NOTES

1 For the different aspects of *Kulturgesellschaft* see the Reader for the conference in Oldenburg 1988 *Das neue Interesse an der Kultur* (Universitat Oldenburg), with speeches by politicians such as Kurt Biedenkopf, former general secretary of the Christian Democrats, Lothar Spath, prime minister of Baden-Württemberg, as well as the influential article by the philosopher Odo Marquard. See also the volume '*Kulturgesellschaft*' of the cultural leftist journal *Aesthetik und Kommunikation*, 1987. The issue is present at meetings of the German Sociological Association, from '*Ende der Arbeitgesellschaft*' in the early 1980s to 'Kultur' in 1988, as well as in common debates on city politics – see Volker Hauft (ed.) *Stadt und Lebensstil*, Beltz Weinheim 1988; and will be part of a future debate on 'modernization' as a key category of the left.

2 For the variety of senses of 'enterprise culture' see the articles in this volume. The material I have studied ranges from the pamphlets of the CPS to popular television programmes, from the theoretical work on the phenomenon of Thatcherism to articles in daily newspapers.

3 Till now, the British debate on the environmental crisis is still one oriented to better consumption, from standard of living to quality of life.

4 The discussion on appropriate education in complex societies can be linked to competitiveness and national curriculum as well as to the shaping of future democratic decision-making process under the conditions of growing cultural uncertainty, and, more than this, both depend on each other.

5 See Fritz W. Scharpf, *Sozialdemokratische Krisenpolitik im Europa*, Campus Frankfurt, 1988.

6 Cp. Hermann Schwengel, *Der Kleine Leviathan*, Athenaeum, Frankfurt, 1988.

Chapter Eight

POST-FORDISM AND ENTERPRISE CULTURE
Flexibility, autonomy and changes in economic organization
PAUL BAGGULEY

INTRODUCTION

The concept of labour flexibility has, in the past few years, moved to the centre of the stage in several social sciences. In particular, there has been a widespread debate as to whether or not advanced capitalist societies are entering a new 'post-Fordist' phase of development. Since the appearance in the *Guardian* of a plain person's guide to post-Fordism (Milne 1988), and the detailed attention being paid on the political left (Murray 1988) and the political right (Hanson and Mather 1988) to the implications of 'flexibility' for political strategy, it is clear that post-Fordism is a concept whose time, as they say, has come.

The terms 'Fordism' and 'post-Fordism' refer to particular forms of economic development and organization in capitalist industrial societies, which are often regarded as existing during relatively long periods of economic growth untroubled by major recessions and crises. The period of Fordism – broadly the 1930s to the 1970s – was characterized by mass production and mass consumption, the rise of the large vertically integrated firm, the Keynesian welfare state and mass trade unionism (see Figure 8.1 (p. 155)). Since the 1970s, it is claimed, Fordist forms of economic organization have entered a period of crisis, and the resolution of this crisis lies in the emergence of a new set of economic institutions, which would ensure further economic growth. This new arrangement, post-Fordism, would be characterized by short-run batch-type production in small or decentralized firms, by the 'rolling back' and partial privatization of the welfare state, and by a decline in the membership of trade unions and of their industrial and political power.

Some writers have explicitly related the development of a post-

151

Fordist economic structure to the emergence and strategy of Thatcherism (Jessop *et al.* 1988). In this chapter I shall be concerned with its relationship to the concept of an enterprise culture, including the question of how far the current political rhetoric of 'enterprise' is consonant with the realities of contemporary capitalist production. For example, the management structures of Fordist production are often associated with an image of the so-called 'organization man', working within rigidly defined bureaucratic rules. It might then be asked whether the new decentralized management structures of post-Fordism give any credence to a corresponding image of 'enterprise man'; and more generally, whether the kinds of qualities typically ascribed to enterprising individuals, such as self-reliance, autonomy, initiative, etc. can plausibly be associated with the conditions of post-Fordist production.

However, there are no straightforward answers to such questions; and this is partly because, I shall argue, there are at least three distinct schools of theory about post-Fordism and flexibility, each with differing implications for the concept of an enterprise culture. The first of these emerges from the work of the French 'regulation school' of Marxist political economy, especially that of Michel Aglietta. The second, which I shall term the 'institutionalist school' is exemplified in the work of Piore and Sabel. Finally, there is the 'managerialist school', which seems to be largely British in origin and is exemplified in the work of John Atkinson and the Institute of Manpower Studies, and his model of the 'flexible firm'.

Despite the considerable overlap between the respective concerns of these theorists, there are a number of important differences between them that justify this division into three schools. First, although they all share some notion of 'labour process' or 'task flexibility' (i.e. workers moving between different kinds of tasks, using different sets of skills), the particular ways in which they conceive of such flexibility diverge from one another. The regulation school writes about neo-Fordism, a new form of economic development that is superseding Fordism, and requires polyvalent, or multiskilled, workers operating as semi-autonomous work groups. The institutionalist school also identifies multiskilled workers as part of the new flexibility, but Piore and Sabel are better known for their account of new, flexible but specialist firms that subcontract much of their productive activities signifying a second industrial transition towards what they call 'flexible specialization'. Atkinson, by contrast, focuses on the 'ideal typical' concept of the 'flexible firm', which employs not only multiskilled core workers, but also part-time employees, subcontractors and temporary employees as part of a growing peripheral workforce.

Second, they differ in their specification of the causal processes that give rise to flexibility. Aglietta, of the regulation school, gives prominence to the new technical innovations in production such as automated production lines, which enable more flexible utilization of machines and labour. In contrast, Piore and Sabel seem to give causal prominence to the increasing diversity and volatility of product markets combined with new flexible techniques of production. These developments tend to undermine mass production and consumption. The managerialist school identifies a rather eclectic range of factors such as technical change, a need to further improve labour productivity and the uncertainty of the economic situation more generally. But what is common to all three causal models is some notion of flexiblity being inherent in, demanded or enabled by computer-controlled production systems, although the prominence they give to this varies.

Third, in relation to enterprise culture and the enterprising self in particular, a reading of these three schools suggests different forms that enterprise culture may take. For the regulation school, this would involve the ideological reassertion of managerial prerogative as a solution to the crisis of Fordism. Piore and Sabel, on the other hand, might see enterprise culture as part of the dynamic industrial cultures of new flexible specialist industrial districts. The managerialist approach would most closely fit the view of enterprise culture propagated by the current British government. This would involve the stress on market demands in shaping companies' production organization strategies, and a change in attitudes and values among management and employees.

Finally, they all have a predictive/prescriptive component to their arguments, but here again they differ markedly. Aglietta's account is profoundly pessimistic, seeing the development of neo-Fordism as a further intensification of Fordism, resulting in increased control over labour by capital. Piore and Sabel, in complete contrast, are highly optimistic concerning the character of flexible specialization. They see it opening up the possibility for a radical democratization of the economy on a decentralized local basis. The British managerialists' prescriptions are, if anything, pragmatic in character. They see the flexible firm as a desirable end, because it is the most efficient solution

153

to the labour problems of British industry. However, this 'pragmatism', arguably, has a strong ideological bent in emphasizing the rights of employers over employees in adapting labour processes and labour markets to needs dictated by the market and new technology.

These three ways of understanding post-Fordism are also clearly related to different political traditions and projects. The regulation approach is self-avowedly Marxist in orientation, and the British Communist Party has made considerable use of its approach in its *Manifesto for New Times* (Communist Party of Great Britain 1989). The institutionalist approach is also related to socialist politics, but of a left-reformist nature. Charles Sabel, for example, was a consultant for the former GLC (Smith 1989: 204); and one of the principal British writers on post-Fordism – Robin Murray – was formerly an employee of the GLC. Finally, the 'flexible firm' model is related to the political right, in particular the labour-market thinking of the Thatcher governments (Pollert 1988: 307);

Thus, what is at stake in these debates is not only a set of theoretical issues about models of economic development and enterprise culture, but also the thinking behind current political strategies and policies. But before exploring these further, I shall now present a more general picture of the main contrasts between Fordism and post-Fordism.

FORDISM AND POST-FORDISM

The notion of Fordism first received a detailed analysis in Gramsci's *Prison Notebooks* (Gramsci 1971). His writings on 'Americanism and Fordism' clearly form the basis of Aglietta's account. However, both Gramsci's original account and Aglietta's concept of neo-Fordism have been elaborated upon by a range of authors, most clearly by Murray (1988) who provides a synthetic idealized contrast between Fordist and post-Fordist economic structures. They can be usefully summarized as two ideal typical economic structures. These ideal types generalize across the substantive claims of each approach, so I am not claiming that each approach is characterized by all of these features. The ideal types are presented in Figure 8.1.

The central element of a Fordist economic structure is mass production articulated to mass consumption. Large volumes of the same product are produced using specialized machinery dedicated to the one product. Jobs are largely semi-skilled or unskilled, arranged

Fordism	Post-Fordism
Mass consumption	Fragmented niche markets
Technology dedicated to the production of one product	General flexible machinery
Mass, assembly-line production	Short-run batch production
Semi-skilled workers	Multiskilled workers
Taylorist management strategy	'Human relations' management strategy
General or industrial unions	No unions or 'company unionism'/no-strike deals
Centralized national bargaining	Decentralized local or plant-level bargaining
Geographically dispersed branch plants	Geographically concentrated new industrial districts flexible specialist communities

Figure 8.1 Ideal types of Fordism and post-Fordism

in complex hierarchies of control and subject to detailed 'Taylorist' organization. Literally thousands of simple, detailed jobs are created in the most extreme forms of Fordist production to create an extremely fragmented division of labour. As Henry Ford himself boasted:

> The lightest jobs were again classified to discover how many of them required the use of full faculties, and we found that 670 could be filled by legless men, 2637 by one-legged men, two by armless men, 715 by one-armed men, and ten by blind men. Therefore, out of 7882 kinds of job . . . 4034 did not require full physical capacity.
>
> (Henry Ford, 1922, quoted in Littler 1985: 15)

To the standard product made using dedicated assembly-line technology under a Taylorist organization of work was allied the phenomenon of high wages and the reshaping of working-class culture. Whilst Ford's 5-dollar day and his 'sociology' department have received extensive comment since the earliest discussions of Fordism (Gramsci 1971), the emphasis on the extensive commodification of working-class patterns of consumption and households examined by Aglietta (1987: 71) amongst others is the more important theoretical point. Essentially, the security of employment and relatively high incomes provide the mass market required for the mass-production system. Under the Fordist regime, large general or industrial unions developed, negotiating with companies nationally on sector-wide, or even on a centralized national basis in some countries.

Furthermore, although Fordism developed in particular sectors and therefore regions, its inherent predictability as an economic system and use of easily trained semi-skilled workers meant that location could be decentralized from old industrial cores. Witness the widespread locations of Ford in the UK – Dagenham (near London), Swansea (in South Wales) and Merseyside – all outside the 'home' of the car industry in the West Midlands. Whilst the UK car market attracted Ford into the country, the location was more driven by the search for pools of trainable semi-skilled workers, than by being close to traditional, car-industry locations.

What, then, are the characteristics of a post-Fordist economic structure? Whereas speciality and fragmentation at work and uniformity in consumption are the central features of Fordism, broad job descriptions and labour flexibility allied with the fragmentation of markets seem to capture the essence of post-Fordism. Attempts are now being made to develop flexible manufacturing systems capable of producing several types of the same general product. Gone are the rigidly defined '7,882' jobs of Henry Ford's era. Now the emphasis is on breaking down rigid job classifications both horizontally between functions and vertically within the hierarchy of authority, implying 'multiskilling' on the one hand, and participation on the other. In the realm of consumption, greater choice and variety are preferred – gone is the option of one version of one model.

Besides these transformations of the techniques of production, the character of product markets and the nature of skills, it is claimed that social relations within production have also been transformed. Post-Fordism ostensibly heralds the decline of the general or industrial unions built up under Fordism. Multiskilling and batch production require a new management strategy in relation to labour, replacing Taylorist-based management strategies with a renewed enthusiasm for human relations and neo-human, relations-based techniques. It is argued that managers are using these new techniques of communication and control to circumvent unions altogether (Bassett 1986; Leadbetter and Lloyd 1987). Where unions remain in place, it is asserted that systems of industrial relations are decentralizing to the plant or workshop level. Finally, the spatial organization of post-Fordist industries operates on a centralizing rather than decentralizing logic. This has been most powerfully argued by Piore and Sabel (1984) and, especially Scott (1988), who see the emergence of new industrial regions as based in the needs of flexible specialist firms to be part of dense highly propinquitous networks of similar firms with which they can collaborate in complex subcontracting arrangements.

A similarly ideal typical model of the causal processes underlying the development of post-Fordism is presented in Figure 8.2. This shows the causal connections between certain of the key elements in the post-Fordist model.

Initially, firms respond to market fragmentation in the form of shorter production runs. From here lie two routes to post-Fordism – flexible specialization or the restructuring of Fordist types of organization. Flexible specialization develops where short production runs are subcontracted among similar small firms. These firms concentrate in densely networked industrial districts in order to obtain the best contacts and deals. Firms are typically small with a few highly skilled workers and low levels of unionization.

The alternative route is perhaps more widespread, involving the restructuring of already existing Fordist forms of organization. These

THE POST-FORDIST CAUSAL CHAIN

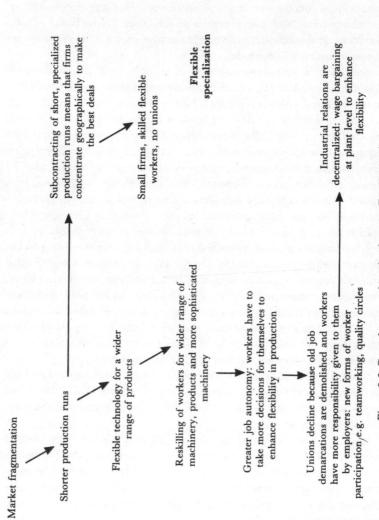

Market fragmentation

Shorter production runs

Flexible technology for a wider range of products

Subcontracting of short, specialized production runs means that firms concentrate geographically to make the best deals

Small firms, skilled flexible workers, no unions

Flexible specialization

Reskilling of workers for wider range of machinery, products and more sophisticated machinery

Greater job autonomy: workers have to take more decisions for themselves to enhance flexibility in production

Unions decline because old job demarcations are demolished and workers have more responsibility given to them by employers: new forms of worker participation, e.g. teamworking, quality circles

Industrial relations are decentralized: wage bargaining at plant level to enhance flexibility

Figure 8.2 Causal connections in the post-Fordist model

previously Fordist firms respond by developing more flexible forms of technology with the capacity to produce a wider range of products. In order to operate this technology and to move between different types of machine, workers develop a wider range of skills. To further enhance flexibility at the point of production, employers introduce greater job autonomy for workers. Allied to this innovation is the development of new forms of worker participation in their firms. Employers are seeking both to utilize workers' detailed and informally developed knowledge of production, and to build a new commitment to the firm among them.

In this model industrial relations in particular are transformed. The breaking down of old divisions of labour in the firm means that traditional skill demarcations are no longer available as objective features around which unions may organize. Further, the new forms of worker participation may even render unions redundant. The pattern of industrial relations also changes with respect to wage bargaining. The search for flexibility often lies behind the attempts of employers to decentralize bargaining from national agreements to the local or plant level. In Britain the public sector has recently taken a leading role in this process. Strikes amongst postal workers, university lecturers, local authority workers, railway workers and the dockers have all, to some degree, been concerned with attempts to decentralize national, collective-bargaining procedures. The aim here is to achieve wage flexibility with respect to variations in local and regional labour market conditions.

I shall now consider in more detail the three schools of theory previously identified (p. 152), and their respective implications for the concept of an enterprise culture.

THE REGULATION SCHOOL

As noted earlier, many of the key concepts in the Fordist/post-Fordism debate were developed during the 1970s by the French Marxist, Michel Aglietta. He saw Fordism as having two principal features as a form of industrial capitalist production. First, semi-automatic assembly lines are developed that move materials between work stations with dedicated machines for specific tasks. Second, semi-skilled jobs emerge where the workers are fixed to a specific narrow range of tasks whose pace and rhythms are set by the machines (Aglietta 1987: 118–19). However, there are definite limits to the continued fragmentation of work that create a crisis for Fordism. Aglietta sees three factors within the labour process that limit the productivity gains that can be delivered by the increased fragmentation of work. First, increases in the 'balance delay time' on production lines, when the constraints arising from the fact that individual tasks take different amounts of time to complete creates serious blockages and delays in the process of production. As tasks are further fragmented, more time is spent by workers simply doing nothing. Second, intensified labour on the production line has deleterious effects on the physical and mental health of the workers. This leads to unpredictable absenteeism and management faces difficulties deploying labour around the plant leading to losses of production. Third, and perhaps most importantly, the collectivization of work breaks the link between individual effort, output and reward (Aglietta 1987: 120–1).

The solution to the crisis is the development of what Aglietta terms 'neo-Fordism'. Machines that control their own operations, organized and planned as a total system, are characteristic of neo-Fordism. Such a system, according to Aglietta requires a more detailed design to deal with variations in the process of production. Furthermore, production norms and the responsibilities of job positions need totally redefining. These changes are made possible by microelectronics and the emergence of numerically controlled machine tools (Aglietta 1987: 123–5). Automation enables a new flexibility within the process of production. This automation enables the centralization of the planning of production, but the decentralization of the units of production. These consequences result in an increasing fragmentation of the working class among smaller units of production (Aglietta 1987: 125–7).

The second feature of neo-Fordism that Aglietta considers in some detail is the 'recomposition of tasks', where management is attempting to reorganize labour in line with the development of the automatic control of production (Aglietta 1987: 128). Job enrichment and the development of semi-autonomous work groups combine component control, preparation and regulation of machines with execution in one operator. Capital then suppresses some categories of skilled workers, maintenance workers, etc. since these tasks are now performed by the semi-autonomous work groups. Nevertheless, the semi-autonomous work group's actions, responsibilities and relations to other work groups are defined by the overall programme controllers (Aglietta 1987: 129). In contrast to the other post-Fordist writers considered here, Aglietta sees the job flexibility that is emerging not as multiskilling, but as a further intensification and extension of deskilling (Aglietta 1987: 129).

These developments entail certain possibilities for the restructuring of both the hierarchies of the capitalist enterprise and the role of trade unions within the regime of accumulation. In particular, Aglietta argues that since workers are to some extent self-managing in semi-autonomous work groups, those employed in monitoring and supervising employees can be 'thinned out'. Furthermore, these semi-autonomous work groups also constitute forms of organization for the working class that are functional alternatives to trade unions (Aglietta 1987: 129–30, 171). Under Fordism, managerial control is centralized in large and complex hierarchy. In Aglietta's model of neo-Fordism the workers partially manage themselves, but within the wider confines of production organization determined by a central management.

The regulation approach stresses the transformation of what it calls 'production norms', that is, the agreed levels of effort and responsibility at work between employees and employers. However, as Aglietta makes clear, these production norms are not simply 'agreements' between management and workers on what levels of effort, output and pay should be, but are the product of bitter struggles between labour and capital. Enterprise culture as we have been discussing it here is clearly a candidate as a new set of production norms in British industry stressing individual autonomy and responsibility at work, in contrast to the old Fordist 'norms' based on hierarchy and centralized disciplinary control. For writers such as Aglietta, enterprise culture would be very much a managerial ideology for post-Fordism, a new, and for him, even more insidious way of controlling the workers. The regulation approach would seem to provide some kind of account of the drive towards the increased use of worker participation schemes at times legitimated in terms of 'enterprise culture'.

THE INSTITUTIONALIST SCHOOL

Piore and Sabel argue for a transition from mass production to 'flexible specialization', which they term 'the second industrial divide' (Sabel 1982; Piore and Sabel, 1984). The major features of this approach are first, their view of the market as the primary causal factor in the development and crisis of Fordism; second, their emphasis on social struggles in shaping technological change and the institutions of regulation in Fordism, such as industrial relations legislation; and third, the important distinction they make between large firms that move towards flexibility and the emergence of small firms producing short batches. This latter case, with its new role for small firms, is what they term 'flexible specialization'.

Their emphasis on the market as the key causal factor in the emergence of Fordism is quite clear and unambiguous:

> Stable demand for large numbers of standard products is the cornerstone of Fordism. It makes possible long-term investment in product specific machines, which encourages the constant, if only partially successful, attempt to decompose skill. Anything that unsettles prospects of manufacturing a certain product in a fixed way and selling it in predictably large numbers for a forseeable price undermines the propensity to invest in the Fordist strategy.
>
> (Sabel 1982: 195)

For Piore and Sabel, then, mass markets are the 'cornerstone' of Fordist mass production. But what of mass-production technology? This they claim was not a necessary outcome of historical change, but rather the outcome of social struggles. Mass production in Piore and Sabel's argument is a 'technological paradigm', a particular perspective on what constitutes efficient productive technology that is dominant throughout society. As long as a particular technological paradigm satisfies competition, it continues to develop along broadly the same lines, but it is not necessarily the only form of technology that could be efficient in the circumstances. The paradigm of mass production was most successful in the new mass markets of the USA, and this enormous success provided the rationale for its emulation elsewhere (Piore and Sabel 1984: 44-8).

There are two further features of the mass production economy that Piore and Sabel consider to be important: the stabilization of markets through the emergence of the large corporation, and the synchronization of production and consumption through Keynesian economic management techniques. The argument in relation to the large corporation is that the mass markets did not just emerge autonomously as some exogenous economic variable, but were in large part constructed by the corporations. Furthermore, the large corporations were also keen to control inputs into the production process, especially labour. Piore and Sabel explain US corporations' hostility to trade unionism in terms of the threat unions posed to the power

of management to redesign and control the fragmented labour processes of mass production (Piore and Sabel 1984: 64).

In Piore and Sabel's account, the key mechanisms of both the
emergence of Fordism and its crisis tendencies operate through the
market, especially product markets. To resolve the world crisis of mass
production, they argue that there are essentially two alternative ways
to reinvigorate mass production. The first involves a restructuring of
large corporate hierarchies, which essentially removes the pyramid of
occupations generated by traditional bureaucracy and Taylorism. The
second involves the development of many small specialized companies
in a new industrial system of flexible specialization, and this is their
preferred strategy (Piore and Sabel 1984: 282). Corresponding to each
of these, it might be suggested, would be different forms of enterprise
culture.

There are four key features to the first strategy of corporate restructuring. First, the introduction of computers makes more feasible
piecework bonuses, and individual workers can be monitored in their
jobs more readily. Second, work stations can be redesigned to enable
workers to carry out a variety of operations, and to control the flow
of work to and from their stations. This increases individual flexibility.
Third, groups of workers might rotate posts regularly, perhaps at their
own rhythm. Finally, work groups could be given responsibility for
inspection, setting up machines and some maintenance (Sabel 1982:
213–14).

There are a number of prerequisites for the development of flexible
specialization. The development and application of computers to
production enables flexibility to develop by responding to and developing the capacities of the user. Flexibility is not inherent in computer
technology according to Piore and Sabel. If the mass markets of the
post-war period had not fragmented, computers would have simply
been used to reproduce the mass production form of economic rigidity.
The flexible possibilities of the computer have only been utilized
because the fragmentation of markets have determined that it be so.
However, competition must be organized in such a way that flexible
specialist firms remain flexible and innovative and do not remain fixed
to their niche markets. The solutions to this problem might be found
in the form of regional agglomerations of firms; federations of firms;
'solar firms', where important parts of the production process are subcontracted to firms with which the core company has a more-or-less
permanent relationship; or 'workshop factories'. What all these share

is a *social* regulation of competition, co-operation, prices, wages and training. In effect, a certain kind of 'enterprise culture' embedded in a set of material institutions.

An important feature of this social regulation is that it limits entry to each industry through some mechanism of a community boundary and informal networks. Within the 'community' certain 'social welfare' provisions are made such that to continue in business in the industry access to the community is crucial. What is provided might be contracts for work, new technology or training, but central to Piore and Sabel's argument is that the community is grounded in prior ethnic, religious or political ties. A further function of these community ties is to limit destructive competition such as low wages or poor work conditions, whilst at the same time the internal hierarchies of the community and intercommunity rivalries encourage competitive innovation to produce new or better quality products. Central to reproducing the boundaries of the community is the acquisition of skill, which generates an internal system of social honour (Piore and Sabel 1984: 274).

Piore and Sabel's model of flexible specialist communities creates an image of a democratically regulated enterprise culture. This community-based enterprise culture is quite different from Aglietta's pessimistic account of semi-autonomous work groups as a new post-Fordist managerial ideology. Piore and Sabel give a very optimistic almost utopian account of flexible specialist communities united in a co-operative competition of continuous economic innovation. And in this markedly 'social' model, typical characteristics of enterprise such as self-reliance, energy and initiative are seen as residing not so much in particular individuals as in the norms and institutional practices prescribing appropriate economic behaviour within the community itself.

THE MANAGERIALIST SCHOOL

Atkinson's model of the 'flexible firm' identifies the emergence of two types of worker, which he terms 'core' and 'periphery' (Atkinson 1984). The core workers are on permanent contracts, highly skilled or multiskilled, and are essential to the organization's activities. These core workers can be deployed by management between different sets of tasks according to the demands of workloads, methods of production or the dictates of technology.

The periphery contains two types of flexibility – numerical flexibility in the form of part-time or temporary work, and what Atkinson (1984) refers to as 'distancing', which is principally the subcontracting of functions previously carried out 'in-house'. Numerical flexibility is primarily concerned with employers' strategies for matching the durations of labour inputs to demands for that labour: part-time employment to cover peak hours of demand in consumer services, for example, or temporary seasonal workers in hotel and catering. Finally, he discusses pay flexibility, which refers to the ability of firms to use pay to encourage functional flexibility, reward scarce skills or tie pay to individual performance.

Atkinson (1984) goes on to explain flexibility in terms of three sets of pressures for change. The first of these is the need to consolidate previous productivity gains, given the effects of the recent recession. Second, there is the development of greater market uncertainty. This refers not to the short-term effects of the recession, but to the greater internationalization of product markets and the greater uncertainty within particular product markets. Third, Atkinson (1984) sees technical change as important in encouraging flexibility. This occurs because new staffing practices are required for new production systems on the one hand, and on the other, because functional flexibility should enable firms to introduce new work practices for the efficient utilization of technology more quickly. This account of the impact of technical change on functional flexibility, it should be noted, is quite different from that found in the work of the regulation and institutionalist schools. There, functional flexibility is seen to reside in some sense *in the technology itself*, rather than being used simply to reorganize labour practices in a more flexible way. This reveals something often implicit in Atkinson's notion of functional flexibility, that this is an expression of management's enhanced control over the deployment of labour in an attempt to improve productivity (Atkinson 1984).

In this model of the flexible firm, the emphasis on the return of managerial prerogative is paramount, and this valorizes particular kinds of managerial culture and strategies in which several characteristics often attributed to 'enterprising' individuals may be discerned. The new managerial style requires energy, initiative and self-reliance in taking decisions quickly to respond to the ever-changing demands of the product market. Flexibility is the key means by which the organization's activities can keep in step with these changes; and managers must constantly seek out aspects of their business that can be made more flexible, and monitor the results to ensure that this is fully and properly implemented. Pay flexibility also plays a central part in this overall strategy, especially in encouraging functional flexibility, matching market rates for skills in short supply, and rewarding individual success (National Economic Development Office 1986).

CONCLUSION

In conclusion I would like to make some rather sceptical remarks about the utility of models of Fordism and post-Fordism as general accounts of recent economic change. Nevertheless, these models do throw some light on the question of whether or not the rhetoric of enterprise culture fits the realities of contemporary capitalist production.

There are now many detailed critiques of the key post-Fordist and labour flexibility theorists I have been discussing here (Bagguley *et al.* 1990; Pollert, 1988; Smith, 1989). I shall note only what I consider to be the most telling criticisms. First, models of Fordism/post-Fordism focus mainly on the manufacturing sector, largely ignoring services. Since in Britain most people in employment work in the service sector, a manufacturing-based model of post-Fordism is surely a narrow and possibly misleading basis for a general account of the changing experience of employment. Second, divisions of gender and race are largely ignored in these models. Women and ethnic minorities generally have very different patterns of employment, labour-market rewards and experiences of work to those of the skilled, white, male workers who are the ideal–typical multiskilled flexible workers of post-Fordism. Finally, the degree and extent of post-Fordist restructuring may be questioned. Many of the post-Fordist writings are based on a few carefully selected case studies. They are probably not typical of most industries in many countries. Indeed, it is almost certainly the case that post-Fordist models of economic organization can only develop under quite specific technological, product-market and cultural conditions.

On a more positive note, it can be argued that post-Fordist forms of organization are most likely to develop in those dynamic leading sectors of the economy such as the so-called 'high-tech' industries, which are of strategic importance to contemporary developed economies. Furthermore, it is in these 'leading post-Fordist sectors' that one is most likely to find the kinds of development discussed by the institutionalist writers such as Piore and Sabel and Scott, whose

166

case studies often focus upon places such as Silicon Valley in the USA, Emilia Romagna in Italy and Britain's M4 corridor. Here the local economic, cultural and political conditions are conducive to flexible specialist forms of economic development, and hence perhaps, also, to the kinds of 'local' enterprise culture sustained by these.

However, one should be careful not to apply such interpretations to whole economies. For example, if one considers the kinds of policies being pursued by the British government in attempting to foster or create an 'enterprise culture', it is not the institutionalist school that seems most relevant, but the managerialist one. In particular, there is an important relationship between its model of the flexible firm and the government's own practices as an employer. The research for this model only examined the private sector. But as critics have pointed out (Pollert 1988) temporary and part-time work are central to many public-sector organizations; and 'flexibilization' in the form of sub-contracting has been strongly pursued in the public sector, especially the NHS (Bagguley et al. 1990; Cousins 1987). In this context, the 'flexible firm' model can be seen as a legitimating device for the marketization of elements of the public sector, and hence for a specific political interpretation of the concept of an enterprise culture.

REFERENCES

Aglietta, M. (1987) A Theory of Capitalist Regulation: the US Experience, London: Verso.
Atkinson, J. (1984) 'Manpower Strategies for Flexible Organizations', Personnel Management, August.
Bagguley, P., Mark-Lawson, J., Shapiro, D., Urry, J., Walby, S. and Warde, A. (1990) Restructuring: Place, Class and Gender, London: Sage.
Bassett, P. (1986) Strike Free, London: Macmillan.
Communist Party of Great Britain (1989) Manifesto for New Times: A Communist Party Strategy For The 1990s, London: Communist Party of Great Britain.
Cousins, C. (1987) Controlling Social Welfare, Brighton: Wheatsheaf.
Gramsci, A. (1971) Selections From Prison Notebooks, London: Lawrence & Wishart.
Hanson, C.G. and Mather, G. (1988) Striking Out Strikes: Changing Employment Relations in the British Labour Market, London: Institute of Economic Affairs.
Jessop, B., Bonnett, K., Bromley, S. and Ling, T. (1988) Thatcherism, Oxford: Polity Press.
Leadbetter, C. and Lloyd, J. (1987) In Search of Work, London: Penguin.

Littler, C. (1985) 'Taylorism, Fordism and job design', in D. Knights, H. Willmott and D. Collinson (1985) *Job Redesign: Critical Perspectives on the Labour Process*, Aldershot: Gower, pp. 10–29.

Milne, S. (1988) 'Post-Fordism', the *Guardian*.

Murray, R. (1988) 'Life after Henry (Ford)', *Marxism Today* New Times issue, 32 (10): 8–13.

National Economic Development Office (1986) *Changing Working Patterns*, London: NEDO.

Piore, M. and Sabel, C. (1984) *The Second Industrial Divide: Possibilities for Prosperity*, New York: Basic Books.

Pollert, A. (1988) 'The 'flexible firm': fixation or fact?', *Work, Employment and Society* 2: 281–316.

Sabel, C. (1982) *Work and Politics: the Division of Labour in Industry*, Cambridge: Cambridge University Press.

Scott, A. (1988) *New Industrial Spaces*, London: Pion.

Smith, C. (1989) 'Flexible specialisation, automation and mass production', *Work, Employment and Society* 2: 203–20.

Part Three

MARKET VALUES AND CONSUMER SOVEREIGNTY

Many versions of enterprise culture insist on the value of markets in elevating the powers of consumers and controlling the worst excesses of producers. The chapters in this section examine the causes and consequences of the introduction of consumer-led production.

Abercrombie argues that there is a shift from producer to consumer in the power to determine the form, nature and quality of goods and services. This shift is actually a double movement comprising a loss of authority on the part of producers on the one hand and, on the other, the appearance of what can be called the 'enterprising consumer'. The decline of producer authority can be seen in a number of ways. For example, producers of many goods and services can no longer deploy detailed knowledge about the product; there has been diminution in the culture of production. Enterprising consumers, on the other hand, make their consumption an active process capable of generating considerable skill and knowledge. In doing so, their tastes may actually run ahead of producers' capacities to satisfy them.

Whiteley's chapter gives a historical perspective on government intervention in design partly through the Design Council. In the immediate post-war period, the emphasis in discussions of good design was on the product rather than the consumer or manufacturer; good design had an educational function. However, in the 1960s this view began to change under the pressures of consumerism. Absolute design values were replaced by plural ones; there could be different views of good design. None the less, even in this partial concession to the consumer's view, the Design Council continued to espouse public values and the virtues of design as education. By the early 1980s though, the emphasis had completely shifted. Good design is no longer promoted because it improves the public mind, but because it maximizes sales and profits.

It is clear that in the 1980s the way that the professions dispense their services is changing as they become exposed to the marketplace. A central question in Stanley's chapter (Chapter Eleven) is to what extent lawyers have been forced to redefine and compromise the principles of justice. He examines changes in the market for legal services, considering the overall increase in the size of the market, greater competition within the market and polarization in certain areas of activity. These changes have meant some transformation in the self-definition of lawyers, who increasingly see themselves as entrepreneurs, suppliers of a commodity in the marketplace, rather than one of the instruments of justice.

The focus of Keat's chapter (Chapter Twelve) is the appropriateness or otherwise of the use of market criteria in 'cultural' activities such as academic research and teaching or the arts. He argues that the use of such criteria undermines the values by which they had been previously, and rightly, judged. The argument makes use of MacIntyre's concept of a 'practice' defined as an activity where goods 'internal' to that activity are realized in pursuing standards of excellence. The difficulty discussed by Keat is that the integrity of practices may be damaged by the pursuit of goods 'external' to the practice such as money, power or prestige. Markets introduce such external goods in that they make producers aim at profit maximization and they locate the criteria of excellence in the preferences of consumers.

Chapter Nine

THE PRIVILEGE OF THE PRODUCER
NICHOLAS ABERCROMBIE

We have got to create a fresh spirit of enterprise in this country and the government has an important role in it.

(Interview with Neil Kinnock *Observer*, 7 May 1989)

I used to have a nightmare for the first six years in office that, when I had got the law right, the deregulation etc., the British sense of enterprise and initiative would have been killed by socialism.

('The Brian Walden Interview', Margaret Thatcher, *Sunday Times*, 8 May 1988)

In these two quotations there is a remarkable agreement about the need to create or renew a spirit of enterprise in the British people.[1] There is feeling in the debate about Britain rather like that expressed in the nineteenth and early twentieth centuries about oriental societies. By contrast with the west, these societies were claimed to be conformist, static, unmoving and authoritarian (Said 1978). In much the same way, Britain in the 1980s needs energy, activity and initiative to move out of her backward, depressed and dependent condition. There the agreement stops, of course. The Conservative and Labour parties have different diagnoses of the disease and very different remedies. The underlying argument of this chapter is that whatever are the apparent political agreements about enterprise, the appearance of enterprise culture is not primarily a function of political interventions. Instead, it is produced by a set of fundamental changes in British society. In this sense Mrs Thatcher and Mr Kinnock are riding a wave, for their advocacy of enterprise merely reflects and accentuates changes that are happening anyway in British society. In this chapter I do not have the space to review all the arguments about the effects of recent social change. Instead, I am going to look at one issue that I believe is crucial to the debate about enterprise – the shift in power and authority from producer to consumer. My argument is illustrated, albeit briefly, by consideration of the book-publishing industry. This example is chosen partly to show the way that enterprise culture is manifested in the private sector and not only in the public services, which are the chief targets of government enterprise policy. Although the publishing industry has some unusual features, the shift from producer to consumer that it manifests is characteristic of many modern economic activities.

FROM PRODUCER TO CONSUMER

The shift from producer to consumer means that the capacity to determine the form, nature and quality of goods and services has moved from the former to the latter. This represents a profound change in social relationships. The culture and institutions of a society in general define the relative positions of consumer and producer, definitions that cut across other forms of social differentiation. This is not to say that the producer/consumer relationship is more funda-mental than any other, but changes in the relation do have society-wide effects. After all, almost everybody produces and/or consumes goods and services and changes in the character of these activities will have effects on large areas of people's lives. Such changes require relatively autonomous developments in production *and* consumption sectors. In this respect both liberal theory, which attributes changes in production to shifts in consumer preferences, and much Marxist theory, in making production the motor of history and consumer wants and needs merely the outcome of manipulation by producers, are misleading. It is also unwise to put too much explanatory weight on the concepts of consumerism and consumer culture,[2] for it is not only a cultural shift in the meaning given to consumption that is at stake, but also a change in patterns of authority between producers and consumers that affects social relations as a whole. Although this change is society-wide, it is less well marked in some sectors than in others. For example, the process moves more slowly in the professions than in commerce, and more slowly in the culture industries, including television, than in consumer electronics. Indeed, some elements of the culture industries, especially book publishing, are only recently showing signs of the move-ment to consumers.

Producers have lost, or are losing, much of their social position.

In some senses, this is a loss of authority. It is loss of authority *as* producer in determining the form and content of production and consumption; it is no longer possible to say with Henry Ford that customers can have any colour of car as long as it is black! However, it is also a loss of authority in a wider sense. Producers, and regimes of production, are associated with the forces of rationalization and order; the activities of production cannot be conducted without high levels of organization. Consumption, on the other hand, especially modern (or post-modern) consumption, is associated with undisciplined play and disorder; it does not require organization and may, indeed, actively deny it. More institutionally, any increase in the importance of consumption and consumers involves a diffusion of authority, which helps to explain the oft-remarked pluralism and fragmentation of the modern world; it is a change from social organization dominated by a relatively small and well-structured group of producers to one consisting of a more diffuse and much larger assembly of consumers.

One way in which the shifts in patterns of authority are represented, particularly in the culture industries, is in the changing relationships of high culture and popular culture. As the traditional relations of authority between producer and consumer break down, so also does the existing relationship between high and popular culture, a relationship that is, as much as anything else, one of authority. High culture represents an authoritative statement of good taste or bad taste, the dominant view of what counts as a good book or film, for example. High culture is a producer culture; production is the problematic and interesting element and consumption is more or less taken for granted. Aesthetic interest focuses on the qualities of the artist and art is an expression of the personality, outlook or talent of the artist. High culture, in other words, is authorial. Popular culture, on the other hand, is a consumer category. In this case, production is routine and uninteresting and the significance of the form lies in the fact of mass consumption.

The boundary between high and popular culture in modern society is breaking down. The exponents of high culture are less disdainful of the popular than, say, in the interwar period. They are less likely to say with Betjeman:

Come, bombs, and blow to smithereens
Those air-conditioned bright canteens
Tinned fruit, tinned meat, tinned milk, tinned beans
Tinned mind, tinned breath
                    (Betjeman 1937, quoted in Skelton 1964)

The suggestion that these cultural boundaries are less secure is a central plank of post-modernist theory, but we do not have to accept the notion that there is a distinctive post-modern culture to acknowledge the force of the view that the boundary between high and popular culture is becoming more diffuse.

The existence of cultural definitions embodied in high culture used to give producers in the culture industries a privileged place. For instance, the key question for editors working for book publishers is: 'What is a good book?' Before the last war in Britain and even for a decade after it, that question could be answered by consulting the editor's taste or instinct supported by a traditional body of knowledge, culture and opinion to which the editor had access by virtue of education and experience. If the editor sought the opinion of others, they would be equally well-endowed, all being participants in a literate culture. In the past forty years these judgements have become less secure as the privilege given to high culture declines. As the next section will argue, editors decreasingly base their judgements on a cultural definition of quality.

THE CULTURE OF PRODUCTION

There is a decline in what one might call the 'culture of production'. It is important to distinguish two possible senses of this phrase. On the one hand, there are cultures specific to particular workplaces, the everyday talk and practices that regulate conduct. I call these workplace cultures. Such cultures prescribe a vast range of activities – who can talk to whom about what, how authority relations work, what is the right way of doing the job, what counts as doing a good job and so on. Academic interest in cultures of this kind has focused recently on corporate cultures – those customs and rules that are characteristic of large, commercial and bureaucratically organized enterprises. It is significant that the cultures of companies can be very different from one another. As Jackall shows, the very quality – bureaucratic organization – that would appear to be the common feature of large companies actually permits different cultures: 'bureaucratic work causes people to bracket, while at work, the moralities that they might hold outside the workplace . . . and to follow instead the prevailing morality of their particular organizational situation' (Jackall 1988: 6). Indeed, the variations in corporate cultures are sometimes invoked as partial explanations of differences in the commercial performance of companies.

It is a second sense of the culture of production that is more important for the present argument. Most producers of any good or service will share technical knowledge of their work, have common standards of what counts as excellence and will be engaged in routine, everyday conversation about the nature and quality of the product. Identities as producers are organized around the importance of being a producer making something worthwhile. This sense of the culture of production – which I will call 'producer culture' – is very similar to the use of the concept of a practice in Keat, Chapter Twelve, this volume.

One of the important features of producer culture is that it can unify practitioners across competing companies. Producers have plenty of opportunities to discuss and judge the quality of what they produce – a set of technical judgements not at all obvious to the consumer. The result can be a certain unification of attitudes and interests of producers *vis-à-vis* consumers. Publishers from competing firms, for instance, may meet fairly often, formally or informally, to discuss market trends, problems in the industry and, at editorial level at least, the kinds of books being produced. My claim is that this producer culture has been undermined: it is no longer so active or detailed and it has had its emphasis shifted from the product to the means of selling.

I have already pointed to the way that the producer culture of publishers is sustained by their wider cultural involvements. The identity of publishers was constructed by their activities as producers of good books that did their job, artistic or educational. Although publishing has, of course, always been commercial, such a producer culture meant that the mission to produce good books would often greatly outweigh commercial considerations. As Sir Stanley Unwin wrote in a book regarded for some time as a definitive statement of the publisher's mission:

> What many people find difficult to understand is our insistence upon complete knowledge of the financial and economic implications of every transaction, coupled with a readiness to act upon other than

economic motives once the full implications of what is being done have been grasped by all concerned. Most people either ignore or act solely upon economic considerations. Our approach is disconcerting because it is unusual; in consequence some catch is suspected.

(Unwin 1960: 312)

Or the more definite statement of intent expressed by Victor Gollancz's biographer:

Victor was, of course, delighted by the commercial success of *The Lost Steps* – how could he not have been? – but his reasons for pushing it with such fervour had little to do with financial considerations and much to do with his passionate belief that Carpentier had something to say which was of vital importance, and that he said it with supreme mastery.

(Hodges 1978: 172)

One of the ways in which this producer culture has been undermined is by the growing importance of commercial considerations, especially those of profit. This, of course, is frequently said not least by authors. Consider the following declaration by Anthony Burgess:

The old cottage publishers never expected to make much money out of books. They loved good writing, even if the general public didn't and they were honoured by serving the art. Such amateurishness could not easily survive. The increased costs of the physical act of getting a book on the market militated against the promotion of the best . . . and enforced the cultivation of the mediocre.

(Burgess 1988)

Publishers themselves also sing a different tune. Here is the author of a guide to careers in publishing writing some sixty years after Unwin:

It should be stressed that the subject matter relates to a highly competitive business concerned with developing and marketing books for profit, and this includes the university presses operating along similar lines. Commercial publishing is not a slow-paced genteel hobby to nurture literature or poetry without reference to the market, or a continuance of academic study, or a vehicle to express and propagate one's own particular views.

(Clark 1988: 1)

So far the idea of producer culture in publishing has been interpreted in terms of content. But the form of the book – the physical form – is also relevent. There is a loss in the craft skill involved in the physical appearance – design, illustration, page layout, typography, paper, binding, quality of copy-editing and proof-correcting. Design is emphasized for its selling properties or the creation of an imprint image rather than its aesthetic contribution (see also Whiteley, Chapter Ten, this volume). Production departments are more concerned with cost control than the aesthetic qualities of the book.

Three further points need a brief mention. First, the creation and maintainance of a producer culture that potentially unifies different companies has an ambiguous relationship to competition and co-operation *between* companies. One way of putting this is that there is a potential tension between producer culture and workplace cultures. Producer culture would seem to be a force that moderates competition and encourages co-operation by identifying producers as involved in a common enterprise – the production of good books, for instance – but is being diminished. At the same time one might expect producer cultures to be enhanced as a consequence of the shift of authority from producer to consumer; a decline in the authority of producers as a group might well lead to a growth in their consciousness as a group. The change in producer culture is therefore the result of a complex of forces not all of which necessarily pull in the same direction. I return to this point later.

Second, one index of the loss of producer culture is the oft-noted shift in authority and power in companies from those people directly concerned with production to those who are essentially concerned with other aspects of the company. Marketing and finance departments grow in importance by comparison to those concerned with production. The same is true of types of companies whose whole orientation may shift away from a producer culture to one based on the perceived needs of customers. As the author of a recent book comparing IBM with other computer companies says: 'Sales-driven companies tend to think in terms of changing the customer's mind to fit the product; market-driven companies change the product to fit into the customer's strategy' (McKenna 1989: 122).

Last, a loss of producer authority is also manifested in the way that the retail sector gains in importance in relation to the manufacturing sector. The retail revolution in the book trade is a relatively late arrival compared with the corresponding changes in food distribution, for instance. However, the appearance of large chains of bookshops able to demand large discounts, to determine print-run decisions and even to influence publishing policy, is a much-remarked feature of book retailing in the 1980s. This undoubtedly represents a shift of power within the book trade generally, and one that ties publishers more directly to consumer preferences. As Tim Waterstone, head of one of the fastest growing book-retailing chains (recently taken over by the W.H. Smith group), said 'the whole balance of power is shifting from supplier to retailer. For decades it was the other way round' (*Observer* 2 October 1988). How much this is a reflection of 'consumer power' and how much it is an outcome of the financial benefits of concentration and conglomeration in book retailing, traditionally fragmented and undercapitalized, is still an open question.

THE ENTERPRISING CONSUMER

In recent years there has been a growth of interest amongst social scientists in the analysis of consumption. Campbell (1987) identifies a peculiarly modern form of consumption, the chief characteristic of which is its insatiability and constant striving for novelty. Modern consumption, he argues, is a hedonistic search for pleasure but pleasure of a particular kind, namely as a potential quality of any experience. The only means of investigating and sampling potential pleasures is by daydreaming and fantasizing. This, for Campbell, explains how the modern consumer's attentions are focused on the meanings and images associated with a product. It also shows how consumption is dynamic, for disillusionment (and moving on) is the necessary concomitant of the acquisition of goods that have been longed for in fantasy.

Campbell's explanation of the sources of the modern identity as consumer is convincing. But there is another feature of the way that consumers behave that contributes to the driving force of consumption. The modern consumer is not only hedonistic, he or she is enterprising. The implied contrast here is between a consumer who is essentially 'passive', who takes whatever is produced *because* the societal culture does not value consumption for its own sake; and the 'active consumer', for whom consumption is a central life activity. One particular feature of this 'enterprising consumer' should be noted. In a society with a strongly marked producer culture and passive consumers there is a sense in which producers are *ahead* of consumers; the innovation and drive lie with producers and their technical inventiveness. In societies with a reduced producer culture and enterprising consumers, the reverse is true. Consumer aspirations and tastes run ahead of producers' capacity to satisfy them. Enterprising consumers are continually trying to give new meanings to their consumption activity. There is a never-ending process of the creation of meaning, which, as Campbell (1987) points out, is a relatively new phenomenon. Instead of, or as well as, revolutionizing the means of production, modern societies are revolutionizing the means of consumption. As a result, producers are faced with the necessity of trying to catch up with innovative consumers. Consumers are giving ever-new meanings to commodities while producers are having to try to 'commodify' new consumption meanings.

One final feature of the autonomous and enterprising consumer deserves brief discussion. Enterprise involves enthusiasm, and the more enterprising consumers are, the more there is a proliferation of enthusiasms.[3] I mean by 'enthusiasm' the dedication of leisure time to the intense involvement in some activity, whether it is gardening or fishing, swimming or collecting antiques, model building or body building. There may also be, within enthusiasms, different relationships between production and consumption. Some enthusiasms, or groups of their practitioners, may be autonomous in the sense that they themselves produce for their own consumption. But others may have commercial activity associated with them: the proliferation of specialist or hobby magazines testifies to this activity. All such enthusiasms invariably involve the accumulation of expert knowledge, the deployment of skill built up over time, the expenditure of considerable amounts of time and money and, often, the involvement with others in clubs and societies.

Of course, enthusiasms have been with us for some time, particularly in working-class communities. My claim is, however, that they are greatly more common in the post-war period. Comparative evidence is lacking. However, one recent study (Bishop and Hoggett 1986) found more than 300 groups organized around hobbies or other activities in a single suburb of Bristol, which is some indication of the widespread involvement in enthusiasms. The important implication of these points is the very great similarity of consumer enthusiasm to producer culture. It is as if the shift from producer to consumer also involves some kind of migration of knowledge, skill, expertise, dedication and the pursuit of excellence from one to the other. The

179

possession of authority seems to carry with it the deployment and recognition of a culture or knowledge and skill.

A society dominated by producers is likely also to be one in which the idea of loyalty is important. Producers set the standards and command a following of consumers. This is, perhaps, most obvious in the case of those delivering a professional service. Thus people will have a certain loyalty to their doctor or solicitor and even to their dentist or bank manager. It has also applied to commodities or particular shops. However, as authority shifts away from producers, the loyalty given to particular producers of goods or services declines. The same process applies within the producer group itself. Consider the habit of referring to publishing companies as 'houses'. This is an almost feudal usage, conjuring up an image of a tightly knit and fiercely loyal group with an equally dedicated wider following. In recent years, however, the imagery has become singularly inappropriate. Authors no longer stay with the same publisher but auction their work to the highest bidder. Editors move frequently, and without visible embarrassment, from firm to firm.

It is an important implication of what has been said so far that there is a relation of conflict and struggle between producers and consumers. All relations of power and authority imply conflict. As Foucault says: 'In effect, between a relationship of power and a strategy of struggle there is a reciprocal appeal, a perpetual linking and a perpetual reversal' (Foucault 1982). The relation between producer and consumer is no exception; there is a potential, if not actual, conflict between the two. This is apparently somewhat paradoxical, for we are accustomed to thinking of relations between producers as competitive. So they are. They are, however, also co-operative. Such co-operation may be obviously manifested in the activities of trade associations. However, it also appears in the very texture of everyday life as a producer. As pointed out earlier, publishers relate to each other, swap notes on authors and exchange advice on market trends whatever the apparently competitive relations of their companies. This co-operation is, in other words, another aspect of the producer culture. At the same time there can be conflict between producer and consumer. I have already referred to one source of such conflict in the struggle over meaning. Active consumers are constantly trying to give new meanings to their consumption, while producers try to 'commodify' those meanings.

The publishing industry depends on copyright. Copyright is the point where art, law and economics meet; it makes artistic or educational objects into properties on which a return can be earned. There have always been conflicts over copyright but these have usually been between producers – between publisher and author over who owns copyright or between publishing firms over the violation of copyright. More recently, however, there are conflicts between producer and consumer as new technologies make copying possible. Particularly in the educational sector, publishers have become very worried about the photocopying of books. This, of course, is a problem, not only for publishing, but for all those industries dependent on copyright including recorded music, video and computer software.

It is an open question what the wider effects of these conflicts are. One might expect that, as the balance of authority shifts from producer to consumer, the producer culture would be intensified in response to an enhanced conflict with consumers, a result precisely the reverse to that described earlier in this chapter. However, this is not necessarily the case, for the balance between competition and co-operation between producers can also alter, in turn moderating the intensification of producer culture.

ELEMENTS OF EXPLANATION

So far I have argued that there has been a shift from producer to consumer that is to be seen partly as a transformation of relations of authority, the mechanisms of which lie in both consumption and production. I want to conclude by making some comments about these mechanisms. I do not have an answer to the question of what causes the shift from producer to consumer. It is worth, however, identifying some of the factors involved. By way of introducing these I consider a commonly advanced argument that locates the causes of change in the production sector and, more specifically, in the capitalist mode of production.

Capitalism, so the argument runs, is an inherently progressive economic system. The forces of competition compel capitalists to innovate, constantly trying new products and new production processes in order to keep ahead. As Marx and Engels say: 'Constant revolutionizing of production, uninterrupted disturbance of all social conditions, everlasting uncertainty and agitation distinguish the bourgeois epoch from all earlier ones' (Marx and Engels 1872: 38). Society as a whole becomes affected by the restless economy – 'all that is solid melts into air'. Specifically, there is pressure to 'commodify', to bring in to the market areas of human life that previously were not bought and sold. At the extreme, all human relationships become commercial transactions. 'Commodification' no doubt helps to account for some of the processes described in the first part of this chapter. Any interest on the part of the producers in the *quality* of their product or service becomes subservient to the need to sell that product as effectively as possible. Since such a commercial aim must involve an interest in consumers, it appears that the authority of producers, given by their capacity to produce something of intrinsic value, declines in relation to consumers. Consumerism is thus apparently engendered by the necessary activities of producers. Last, as Marx observed, all ties of loyalty are destroyed by 'commodification'; 'there is left remaining no other nexus between man and man, than naked self-interest, than callous cash payment' (Marx and Engels 1872: 38).

Commodification cannot be a complete explanation, however, chiefly because it treats consumers as passive. The whole society is seen as production-driven, with consumer behaviour simply trailing along behind. As a theory, then, this is itself a reflection of a society in which authority goes to producers and has failed to keep up with real social changes that have shifted the balance to consumers. There are other reasons for being doubtful of a simple commodification approach. Thus the producer–consumer shift occurs in sectors other than those affected by market or commodification pressures. Education, for instance, has shown a greater interest in treating pupils or students as consumers or clients, yet it is not a sphere of activity directly affected by commodification. Again, commodification is not a uniform or even process. It can take different forms and can even be reversed. For example, book publishing in the early nineteenth century was a highly commercial activity, certainly by comparison with what followed. In its early stages publishing was in the hands of market-oriented booksellers and, if anything, the period from 1820 to 1940 represents a relative decommodification.

If, therefore, commodification has limited value in the explanation of the shift from producer to consumer, what other forces are at work? Very briefly, I pick out four. First, there has been a change in class structure since the Second World War. A rise in demand for highly qualified workers has led to an increase in social mobility from middle and lower classes creating, or enlarging, what has become known as the 'service class' (Goldthorpe 1980). One could hypothesize that this class, members of which occupy strategic producer locations, will give producers a different orientation; the internal culture of the producing class is changed significantly. Two points are important here. First, service-class members see their own consumption as a significant life activity (see, for example, Bourdieu 1984) and hence are more likely to take it seriously for others. Second, the working-class origins of many members of the post-war service class may predispose them against the high-culture orientation that is both a product and a support of the authority of the producer. Indeed, one could go further in suggesting that new service-class members have an interest in displacing producers whose social origins and outlooks derive from an older established capitalist class and one strategy would be to undermine the authority of producers in general.

A shift in authority from producer to consumer is therefore in part due to conflicts within the producer sector. That, in turn, might imply that, once the service-class producers are established in industry, commerce and the professions, they will attempt to reassert the authority of producers as a group.

Second, however, the production and marketing policies of companies are also changing. Large-scale, mass-production methods are giving way to smaller batch production. At the same time, mass-marketing methods, which effectively treat consumers as an undifferentiated block, are being replaced by a greater awareness of market segments, each of which has different requirements. This change in policy is usually referred to as a movement from 'Fordism' to 'post-Fordism' and is discussed in much greater detail in Bagguley, Chapter Eight this volume. The net effect of post-Fordism, together with the internationalization of consumer markets that has come with it, is an *enabling* of consumer choice.[4]

Third, there is the question of cultural citizenship. Distributions of power and authority not only involve the use, actual or potential, of force, and a range of other sanctions including those of social honour, but are also invested with symbolic power. Authority relations are partly constituted by boundaries, breach of which is like violating a taboo. I have argued that one form of the authority of producers over consumers is the dominance of high culture over popular culture. High-culture concerns set the cultural agenda, define the criteria of aesthetic excellence and, more importantly, determine the appropriate modes of cultural response on the part of consumers. The division between high culture and popular culture is also a boundary that is

183

partly sustained by taboo; when the boundary is reasonably solid, people feel awkward about mixing the cultures and prefer to stay with their 'own'.

The breakdown of the producer/consumer and high culture/popular culture boundaries, and of the authority of the producer, can be seen as a process of acquiring 'cultural citizenship'. These boundaries functioned to exclude people from certain cultural rights; correspondingly, then, the acquisition of these rights entails a reorganization of the boundaries. Marshall (1950) has argued that the eighteenth century saw the acquisition of civil citizenship, the nineteenth century the development of political citizenship and the twentieth century the formation of the welfare state, giving social citizenship. Cultural citizenship is simply an extension of the citizenship process, a democratization that undermines the authority of the producer as surely as the extension of the franchise undermined the political authority of the ruling class.

Finally, there is a certain ironic continuity between the radical attitudes (and actions) manifested by certain groups in the 1960s and the shift from producer to consumer increasingly apparent in the enterprise culture of the 1980s. This may actually be a continuity of persons – the very same people who embraced the 1960s are sometimes the active promoters of the 1980s. More significantly, there is also a cultural continuity. It is true that 1960s radicalism was hardly consumerist but, in essence, it was an opposition, in various modes, to traditional forms of authority. In a sense, as I have implied, 1980s enterprise culture is anti-authority; and at the very least, market relations are themselves corrosive of traditional authority. United by a distaste for authority, the 1960s paved the way for the 1980s. That the latter also encouraged consumerism is simply an ironic twist.

NOTES

1 I am grateful to Paul Bagguley, Russell Keat and Alan Warde for their comments on earlier versions of this chapter. I am also indebted to many members of the Centre for Cultural Values at Lancaster University and to Scott Lash, Celia Lury and Dan Shapiro for many discussions of the relationship of enterprise culture to the culture industries.

2 Featherstone suggests that consumer culture points to:

the impact of mass consumption on an ever-increasing range of goods and experience. New modes of cultural representation ensure the proliferation of images which saturate the fabric of social life with a melée of signs and messages which summon up new expressive and hedonistic definitions of the good life.

(Featherstone 1983: 4)

3 The term is borrowed from Bishop and Hoggett (1986).
4 I owe this point to Paul Bagguley (Chapter Eight, this volume).

REFERENCES

Betjeman, J. (1937) 'Slough', in R. Skelton (ed.) *Poetry of the Thirties*, Harmondsworth: Penguin, 1964.

Bishop, J. and Hoggett, P. (1986) *Organizing Around Enthusiasms*, London: Comedia.

Bourdieu, P. (1984) *Distinction*, London: Routledge.

Burgess, A. (1988) 'The Literature Industry', the *Observer*, 28 August 1989.

Campbell, C. (1987) *The Romantic Ethic and the Spirit of Capitalism*, Oxford: Basil Blackwell.

Clark, G.N. (1988) *Inside Book Publishing*, London: Blueprint.

Featherstone, M. (1983) 'Consumer culture: an introduction', *Theory, Culture, and Society* 1(3).

Foucault, M. (1982) 'The subject and power' in H.L. Dreyfus and P. Rabinow (eds) *Michel Foucault*, Brighton: Harvester Press.

Goldthorpe, J.H. (1980) *Social Mobility and Class Structure in Modern Britain*, Oxford: Oxford University Press.

Hodges, S. (1978) *Gollancz: the Story of a Publishing House*, London: Gollancz.

Jackall, R. (1988) *Moral Mazes*, New York: Oxford University Press.

McKenna, R. (1989) *Who's Afraid of Big Blue?*, Massachusetts, Addison-Wesley

Marshall, T.H. (1950) *Citizenship and Social Class*, Cambridge: Cambridge University Press.

Marx, K. and Engels, F. (1872) *The Communist Manifesto*, in *Selected Works*, London: Lawrence & Wishart.

Said, E.W. *Orientalism*, London: Routledge.

Unwin, S. (1960), *The Truth About a Publisher*, London: Allen & Unwin.

Chapter Ten

DESIGN IN ENTERPRISE CULTURE

Design for whose profit?

NIGEL WHITELEY

> Good design has never been more important for the success of the British economy.
>
> (Margaret Thatcher, quoted on the cover of the Design Council's annual report and accounts, 1985/6)

With the explosion of consumerism, the 1980s has witnessed a boom in the growth and newsworthiness of design: the High Street has been visually transformed; design consultancies have mushroomed and some have even gone public; the press has revelled in the epithet 'designer'; and television programmes have celebrated design awards for an increasingly design-conscious public. Design has also become an important component of the Conservative government's industrial policy. A huge increase in public money – more than a threefold rise from just over £4 million to nearly £14 million – has been put into design via the Department of Trade and Industry (DTI) between 1982 and 1988. And this from a government ideologically hostile to increasing public sector spending. Perhaps even more surprising, the direct funding from the DTI to the Design Council – one of grant-aided quangos that have been so berated by the government in the last decade – has also substantially risen by nearly 40 per cent in the same period.

This chapter offers a historical perspective on governmental intervention in design over the last century and a half. Such a perspective enables us to understand the Conservative government's policy and pronouncements on design. Just what does the Prime Minister *mean* when she refers, as in the quotation at the head of this chapter, to 'good design'? Is the Government's design policy – whether implemented directly through the DTI or indirectly through the Design

Council – a radical expression of enterprise culture, or is it merely a logical development of post-war consumerist tendencies? How has the Design Council's definition of 'good design' changed since its inception in 1944? Has it been forced, through government policies, to neglect what would once have been considered its proper responsibilities? Has a 'public' body, such as the Design Council, a duty to provide a balanced critical perspective on governmental policies?

The reason for the Government's championing of design has been stated many times in recent years, principally by John Butcher who, between 1982 and 1988, was the Undersecretary of State for Industry at the DTI with special responsibility for design. According to Butcher, the 'British Government regards design as a dominant factor which lies at the heart of product success. Product success creates wealth for companies and economies – that is why we have a policy for design' (*Design* 1985: 17). Design, therefore, becomes for the nation 'a competitive weapon . . . in an industrial and economic war' (*Design* 1987: 5). The Design Council was seen as the main means, as we shall see, for spreading the DTI's word and providing design resources. Eric Forth, who took over from Butcher in the summer of 1988, subscribed to the same values, reaffirming that 'the Design Council is the main vehicle we have for promoting the idea that design is an integral part of the wealth creation process' (*Designers' Journal,* 1989: 18).

DESIGN FOR SOCIETY

Governmental intervention in design with a view to generating wealth and enhancing the country's financial wellbeing is not a recent phenomenon and dates back to 1835 when a parliamentary select committee was set up 'to inquire into the best means of extending a knowledge of the arts and principles of design among the people (especially the manufacturing population) of the country'. The intention and the need was to improve the quality of British goods so they would be more exportable. The outcome of the committee's report was the formation of the Normal School of Design (which later evolved into the Royal College of Art), established under the auspices of the Board of Trade in 1837. By 1846, eleven branch schools were also receiving government support. But, while the government had a clear idea of the role and purpose of the schools – namely a training in wealth creation – others argued that they should be more liberal and roundedly educative. An argument developed as to whether the schools should be uncompromisingly commercial in their orientation, or teach design as an adjunct of fine art, which was seen as morally and culturally uplifting. Should design be at the service of commerce (a position held by Henry Cole, for example), or should it facilitate the wider wellbeing of society (as John Ruskin continually hoped)? The conclusion – for optimists, an inspired British compromise and, for cynics, a typical British fudge – was to try to accommodate both points of view.

This dual role for design set the tone for government intervention for some considerable time. It was reasserted at the time of the second burst of government involvement in design in the 1930s (most notably the Gorrell Report of 1932 and the Council for Art and Industry, formed in 1934), which emphasized both the commercial role of design *and* the social and cultural improvement of the individual through an enlightened design policy. At no time were these two objectives more suited to their time than immediately after the Second World War with the combination of the desperate need to win export markets at a time of rationing and austerity, and the commitment, epitomized by Labour's 1945 election victory and the establishment of the Welfare State, to an egalitarian and caring society.

Hugh Dalton, President of the Board of Trade, set the tone for the (as it was then called) Council of Industrial Design's endeavours when he addressed it at the time of its inception in 1944:

> We must . . . make a sustained effort to improve design, and to bring industry to recognise the importance of this task. You have to arouse the interest of ordinary men and women. . . . If you succeed in your task, in a few years' time every side of our daily life will be better for your work. Every kitchen will be an easier place to work in; every home a pleasanter place to live in. Men and women in millions will be in your debt, although they may not know it; and not in Britain alone but all over the world. . . . Industry itself will have much cause to thank you. Our export trade, and our volume of business at home, will both be the greater if our goods are planned and made, with skill and imagination, to meet the user's real need, to give pleasure in the using.
>
> (MacCarthy 1979: 74)

The ethos of the Council was clearly to benefit the lives of the wider public through design. There would be less drudgery at work, and more pleasure at home because goods – the Council's remit has always been to 'promote by all practical means the improvement of design in the *products* of British industry' – would be designed to perform better and more easily.

From the vantage of the sophisticated consumerism of the present day, it is easy to see the Council's initial beliefs as naïve and oversimple, a rosy vision of the new democratic Britain that had dominated the propaganda of the latter part of the War, but the genuine sense of egalitarianism (albeit one in which experts know best) and altruism (rather than the profit motive) is undeniable. In this vision, manufacturers' profits resulted from meeting the 'real need' of the public through 'good design', not from creating and satisfying unnecessary materialist desires. A definition of good design was attempted by the director of the Council, Gordon Russell, in the very first issue of *Design*, the Council's own monthly magazine, which commenced publication in 1949. Russell rhetorically asked what the consumer demands (which really meant what he or she *should* demand) of a product: 'He demands something which is well made of good and suitable materials, which does its job efficiently and gives him pleasure, at a price he can afford to pay. So the first design question is "Does it work?"' Russell continued that: 'Good design always takes into account the technique of production, the material to be used and the purpose for which the object is wanted' (Russell 1949: 2). This was a definition that married functionalism (e.g. form follows function; fitness to purpose) and the aesthetico-moral principles (e.g. truth to materials; integrity of surface) derived from Ruskin and other design 'reformers' of the mid-nineteenth century. Standards were presumed to be objective and transcendent, so a definitive judgement about a product could be made so long as one knew the task for which it was designed – its 'primary' function – and recognized the manifestations of the supposedly timeless aesthetico-moral principles. During this period the emphasis in the definition of 'good design' was thus largely on the product rather than the consumer or manufacturer (e.g. the social role of products; market segmentation; ease of manufacture; profit motive).

The Conservatives were returned to office in 1951 with an electioneering promise to 'set the people free' from state intervention and interference. For the next thirteen years the majority of Britons personally became decidedly more affluent as society followed increasingly consumerist tendencies. And yet the Council of Industrial Design remained, throughout the 1950s, committed to and, more significantly,

189

able to preach 'public-spirited' values in design. Under successive prime ministers including Winston Churchill and Harold Macmillan, Conservative governments largely adhered to the 'arm's length' convention (which applied to other 'public realm' institutions such as the universities and the BBC), so effectively maintaining the ideological independence of the Council. The vision of a Britain designed for the common good remained intact and was occasionally described in *Design*:

> Suppose we go on a bus ride through London or any large town. We would traverse street after street of buildings conceived in harmony, elegant in proportion and lively in colour, unsullied in urban grime and smoke; all lettering would be a work of art, all the vehicles we passed as fine as the farm waggon or the phaeton, the street lighting graceful and efficient. Even the displays in the shops would all be the work of masters in their art working with material of impeccable quality. When we reach the outskirts of the city there would be no untidy fringe, but a clearly marked green belt of unspoilt landscape, pasture, arable and woodland, with all the necessary buildings carefully sited, constructed and coloured so that they melted into or contrasted with the countryside in the most sensitive way.
>
> (*Design* 1952: 17)

In this utopian vision of community responsibility and care, even the vehicle of perception is publicly owned!

This is not to imply that the commercial role of design was ignored – from the very first issue of *Design*, Council spokespersons acknowledged the economic importance of design – but this was *never* to be at the expense of standards of good design. The Council believed – and if they didn't believe they prayed – that the public would purchase good design rather than bad design. In fact, if ever it came down to a situation of one or the other – of good design or commercial success – the Council's sympathies were with the former. Michael Farr, editor of *Design* from 1952 to the end of the decade, analysed *Design in British Industry* in book form in 1955. Addressing the much-bandied motto (which emanated from the Council) that 'good design is good business', Farr retorted that: 'I am convinced that it is scarcely a half-truth and never susceptible to generalization. The great mistake that propaganda can make is to lure manufacturers and retailers into improvements of design by promising them an increase in sales' (Farr 1955: 288).

It was more honest, he remarked, to admit that 'successive improvements in design *can* maintain sales at their normal level. And that,
I suggest, is the balance between private business and social duty that
every manufacturer and retailer should strive to attain' (Farr 1955:
289). Lest anyone was unclear about the true purpose of design, Farr
proclaimed that the question of design was essentially 'a social question,
it is an integral part of *the* social question of our time. To fight against
the shoddy design of those goods by which most of our fellow men
are surrounded becomes a duty' (ibid: xxxvi).

DESIGN IN A CONSUMERIST SOCIETY

Although there were traces of these values in the Council's pronouncements in the 1960s (and even into the following decade), a shift
towards what eventually was transformed into enterprise culture was
beginning to take place. The reason, of course, was the change being
brought about by consumerism. In the present author's view the term
'consumerist society' is subtly but significantly different from 'consumer society'. The latter term is roughly synonymous with capitalist
society and so has been in existence for some centuries: 'consumer*ist*
society' signifies an advanced state of consumer society in which private
affluence *on a mass scale* is the dominant force in the marketplace.
Terence Conran talks about the time around the mid-1960s when
'people stopped needing and need changed to want. Designers became
more important in producing "want" products rather than "need"
products, because you have to create the desire' (Brand New n.d.: 22)
  Almost inevitably, therefore, the 1960s – criticisms of decadism
apart – really were a transitional period for the Council. In an article
in *Design* in 1960, L. Bruce Archer tackled head-on a definition of good
design in the consumerist age. Archer admitted that the old definition of good design was too narrow: a wider view of 'function' was
needed, which was less product-based and more socially constructed.
'Instead of taking the purpose of a product for granted', Archer argued,
'more and more designers are examining the human needs behind the
use of the product' *Design* 1960: 29). At one level this placed greater
emphasis on ergonomic considerations, and at another 'the product
should give rise to a certain amount of pride in possession, so that it
is fully employed and properly looked after' (ibid: 30) A degree of
fashionability was tolerated by Archer because the 'study of the nature
of fashion changes indicates that it is related to something basic in

human nature, and is not often imposed by unscrupulous designers or manufacturers' (*Design* 1960: 30).

Archer's definition is interesting because it represents a move away from the exclusivity and timelessness of the old definition towards a tentative pluralism, which takes into account social factors of needs and desires. His reference to 'unscrupulous designers and manufacturers' does, however, betray Archer's commitment to higher motives than mere profit. In fact, the old principles should not, he argues, be cast aside: 'even now, a product which grossly offended one or more of the old principles would almost certainly be regarded as poor design' (ibid: 28). There are other telling phrases in the article that underline Archer's commitment to the 'public' role of design. For example: 'in order to serve the interests of progress in the community *as a whole,*¯ [a product] should contribute something towards raising the standards of discrimination of the ordinary user' (ibid: 30). He also urges the reader to distinguish between short-term fashion oscillations and 'aesthetic standards in human society as a whole' (ibid: 31). There are standards, in other words, that can be upheld in the age of consumerism, even if a new definition of good design has to be expanded to incorporate 'human' and social values.

This shift from absolute to plural values was taken a stage further by Council chairman Paul Reilly in 1967. The Council had been caught hopelessly wrong-footed by the explosion of pop and youth culture, and appeared anachronistic and out of touch. Reilly perspicaciously concluded that good design had to be defined in largely social (and therefore plural) terms:

> We are shifting perhaps from attachment to permanent, universal values to acceptance that a design may be valid at a given time for a given purpose to a given group of people in a given set of circumstances, but that outside these limits it may not be valid at all. . . . All that this means is that a product must be good of its kind for the set of circumstances for which it has been designed.
>
> (Reilly 1967: 256)

The implication for design of the social changes that had occurred in Britain was that a hierarchical single design structure based on universal and changeless values had been replaced by values that were relative to time, place, group and circumstance. An important point to note is that Reilly was not claiming that the question of standards had been negated by total relativism, but that standards were contingent upon what I have elsewhere termed a 'plurality of hierarchies' (Whiteley 1987: 227–9). Reilly is in no doubt that standards are still pertinent. Lest the reader felt that he was slipping into total relativism he reassures, in language redolent of the previous decade: 'And so we come back almost to moral judgements. The need is again for discipline, for function . . . only then shall we sift the contributors from the charlatans when confronted with the challenge of Pop' (Reilly 1967: 257). Or, presumably he would have agreed, the challenge of consumerism and commercial exploitation.

A significant symptom of the Council's sharper thinking about design in society was the subdivision, in 1966, of products into either capital goods or consumer goods. The Council was acknowledging that both types of goods performed different *types* of function: we expect invisible and efficient performance from capital equipment, whereas consumer goods, especially if personal items, often have to meet complex psychosocial aspirations.

DESIGN AND SOCIAL CONSCIENCE

A final major factor that informed the Council's thinking in the 1960s was the broad issue of what was often referred to as 'the environment'. The pollution caused by the grounding of the Torrey Canyon; industrial waste and the stagnation of rivers; the destruction of the countryside; the problems of traffic and noise in cities; and the loss of faith in design (and other) 'experts' following the collapse of Ronan Point all contributed to a reappraisal of the role and status of the designer in society. In the wake of the politicization of 1968, socially responsible thinking gathered momentum. In 1968 the editor of *Design* was of the opinion 'it would seem the right time for a major rethink of what people really want' (*Design* 1968: 19), and in the following year in a statement entitled 'Design in its Context', the editor argued it was a 'crucial' time to look at the wider environment' (*Design* 1969a: 15). Paul Reilly wrote (in *New Statesman*) of the need for a 'thorough reappraisal of attitudes to design across the whole span of British industry' (Reilly 1969: 303). Much of the debate centred on the role and status of technology in society. As the editor of *Design* in 'A Choice of Tomorrow' pointed out:

> If we are to avoid mistakes similar to those of the first industrial revolution, then we have to make sure that modern technology

is geared to take us where we want to go, and not just where the next steps happen to place us.

(Design, 1969b: 25)

The Council was contributing to the politicization of design and designers as it helped to make explicit the fact that design was part of the social, economic and, most importantly, the political system of a country.

Regardless of how effective the Council was in its propaganda – in its work in education it had many successes; with manufacturers, retailers and the public, considerably fewer – the fact of the matter remains that the Council upheld a role that promoted *public* values and social duty and responsibility. At no time did it commit itself to a simply commercial argument for design. Nor was governmental pressure such that policy was dictated centrally. Successive governments accepted an 'arm's length' approach that permitted the Council to broadcast views that were sometimes anti-commercialist and certainly critical in a broader cultural sense. We have identified three phases of Council propaganda: the period from 1944 to 1960 when the Council was preaching the role of design as a moral and social improver; 1960–1967 when the Council acknowledged the changing nature of society and attempted to formulate a notion of good design based on consumerism and pluralism; and the period at the end of the 1960s when the Council adopted an environmental conscience that verged on the anti-consumerist. It is interesting to note that the majority of the first phase of Council propaganda took place under a Conservative government albeit, significantly, a consensus-oriented one with a social conscience – the old-fashioned 'one nation' Tory Party. Half of the second and all of the third phases were under Labour (including, at the end of the third phase, the 'Lib/Lab pact'). The increasing impact of consumerism makes the second and third phases more relevant to our own age, and it is revealing to analyse the changes in attitudes and values that have occurred.

FROM ONE NATION TO ONE NOTION

The major shift for the Design Council – its name was altered in 1972 so it could place greater emphasis on engineering design – towards becoming a largely uncritical mouthpiece for enterprise culture took place in the early 1980s. In the 1970s, the Council, according to Keith Grant, director from 1978 to 1988 'was benignly supported by the

Labour government of the time but it was low-key support, and there was a feeling in the Department of Industry that design was peripheral' (*Design* 1988a: 9). The Council was granted a royal charter in 1976 with a restated aim to pursue the 'advancement of British industry by the improvement of design' and, according to Viscount Caldecote, chairman of the Council:

> we became involved in the whole spectrum of design, from appearance at one end to technical performance at the other. We have consistently preached that a well designed product will look right, will perform according to the specification, will be reliable and easy to maintain, will be ergonomically correct and economical to make: it will thus be suitable in every way for the market for which it has been designed, and will be saleable at a profit.
>
> (Design Council 1980: 4)

Caldecote's definition drew on previous Council ones combining product-, social- and consumer-based criteria. Wealth creation formed a part, but only a part of the definition.

There was little immediate change during the opening years of the Conservative Government's office. Following Viscount Caldecote, Sir William Barlow was appointed chairman in 1980. A year later, in response to a question about his future plans for the Council now he had settled into the post, Sir William replied: 'I've no ideas for rapid change. The Council has triggered a lot of interest in design in the past; I think it should continue to do the job it's doing well now' (*Design* 1981a: 9). Both Caldecote and Barlow argued that the deepening economic recession of the early 1980s made the design 'message' more urgent, and Barlow regretted that much of his time was spent 'in persuading the Government to support its public statements and improve the Council's financial position' (*Design* 1981b: 31).

The crucial change came about in 1982. On the evening of 25 January the Prime Minister invited about seventy people to 10 Downing Street to discuss design. The briefing notes that accompanied the invitation to the occasion promised a 'discussion on product design and market success'; the guest list comprised eight ministers, eight MPs, one member of the Lords, eight individuals listed as designers, eight representatives from industry and commerce, twelve from professional or relevant bodies, six from education, five 'advocates of design' and fourteen Government officials from six departments – a high-status and influential group that signalled that the Government had decided to take design seriously as a part of its industrial policy.

Margaret Thatcher's definition of design around that time seemed greatly influenced by Design Council thinking. In an article supposedly written by the Prime Minister for *Design* in 1982 she stated:

> By 'design' I do not just mean 'appearance'. I mean all the engineering and industrial design which goes into a product from the idea stage to the production stage, and which is so important in ensuring that it works, that it is reliable, that it is good value, and that it looks good. In short, it is good design which makes people buy products and which gives products a good name.
>
> (*Design* 1982: 3)

She also had a dualistic 'science/art' or 'rationalist/anti-rationalist' attitude to design: 'At present, design is too often taught in secondary schools as an art subject. It is rarely taught as it should be – as a practical, problem-solving discipline that is ideal for preparing young people for work' (ibid: 3). To view design as a 'hard' subject concerned with objective 'problem-solving' is to adopt a narrow view often held by unreconstructed engineers. Certainly, it is at odds with consumerist desires and design for the market that the Government was soon to adopt. The Prime Minister's advice to designers was direct: 'The profit potential of product design and development is considerable. Designers themselves should be more aggressive in selling themselves to industry as wealth creators' (ibid). This would require integrity on the part of the designer otherwise a possible conflict could result: should he or she design reliable, etc. products, or profitable products even if they are badly designed?

As a result of the 1982 seminar and the increasing belief in the wealth-producing potential of design, the Government initiated a number of projects that prepared the ground for design's place in enterprise culture. Most innovative was the 'Funded Consultancy' scheme, launched in June 1982 and operated by the Design Council on behalf of the DTI. Initially, government funding of £3 million was granted for three years: this was increased almost immediately to £10 million because of an enthusiastic response. In its earliest form, manufacturing companies were offered fifteen days of product design consultancy time free of charge. Further consultancy was available, either as a follow-on from the first or for a new project, for which half the cost would be met. Modifications to the scheme relating to the amount of funding and size of manufacturing company were brought in in 1984 and these are detailed elsewhere (Department of Trade and Industry 1988). The aim remained the same: to convert manufacturing companies to using design as a part of their product and marketing strategies. The Council's role was also clear: to act as 'marriage broker' between design consultancies and companies. The scheme proved popular and, between 1982 and 1985, 1,590 companies employed it. Sixty-two per cent of the companies used an external design consultant for the first time; and 94 per cent of all participating companies found the consultancy work 'worthwhile' or better. By 1988, when the Council's role was changed, more than 5,000 companies had commissioned design groups, fuelling the rapid expansion of British design consultancies.

DESIGN FOR PROFIT

One of the most significant of the Government's projects was the 'Design for Profit' campaign, run from 1983 in conjunction with the Design Council. Its aim was 'to reach the decision-makers in industry and to change their attitude to design' (*The Designer*, 1983: 1). To reinforce the message, the Design Council published a 40-page booklet entitled 'Design and the Economy: the role of design and innovation in the prosperity of industrial companies' (1983). It provided the arguments, supported by detailed statistics and case studies, about the commercial potential of design in company strategy.

With 'Design for Profit', the Government's attitude came into sharp focus. The title of the campaign was unambiguous about the perceived role of design; and the target group – industrialists or, in other words, producers – signified clearly to whom the Government was addressing the design message. From 1983 the Government's ideology begins to change too, from the more liberal, Design-Council-derived definition of good design to one that is almost wholly concerned with profit. A 'Profit by Design' brochure published in 1986 hammers home the profit motive: 'To put it simply, the design process is a planning exercise to maximize sales and profits.' No reference to social duty or wider cultural (or environmental) concerns here.

The change can be perceived directly in the pronouncements of John Butcher, the Government's 'minister for design'. At the time of the launch of 'Design for Profit', Butcher was describing good design as

one of the key factors in re-establishing the competitiveness of existing product lines and in entering new product areas. By taking an integrated approach, having regard to ease of manufacture, ease of maintenance, reliability, ergonomics and appearance, a company can transform its product's prospects in the market'

(*The Designer* 1983: 1)

By 1987 Butcher's more inclusive definition had been replaced by one fully in keeping with what the Government would claim to be the 'consumer-orientation' of enterprise culture. In a seminar paper he presented to the London Business School, Butcher defined good design in consumerist terms: 'good design is the planning process for products or services that fully satisfy the aspirations of the customer' (Butcher 1987: 218). However, as Russell Keat argues in the Introduction to this volume, consumer sovereignty is not straightforward. The consumer has to be manipulated: 'it is no good producing something that responds to what the customer thinks he wants now – you have to aim for what he will discover he wants in the future' (ibid). It is hard to imagine this dubious definition being acceptable to the Design Council at any stage of its history.

Design, Butcher argued, should serve the 'national interest'. A national interest that promoted wellbeing and awareness in both materialistic *and* non-materialistic terms would have been acceptable to more liberal design propagandists but, for Butcher, the national interest could – or, rather *should* – be defined simply as 'the creation of wealth' (ibid). This hardly promoted design's role in improving the quality of life on planet Earth. Butcher praised the approach to design of several successful companies: 'Here is design at work. Improving competitiveness. Winning markets. Increasing profitability. . . . That's what design is about' (ibid: 221). The competitive, 'enterprise culture' ethos of design was summed up in his comment about the role of design in society: 'Stripped down to its basics it's about the survival of the fittest' (ibid: 218). The 'law of the jungle' mentality is applied to national prowess: successful design is a way of giving: 'the international competition a sound drubbing' (ibid: 223). The language of war reappeared in the concluding comments: 'we are at war in both our domestic and export markets. There's a weapon which can help us win. It's not a secret weapon. Nor, by itself, is it so potent that we can throw all our other competitive weapons away. . . . That weapon is design' (ibid: 225). Whether design would be included in any arms negotiations is, however, unlikely.

The Government's attitude to design had begun to crystallize after the 1982 seminar. Understandably, given its vested financial interest, the design profession heaped praise on the Government's policy. In 1985 the International Council of Societies of Industrial Design awarded the Conservative Government an international design prize, – the first time the prize had ever been awarded to a Government. Margaret Thatcher was singled out for special praise and John Butcher collected the award. The following year Butcher received the Royal Society of Art's 'Bicentenary Medal for 1986' for his 'exceptional influence in promoting art and design in British industry'. Although less 'design-conscious' as individuals, John Butcher's successors have had no difficulty confirming the Government's attitude: Eric Forth, Butcher's immediate successor, for example, declared his commitment to design as an 'integral part of the wealth creation process'.

WHITHER OR WITHER THE DESIGN COUNCIL?

With an attitude to design such as the Government's, what hope for a view of design that promotes social responsibility and the public good? In fact, what hope for the Design Council in its traditional role? The Conservatives' approach does not accord with the recommendations presented in their 1984 'Policies and Priorities for Design' strategy group report. The strategy group was set up by John Butcher and was chaired by Sir William Barlow, chairman of the Design Council. It included Keith Grant, the Council's director, and five other members of the Design Council in a total membership of eleven. A further member was the deputy director of the Consumers' Association. Its recommendations were wide-ranging and inclusive. Although the role of design in wealth creation was underlined, 'priority' status was given to the establishment of a 'national product approval scheme' like the Design Council 'label' scheme: 'under which approval is based on expert assessment, user reports and technical checking – all in relation to published criteria' (Design Council 1984: para. 5.6).

It followed from this criterion that successful (or wealth-creating) design might be adjudged bad design, so presenting the Government with a dilemma. It would also imply a radical re-evaluation of priorities from market-led design, which favours producers, to consumer-protection, which genuinely favours the wellbeing of consumers. Even more radical was the proposal that: 'The Government should initiate and support design competitions leading to the development of economically significant or *socially* desirable products' (my italics) (Design Council 1984: para. 5.4). Perhaps some of the spirit of the late 1960s lived on at the Design Council! No reference was made to directly educating consumers, or raising their awareness about design. It seemed to be felt that the consumer-protection measures, and the design education input into formal education (primary, secondary and tertiary) and courses (industrial, business and management courses, and post-experience education) were all that was necessary.

The strategy document has never been fully adopted, partly because of senior management changes at the Council. In 1986 the 'discreetly aggressive' and 'ambitious' (*Blueprint* 1986: 8) Simon Hornby (knighted in 1988), a personal friend of Conservative ex-minister Paul Channon, replaced Sir William Barlow as chairman. Following an outspoken and controversial interview that appeared in *Vogue* in February 1987 in which Hornby attacked many aspects of the Council's performance, Hornby faced and survived a vote of no confidence. But changes became inevitable. Both director, Keith Grant, and deputy director, Mervyn Unger, resigned abruptly around the end of 1987. Unger was not replaced; Grant was replaced by Ivor Owen, a former chairman of Thorn EMI's lighting and appliances group of companies. The design magazine, *Blueprint*, welcomed the appointment, contrasting 'the careful civil servant', Grant, and the 'real-life businessman' (*Blueprint* 1988: 3), Owen, who was quick to prioritize the industrialist as the Council's main target. This echoed the sentiments emanating from the second Downing Street Design Seminar, hosted by Margaret in 1987.

Decisions were made by the chairman and director to phase out some of the Council's activities in 1988, the most significant of which was the 'label' scheme which the 1984 strategy group considered should be boosted so it became an important guarantee of objective quality for the consumer. June Fraser, head of industrial design at the Council and responsible for the scheme, resigned over the matter complaining: 'Ivor Owen appears to have no historical knowledge of design culture and no long-term view of the future of the Design Council' (*Design Week* 1988: 3). Morale at the Council was very low throughout 1988 and in an interview with Hornby in *Design* the interviewer reported: 'The gossip going around is that the Design Council won't exist in three to five years time; in fact that Owen's brief may have been to close it down. Is there any truth in that?' Hornby strenuously denied the rumour but warned: 'The problem is simply that the Design Council hadn't changed for a very long time, and it did need a thorough review. I couldn't just let it trickle on' (*Design* 1988b: 5). The strategy review had been made all the more urgent because the DTI had decided to end the Council's role in the 'funded consultancy' scheme. From 1988 the DTI had integrated design into the broader 'Enterprise Initiative', which included marketing and management. This had led to a cash shortfall for the Council causing about thirty redundancies. By scrapping the 'label' scheme the Council anticipated saving £700,000 a year.

During the first year that Owen was director (1988), eighty of the Council's 330 staff had been made redundant or left without being replaced. In a bid to dispel pessimistic rumours and lift morale, Owen announced that the Council was seeking greater independence from the DTI. This was partly the result of Government pressure for income generation. Sir Simon Hornby, in the 1988 annual review, announced:

> It is . . . our intention to find ways of increasing the amount of money which the Council can raise both by sponsorship and by charging for services. Although we recognise that we are set up as a public body and cannot exist without a significant measure of public funding, both the Council and the government believe it to be desirable to achieve a greater degree of self-reliance and independence.

> (Design Council 1988: 14)

The language of 'self-reliance' and 'independence' is 'enterprise culture'-speak for the cuts in public funding that have also so drastically affected the universities. In 1987–8 the greater part of the Council's income comprised sales, commercial sponsorship and contract fees – as opposed to the DTI grant – for the first time ever. Like the universities, the Design Council is left, in spite of its undeniable shift towards Government thinking, with the dilemma of the gulf between what it feels its broader role should be, and how it can most easily raise funds. The concluding paragraph of the 1988 annual review contains a heart-felt warning to the Government:

> The Council does not, however, see itself as self-financing. Its main aims must not be subverted by only developing its most profitable activities. The Design Council's original aims when set up by Churchill's wartime government all those years ago remain pertinent and paramount to this day: 'to promote by all practicable

201

means the improvement of design in the products of British industry'. The Design Council is a servant to the nation first and foremost. This will continue to be the priority in the new directions it takes for the future.

(Design Council 1988: 20)

The last sentence must have been uttered with rapidly dwindling hope rather than with any confidence or belief. The Design Council is becoming in effect 'semi-privatized', a consequence of which is the demise of broader public values in favour of what Eric Forth referred to as the improvement of the economic performance of 'United Kingdom Limited'. Forth believed the Council was now providing the tax payer with good value for money and so 'Privatisation at this stage is not a serious option' (*Blueprint* 1989: 16). The phrase 'at this stage' could well be significant.

BLUEPRINT FOR A CRITICAL DESIGN COUNCIL

It seems there is no chance of developing a Design Council whose first priority is the public good while the values of 'enterprise culture' dominate our political agenda. But, as history demonstrates, there is an alternative. We could have a Design Council that, along with other 'public' bodies, has an important role to play in a more egalitarian and democratic society. First, it would distinguish between consumerist design and, as it has done in the past, the wider issues and values in design that are to the benefit of society as a whole. Few would want a return to the dogmas and patriarchal values of the 1940s and 1950s when good design was often confused with a professional, middle-class, exclusive notion of 'good taste': we would want a more critical description of good design that was based on performance and ergonomics. At present, there is all too often a conflict between the criteria of the Design Council and the Consumers' Association. For example, Ross Electronics' stylish and fashionable RE5050 radio of 1985 met the Council's late-1980s consumerist criterion of 'good design' and was included in their 1986 'Design by Profit' brochure. Yet when tested in *Which?* in September 1986, it was found to have some serious defects of both reception and volume. A design-led policy may have helped Ross move from a loss of £31,000 to a surplus of £525,000 over a 4-year period but it does not necessarily imply the company was producing anything but commercially successful design.

Second, the Council should take the lead on lobbying for design for disadvantaged groups. In the strategy group report on 'Policies and Priorities for Design' (Design Council 1984), lip service was given to the need to promote 'socially desirable' products, but this has been overtaken by the Council's revised refocusing on industry and designers. It would be crucial for the Council to distinguish between consumers and users in this respect. A consumer group is one that has power in the marketplace; a user group may have no financial clout. In a recent interview with a senior member of the Council's staff this year, I asked about the Council's attitude to consciousness-raising campaigns about design for the disabled. I was told that, while once the Council would have mounted an exhibition that appealed to a manufacturer's sense of social duty, now it would start by trying to entice a manufacturer by emphasizing potential profit. More should be done on behalf of those whose needs are genuine but whose wealth is limited or non-existent.

Third, the Design Council should have a duty to raise the public's awareness about macro-environmental issues. 'Green' issues have now entered the public's consciousness and the Council should make the active promotion of environmentally responsible design one of its chief priorities. The design profession is already becoming attuned to marketing goods aimed at the 'green consumer'. The Design Council would need to differentiate between 'green' merely as a marketing strategy, and *real green* concerns. It should praise and criticize relevant products for their uses and abuses of materials, packaging and environmental effects, so contributing to the public's understanding of the implications of design and technology.

Finally, the Council should adopt a socially conscious role that promotes genuine social pluralism. Feminist critiques of design ought to inform the Council's pronouncements with the ultimate aim of establishing a socially and politically aware culture. The guiding ideal was stated as long ago as 1960 by the artist Richard Hamilton: 'An ideal culture, in my terms, is one in which awareness of its condition is universal' (Hamilton 1983: 151). This is the vision, acknowledged by Paul Reilly in 1967, of a plural culture in which: 'each of its members accepts the convenience of different values for different groups and different occasions' (Reilly 1967: 151).

This utopian blueprint for the Design Council is, of course, idealistic. It requires a drastic change of social and political priorities and values. But the demise of the Design Council into what is often little more than a limp organ of governmental policy seems a misuse and a waste. The blurring of roles between the DTI and the Design Council is regrettable. The DTI is an arm of government and it is bound to express and reflect central policy decisions. Its role is to facilitate wealth creation. The Council's role should be a broader, educative one, championing social and environmental responsibility. This is not anachronistic sentimentalism. It is because consumerism is growing without apparent check that this role is not only necessary but increasingly urgent. The Design Council has been criticized from many quarters during the last decade, including the design profession and press. But the Council does not exist for the benefit of designers; they do not need the Council because they now have a highly conducive marketplace. Some of the criticisms have been valid; others miss the Council's dilemma. While the Council cannot be excused for bad management or sloppy practices, it has had to cope with the daunting pressure applied to all public-sector or grant-aided bodies by a Government that has attacked not only the 'welfare-statist' understanding of social duty, but the very notions of public values and, indeed, of society. The recent history of the Design Council seems to show that Thatcherite 'enterprise culture' and 'the public good' are mutually exclusive. We need public institutions that critically and openly question enterprise culture if we are to retain our much-vaunted British 'freedom'.

REFERENCES

Blueprint (1986) J. Woudhuysen, 'New boss for Design Council', September.
Blueprint (1988) editorial, February.
Blueprint (1989) 'Sour grapes', March.
Brand New (Product Origination) (n.d.) *Innovation in Consumer Markets*, a report.
Butcher, J. (1987) 'Design and the national interest' 1988 in P. Gorb (ed.) *Design Talks!* London: Design Council.
Department of Trade and Industry (1988) *Support for Design: Final Evaluation Report*, London: DTI.
Design (1952) A.B.R. Fairclough, 'Designers' paradise', December.
Design (1960) L.B. Archer 'What is good design?' May.
Design (1968) editorial 'Designing for satisfaction', March.
Design (1969a) editorial, 'Design in its context', January.
Design (1969b) editorial, 'A choice of tomorrow', May.
Design (1981a) 'Sir William takes the helm', January.

Design (1981b) J. Lott, 'The Chairman speaks', November.
Design (1982) M. Thatcher, 'Take it from the top', May.
Design (1985) 'Glittering prizes for UK design', December.
Design (1987) C. Gardner, 'Accentuating the negative', February.
Design (1988a) 'The fourth director', February.
Design (1988b) M. Hancock, 'And now, a word from the chairman', August.
Design Council (1980) Annual report for year ending 31 March 1980.
Design Council (1984) *Policies and Priorities for Design Strategy*, group report, London: Design Council.
Design Council (1988) Annual review.
Designers' Journal (1989) A. Best, 'Forth Bridges', February.
Design Week (1988) 'Major council cuts loom as Fraser quits top post', 22 April.
Farr, M. (1955) *Design in British Industry*, Cambridge: Cambridge University Press.
Hamilton, R. (1983) 'Popular culture and personal responsibility' (1960) in *Collected Words*, London: Thames & Hudson.
MacCarthy, F. (1979) *A History of British Design 1830–1970*, London: Allen & Unwin.
Reilly, P. (1967) 'The challenge of pop', *Architectural Review*, October.
Reilly, P. (1969) 'Design for survival', *New Statesman*, 5 September.
Russell, G. (1949) 'What is good design?' *Design*, January. London: Design Council.
The Designer, (1983) 'Design for Profit', 'extra' supplement, February.
Whiteley, N. (1987) *Pop Design: Modernism to Mod*, London: Design Council.

Chapter Eleven

JUSTICE ENTERS THE MARKETPLACE

Enterprise culture and the provision of legal services

CHRISTOPHER STANLEY

It is the purpose of this chapter to analyse the effect of enterprise culture upon the provision of legal services in contemporary Britain. A central question will be to what extent lawyers have been forced to redefine and compromise the previous governing tenets of legal ethics and the principles of justice in order to reconcile them with the demands of the market. By way of introduction I want to make three points: (1) Thatcherism and the enterprise culture are not the same thing; (2) There are identifiable historical parallels between the current emphasis on enterprise and features of nineteenth-century legal practice; (3) The enterprise culture contains a significant self-ethic for the governance of individual conduct.

Although often associated, Thatcherism and enterprise culture are different conceptually. Under certain circumstances the 'motives' of the two are similar but in other circumstances they are different and even, on occasion, contradictory. What is more important is that there has been a sea change in attitudes affecting the legal profession occurring at a far deeper level than the transitory emergence of Thatcherism. A fundamental transformation in the nature of the legal profession has occurred that is not simply the result of the policies of the Conservative Government. This is a transformation based on an organic reaction to the market, gradually emerging over a number of years as global market behaviour has developed to increasing levels of sophistication.

The enterprise culture, as a political initiative designed to foster personal qualities such as initiative, independence and self-reliance, is not new. The echoes of certain periods in the Victorian age are clear, particularly in the two decades of the 1840s and 1850s. The 'self-ethic' or philosophy of the 'good, industrious citizen' achieving success by the virtues of hard work and living independently of state largesse was the theme of Samuel Smiles' *Self-Help*, published in 1859, with a later edition in 1863. This book encapsulates the enterprising spirit as the industrial revolution reached fruition. With the support of government policy through diverse statutory measures, the development of trade was encouraged. For example, the Companies Act 1856 permitted the association of seven or more to incorporate and to adopt the corporate legal form with limited liability. Share ownership was encouraged and it was the duty of the lawyer and the citizen: 'to give his best assistance toward accomplishing the objectives of the law . . . the encouragement of speculation, by the introduction of an unlimited chance of gain with only limited risk of loss' (Ireland 1983: 36)

The promotion of self-reliance was also achieved through the removal of state support in the form of the harsh Poor Laws. As the enterprise culture in Thatcher's Britain has in part been paid for by the dismantling of the welfare state, so, in the nineteenth century, the problems of poverty were to be dealt with by private philanthropy. As a result of massive economic expansion, the legal profession increased in size with the benefit of corporate work, the rapid transformation in land ownership and the deluge of statutory provisions that occurred. Witness the 'enterprising lawyers' at work in the novels of Charles Dickens and in the finely drawn portrait of Soames in Galsworthy's *Forsyte Saga*.

Whereas in Victorian Britain the spirit of enterprise was encouraged in order to achieve industrial expansion, the contemporary implementation of an enterprise culture has developed to tackle the problems of the collapse of the industrial base and the economic regeneration of a post-industrial technological revolution. There is a cyclical logic in the analysis of enterprise culture phenomena.

Enterprise culture makes assumptions about personal conduct. It includes an ethic for the individual in promoting the personal qualities of industry and initiative, endorsing success, whilst encouraging a willingness to accept the penalties of failure in a competitive world. The 'enterprising self' takes responsibility for his or her own life, acquiring and exercising the personal and practical skills necessary for effective action. Such attributes are founded upon an authoritative, disciplined self-judgement of resolute, although ambiguous morality (cf. Heelas, Chapter Four).

The primary means through which enterprise values are made possible is through the development of competition and institutional reforms geared toward increasing the influence of market forces. The commercial enterprise (a collective of enterprising individuals) provides a model for the organization of any institutional provision of goods and services. The virtues of competition achieved through deregulation, deprofessionalization and demystification are the central tenets of the Government's proposals for the future of the legal profession: 'The government believes that free competition between the providers of legal services will, through the discipline of the market, ensure that the public is provided with the most effective network of legal services at the most economic price' (Mackay 1989, para. 1.2).

This statement introduces a final element into the definition of enterprise culture: the primacy of the consumer. Since the world of enterprise is one in which 'competition rules', responsibility is placed upon the consumer to likewise be 'enterprising' with regard to the acquisition of goods and services.

I now turn to an examination of the practical effect of the enterprise culture on legal practice by looking first, at the market for legal services and second, at the nature of the 'enterprising self' as applied to the lawyer.

THE MARKET FOR LEGAL SERVICES

There are three significant changes in the market for legal services: the increase in the size of the market, greater competition within the market, and contraction/polarization in certain areas of market activity.

The increase in the size of the market for legal services is caused by a number of factors. The number of lawyers has grown. Since the mid-1970s, firms of solicitors with a corporate work bias have greatly increased in size. For example, the largest City firm has doubled the number of its partners to over 150 in under 10 years. Even after the oil price collapse in 1974 the size of these firms did not contract as with other City-related activities, but went on to a plateau in growth terms and then steadily continued to grow sometimes by merger with other firms. A leap in growth followed the 'Big Bang' in the City in 1986 with the following year's 'Black Monday' having little real effect, with continued expansion since then. There has been an organic growth factor due to a number of firms operating overseas, notably in America and the Far East and competing in world markets representing UK commercial interests. Preparation for the removal of trading barriers in Europe in 1992 has also provided a source of growth. It is now common for City-based firms to have offices in all the major financial centres of the world.

There has also been an increase in the number of in-house lawyers. Upwards of 2,000–3,000 lawyers are now employed by the corporate sector, acting as counsel for one client. The type of work such lawyers undertake is varied, ranging from commercial conveyancing and the drafting of contracts through to work that is based on participation in the general business of the company.

A major external factor that has effected change in the market for legal services has been the policy of the Thatcher administration. One of the ironies of the enterprise culture has been that to implement it, the Government has had to introduce a massive statutory programme, which has provided much work for the lawyers. In 'rolling back the frontiers of the state' through legislative reform, a vast area of work has been created for the legal profession. This legislation is complex in nature, requiring real advice on interpretation and scope. In addition, policy is increasingly being implemented by quasi-legislation (delegated legislation that does not pass through the formal parliamentary process). Every session, pressure is placed upon the draftsmen to produce statutes rapidly with the consequence that many are often inadequately or incompetently drafted. The ambiguously worded statute offers the potential for manipulation and exploitation by lawyers, and can also result in considerable litigation.

Within these new statutes there is often a shift from what were formerly rights-based issues toward a reliance on discretion exercised by the officers, quasi-officers and new regulators of the state. Even though the right to challenge discretionary justice is being removed, lawyers are often called upon for advice on the interpretation of possible outcomes in the exercise of discretion. Further, it has been a major feature of current economic policy to encourage the establishment of free markets. Deregulation in the City has led to the introduction of self-regulatory bodies, such as the Securities Investment Board, which require legal expertise on the problems involved in implementing the new rules governing market activity.

In private practice, the changes in the market following 'Big Bang' led to clients requiring similar advice on regulation so as to be able to negotiate the reformed market. The demolition of the barriers between trading, stockbroking and consequent advising on flotations, privatizations, new issues, rights issues and takeover bids led to a year-long explosion in legal work, with lawyers barely able to cope.

The subsequent replacement of equity by debt financing resulting from 'Black Monday' can involve complex legal procedures: for example, the securitization of debt is now normal rather than exceptional. UK lawyers have readily adapted to many of these new ideas, but the consequence is that each deal is legally more complicated while still having to be undertaken in the same or even a shorter time scale. These were important developments, separate in themselves from the movement towards more investor protection (though the two are connected) both conceptually and in practice. Likewise the 'legalism' of the Financial Services Act has generated work, the proportion of growth attributable either to 'Big Bang' or to the FSA regime being obscured by the overlap. The overall rate of growth by any measure has been remarkable. In the future, no matter what the effects of the government's proposed reforms may be, continued growth is inevitable. Having developed a sophisticated and highly skilled package for the marketplace and secured their niche in the corporate sector, the City law firms will continue to dominate.

The increase in size of the market has been paralleled by an increase in competition between lawyers at various levels: solicitors–barristers, solicitors–solicitors and the opening of the market to allow legal services to be offered by specifically non-legal concerns. In particular, changes in the corporate sector require lawyers with particular skills and abilities and 'headhunting' amongst the larger firms is not uncommon. The law governing financial and corporate transactions did not ostensibly change. The change for legal practice has come from the new institutional element, regulation and the development of new tactics. Much of this work can be undertaken by the overseas-based firms and through the use of in-house counsel, who have the additional advantage of being able to benefit from other specialist resources within the corporation (accountants, economists, management consultants), and often become part of an overall project team. But this threatens to make commercial clients question the need for external legal advice and the payment of high fees. The largest firms have countered this threat by marketing their services as 'client specific', offering a package drawing upon all areas of their specialist departments and building a continuing relationship with the client with a consequent restructuring of fees.

The third change in the market for legal services is the contraction in some areas, often largely as a consequence of the growth in others. The legal profession is now polarized between the huge City firms of solicitors and 'the rest'. There are fewer lawyers willing to specialize

210

or to develop alternative forms of legal skill. The nature of the problem is that certain areas of work are far less attractive than others, primarily because they can be loosely described as 'anti-enterprise' and because the policy of the Government has been to cut the available resources for previously state-funded legal activity such as legal aid work. Further, the erosion of welfare state, union rights, civil liberties and other 'public sector' areas of legal practice because of statutory change post-1979 has effectively removed large areas of work.

The reliance on fees from government agencies, for example, the legal aid fund, is unattractive since the level of remuneration compares unfavourably with private sector fees. The period 1987–9 witnessed an exodus from criminal work, which has resulted in a backlog in cases, unrepresented defendants and a decline in standards in an already overloaded system. As a result, informal, dispute-resolution procedures have evolved. The Government's proposals are widely assumed to mean the development of different, community-oriented solutions to what are, at present, regarded as 'legal problems' requiring 'professional' attention. In short, what is emerging is a range of non-legal and quasi-legal forums for dealing with dispute (Matthews 1989). However, the problem with reliance upon informal justice procedures is that the opacity of these processes has led to the creation of new layers of administration and bodies of professionals. The rationalization of legal services in such a way leads to minor cases being hived off, leaving the expanding legal profession to concentrate upon the more prestigious and lucrative sectors of the market.

Finally, in relation to the increase in competition in the market for legal services, the position of the general consumer has to be examined. Given the primacy of the consumer in the enterprise culture and the strategies that have developed to accommodate consumer demand, what effect has this had on the provision of legal services? The general consumer can be characterized as being the person who will see a solicitor for the purpose of house sale and purchase, the drawing up of a will or a divorce. The provider of these services continues to be the 'general practice' solicitor in the High Street. Such a practice will have a staple diet of conveyancing, probate and wills, matrimonial, small-crime and some commercial work in relation to small businesses. But the development of consumer awareness with regard to these legal services has meant that the consumer is now more than likely to question both the nature of the provision of the service itself and the cost, and often to turn to alternative sources of expertise. The former

211

awe in which solicitors were held until relatively recently has gone along with the tradition, particularly among the middle classes, of having the same firm conduct all legal matters: the consumer now is more likely to pick and choose between firms.

THE ENTERPRISING LAWYER

The idea of the self within the enterprise culture has been suggested as incorporating such characteristics as initiative, self-reliance and the pursuit of success at the expense of benevolence, altruism (and possibly justice). The enterprising self operates independently of the largesse of the state and in an economic–competitive relationship with the community in which he or she operates, whilst at the same time being a responsible and accountable member of that community. The central question is: when enterprising lawyers are functioning in a market for their services, how do they understand the nature and purpose of their activities?

The lawyer is the producer and supplier of legal services. As opposed to conceptualizing consumption as the antithesis of labour, as if the two activities demanded completely different mental and emotional qualities, it is necessary to see them as two sides of the same process. The transition in the ethos and values of the legal profession caused by the commodification of legal services is premised upon the idea that: 'Commodities are produced for immediate consumption. Their value lies not in their usefulness or permanence but in their marketability' (Lasch 1985: 21). Although legal services are not objects in the sense just implied, the provision of legal advice and skill is increasingly seen in terms of its marketability as opposed to being a device in the negotiation of justice. Traditional services are marketed to both types of client: individual (for example, the conveyancing package) and corporate (for example, the financial restructuring of the firm). In addition, new services are being developed in response to market demand, such as regulatory advice. Lawyers remain specialists, but in addition, they now act as professional producers and suppliers of a commodity within the framework of the marketplace. As one solicitor commented on the Government's recent proposals: 'Like it or not, we are in a consumer age where it is crucial for suppliers of services to think carefully about their potential clients and how to reach them' (quoted by Berlins 1988).

There are undoubtedly positive aspects of this gradual commodification of legal services. No longer the traditional awesome figures of the recent past, revered as the guardians of the law, a misunderstood professional clique surrounded by a mystical aura of ritual, the lawyers of today trade their skills in a business environment in which respect is earned by success. Law firms are less like clubs and more like businesses in which patrician airs and professional noblesse have been replaced by the survival tactics of the market. Further, the democratization of manners and a shift to a meritocratic appointments system has enabled sections of society previously excluded from the profession (women and ethnic minorities in particular) to enter it, and to be rewarded by progress through skill and ability rather than social graces and connections. As one lawyer commented:

> I maintain that this is a very good thing because we have to remember that gentlemanliness is often a euphemism for the club syndrome. It is also an excuse for keeping things the way they were and is also very often an excuse for maintaining inadequate standards of competence.
>
> (quoted by Flood 1989: 587 n. 74)

The exposure of the legal profession to market forces has resulted in the provision of legal services that are consumer-oriented. Advertising and increased diversification have forced lawyers to offer competitive packages. The sophistication of the consumer client ensures that the technical legal skill that is supplied is of a high quality, since remuneration is by 'results'. Business clients are willing to invest enough in their lawyers to permit them to develop the highest levels of professional skill and this, together with complex legislation, regulatory provisions and the harnessing of information technology, has combined to produce a distinctive style of practice. It is a style that is dynamic and diverse and very much removed from the traditional image. It is a practice that relies on maintaining a relationship with the client and thus is subject to a higher degree of accountability than before. This transformation, which has occurred in recent years, is often described as the advent of 'megalawyering' or the 'Americanization' of legal practice and this has contributed to redefining the relationship between lawyers and the wider economic and political order.

'A protean entrepreneurial quality' (Galanter 1983) is a major characteristic of the 'megalaw' firm. The demands of the market, and the centralization of technical legal skills in the corporate financial sector, have ensured that the ethics of the legal profession have changed. Lawyers have become more businesslike, client oriented and sophisticated, and more innovative in the provision of legal services. However, these new skills and innovative tactics involve *inter alia*, the development of takeover strategies, asset stripping and taxation 'planning', operations requiring a manipulation of existing laws via meticulous research and the painstaking assembly of data. As law becomes commodified, the boundaries of acceptable behaviour between the legal and illegal become blurred. The desire for profit as an arbiter of success in the enterprise culture has encouraged corporate crimes such as fraud. Although such crimes appear as such on the statute book (carrying comparatively low penalties), they have arguably become increasingly '*normalized*' standards of commercial behaviour in the corporate climate. Indeed, it can be argued that in popular consciousness, they have attained a quasi-respectable status due to the high level of technical skill required to perpetrate them and the fact that the loss and the losers are often seemingly unquantifiable, involving amounts beyond the common imagination. Such crimes appear to be a test of the legitimacy of the economic climate of 'enterprise', just as disputes are often apparently now not so much concerned with justice as with a division of the profits.

The aim of successful law reform must be to balance the requirements of efficiency and quality. In the past, the former has been subordinate to the latter. In the future, there is a legitimate fear of too great a swing in the opposite direction. Innovation and industry may be adjudged as positive virtues but the gradual commodification of legal services tends to undermine the possibility of the alleviation of human suffering through the administration of justice. This point was echoed in a report published by the legal profession, which attempts to determine its future configuration: 'the ordinary commercial consideration cannot always be decisive if the traditional character and functions of an independent legal profession are to be preserved' (Marre Report 1988: 39). There is a real risk that justice will be sacrificed to the market. But we may all be too busy being enterprising to notice.

NOTE

My thanks to Lynne Williams who commented upon and supported my work on this chapter.

REFERENCES

Berlins, M. (1988) 'Survey of the legal profession', *The Financial Times*, 20 October.

Flood, J. (1989) 'Megalaw in the UK: professionalism or corporatism?' *Indiana Law Journal*, 64 (3): 569–92.

Galanter, M. (1983) 'Mega-law and Mega-lawyering in the contemporary United States', in R. Dingwall and P. Lewis (eds) *The Sociology of the Professions*, London: Macmillan.

Ireland, P., (1983) 'The triumph of company legal form: 1856–1914' in J. Adams (ed.) *Essays for Clive Schmitthoff*, London: Butterworth.

Lasch, C., (1985) *The Minimal Self*, London: Picador.

Mackay, Lord (1989) *The Work and Organisation of the Legal Profession*, Lord Chancellor's Department, Cm. 570.

Marre Report (1988) *A Time for Change*, Report of the Committee on the future of the Legal Profession under the Chairmanship of Lady Marre, CBE, London: The Law Society.

Matthews, R. (1989) 'Green Paper recipes for a second class service', the *Guardian*, 24 February.

Smiles, S. (1863), *Self-Help*, London: Murray. First published 1859.

ADDITIONAL SOURCES

Economides, K. (1987) 'Critical legal practice: beyond abstract radicalism', unpublished paper, University of Exeter.

Levi, M. (1987) *Regulating Fraud*, London: Tavistock.

Mansfield, M. (1989) quoted in 'Justice that may go out of the window', the *Guardian*, 22 February.

Scheingold, S. (1988) 'Radical lawyers and socialist ideals', *Journal of Law and Society* 15 (1): 122.

Chapter Twelve

CONSUMER SOVEREIGNTY AND THE INTEGRITY OF PRACTICES

RUSSELL KEAT

THE PROBLEM OF BOUNDARIES

A central feature of current attempts to construct an 'enterprise culture' in Britain has been a series of institutional reforms designed to introduce market principles and commercially modelled forms of organization into a wide range of activities previously conducted upon different principles, and 'protected' by means such as public funding or subsidy from the forces operating in a free market economy. These extensions of the market have raised, in an often acute and practical form, an important set of theoretical issues about what kinds of activities are, and are not, appropriately governed by market mechanisms: about how, and upon what basis, the boundaries should be drawn between market and non-market domains.[1]

In this chapter I shall consider some of these issues by exploring a particular kind of critical response often voiced by those whose activities are affected by such extensions of the market domain; and in doing so I shall focus upon activities that might loosely be described as 'cultural' in character, such as academic research and teaching, broadcasting, the arts and so on. The general form of this critical response is that such activities are not appropriately judged by 'market criteria'; and hence that their subjection to the kinds of forces operating upon and within commercial enterprises tends to distort or undermine the values and standards by which they had previously, and rightly, been judged.

Thus, for example, academics complain that the pressure to compete for students undermines their own conception of what is educationally worthwhile, and that the value of their research is now being judged by intellectually facile considerations of 'marketability'; television programme-makers argue that government-initiated reforms of broad-casting will lead to a decline in the quality of programmes; theatre directors, dance companies and musicians claim that the new criteria for funding imposed by the Arts Council make it increasingly difficult to nurture innovation or to maintain artistic integrity; museum curators protest that by being reduced to the status of a leisure industry, the purposes properly served by their collections are put at risk; and so on.

As an initial step in analysing the nature of such claims, and their possible rationale, it may be helpful to consider the implications of a powerful and influential argument often employed to support the use of free markets. According to this, markets are the most efficient means of producing goods and services whose 'value' is determined by their satisfaction of people's wishes or preferences: that is, they generate a greater total amount of individual 'want-satisfaction', from a given set of inputs, than any alternative economic system.

This argument derives its justificatory force from an essentially utilitarian standpoint, being both 'aggregative' and 'want-regarding' in character.[2] For on the one hand, it focuses exclusively upon total amounts of want-satisfaction, without attending to their pattern of distribution between individuals or groups; and on the other, it 'takes people's wants as given', in the sense that it rules out any judgements about the respective merits of some kinds of wishes or preferences as against others. The satisfaction of people's wishes is taken to be intrinsically desirable, whatever the character or content of those wishes may happen to be: one is not permitted to discriminate between more-or-less valuable, desirable or acceptable forms of satisfaction. To do so would involve adopting instead what may be termed an 'ideal-regarding' standpoint.

Suppose now that markets do, in fact, maximize aggregate want-satisfaction. Then one might object to their use either on distributive or on ideal-regarding grounds: by arguing, with respect to particular kinds of goods or services, either that they should not be distributed in the ways that would result from market mechanisms, or that they are not suitably judged solely by reference to their satisfaction of people's preferences.

The former, 'distributive' argument against the use of markets can be illustrated by the kind of objection that might be made to the privatization of education and health care: to transforming them from freely provided, publicly funded services, into purchasable commodities like any other market product. Since the operation of

217

market economies tends to generate major inequalities of income and wealth, the relative ease of people's access to these services (and indeed the relative quality of the services thereby received) would then broadly reflect these inequalities, and hence be unrelated to people's need for them. Whatever the merits of market economies, their distributive consequences clearly do not satisfy need-based criteria of justice; and hence their obvious unsuitability for the provision of goods and services where such criteria are regarded as relevant.

Yet, this is not what is at issue in the kinds of criticism of market principles with which I am concerned, where the objection appears to be not that markets make the quality of what is available to people dependent upon their (unequal) income and wealth, but rather that they operate in ways that fail to meet the appropriate criteria for judging the 'quality' or 'value' of what is provided, whether or not this is justly distributed.

This objection would seem then to be 'ideal-regarding' in character; and it therefore depends, *inter alia*, upon the claim that the value or quality of what is 'produced' by these cultural activities cannot properly be assessed by reference only to their satisfaction of consumer preferences. And if this is so, it might partly explain – though not, I believe, justify – such criticisms often being met with the charge of 'elitism': if the participants in such activities are unwilling to subject themselves to the judgements of the market, this must be because they accord to themselves some 'privileged' status or authority in judging what they produce, and regard the wishes and preferences of at least many of their potential consumers as ill-informed, undiscriminating, philistine and the like.

Of course it may be argued, against the preceding supposition, that market mechanisms do *not* in fact maximize aggregate want-satisfaction; or alternatively, that they do so only by virtue of the ability of producers to shape and control the preferences of their consumers, thereby making this justification for the market quite vacuous. But such arguments will not be examined here. Indeed, if the latter were correct, participants in cultural activities would presumably have little to fear from their relocation in the market domain, since they would then be able to impose their ideal-regarding criteria of value upon their new-found consumers. But it is not this prospect that they seem to find so alarming.

Having now indicated what may be involved in these criticisms of the extension of market boundaries, I shall explore one particular direction in which they might be developed and substantiated. I shall start by outlining the account of 'practices' presented by Alasdair MacIntyre in *After Virtue* (1981, esp. ch. 14), and will then go on to develop this in a way that may explain the potentially antithetical relations between the conduct of cultural activities (understood now as 'practices'), and the forces operating in a free market economy. I shall conclude by addressing a certain problem about the nature and status of value judgements that face those who wish, not only to exclude such practices from the market domain, but also to argue for their support by public means.

PRACTICES AND INSTITUTIONS

MacIntyre defines the concept of a 'practice' in the following way:

> By a 'practice' I am going to mean any coherent and complex form of socially established cooperative activity through which goods internal to that form of activity are realised in the course of trying to achieve those standards of excellence which are appropriate to, and partially definitive of, that form of activity, with the result that human powers to achieve excellence, and human conceptions of the ends and goods involved, are systematically extended.
> (MacIntyre 1981: 175)

And from the examples that he provides – farming, architecture, portrait-painting, chess, football, the sciences and humanities, music and so on – there is clearly a wide range of activities that might display the characteristics of a practice, including amongst others those of a 'cultural' nature.

Two elements in this definition require some elaboration. First, 'standards of excellence'. Every practice involves a set of standards that serve to identify what counts as a good or bad (genuine or spurious, exemplary or worthless, etc.) instance of the activity concerned, and by reference to which the success or otherwise of attempts by individuals to perform these activities is thus to be judged. In 'entering' a practice one must (at least initially) be willing to subject one's own attitudes, choices and tastes to the authority of its standards. Thus:

> If, on starting to listen to music, I do not accept my own incapacity to judge correctly, I will never learn to hear, let alone to appreciate, Bartok's last quartets. If, on starting to play baseball, I do not

219

accept that others know better than I when to throw a fast ball and when not, I will never learn to appreciate good pitching let alone to pitch.

(MacIntyre 1981: 177)

However, this is not to imply that the standards accepted at any one time are beyond criticism or impervious to change; and the history of particular practices is thus in part a history of such criticisms and of consequent changes in those standards. This itself is one reason why practices never consist merely in a specific set of 'techniques', of ways of achieving some fixed and pre-established goal. For part of what is involved in a practice is a continuing process of critical reflection on existing goals, and the development of new ones whose content cannot be articulated in advance (ibid: 180–1).

The second element to be considered in MacIntyre's definition of practices is the concept of 'internal goods', and the related contrast with what he terms 'external' ones. The internal goods that are realized by engaging in a practice are such that their character can only be identified by reference to the specific nature of the practice concerned, and its particular standards – for example (mine, not MacIntyre's), the elegance of a scientific theory, or the truthfulness of a theatrical performance; and they are achievable only through the experience of involvement in its activities.

By contrast, the character of an external good is not thus dependent upon the particular nature of the practice through which it may be achieved. The prime examples of external goods are money, power, prestige and status. When the reasons for which people engage in a practice refer predominantly to such external goods, what counts as success in terms of the practice's own standards becomes valued only instrumentally, as a means to achieving other goods that might equally well be acquired by some other means; and not intrinsically, as is the case with internal goods.

Further, it should be noted that this contrast between internal and external goods, and the ways in which they operate as reasons for engaging in the activities of a practice, does not imply or rest upon any simple distinction between altruistic and egoistic motivations. Both types of goods are potential sources of pleasure or satisfaction for those who experience them: they are both 'good' *for* their recipients. Hence orientation towards the internal goods of a practice is not to be seen as involving some kind of self-sacrifice on the part of those concerned, acting 'for the good of the practice' at the expense of their own interests. Rather, their form of involvement in the practice is such that their own identities, and hence interests, are at least partly bound up with those of the practice and its standards.[3]

None the less, whilst both external and internal goods are beneficial to those who achieve them, they differ in the 'exclusivity' of the benefits they produce. Those who possess external goods do so to the exclusion of others who do not; and in the competition for external goods, there are necessarily both winners and losers. By contrast, although competition with others may also be involved in achieving internal goods, such competition is itself conducted in relation to the shared standards of the practice concerned; and because of this, success comes at least partly in a non-exclusive form. Thus:

> Internal goods are indeed the outcome of competition to excel, but it is characteristic of them that their achievement is a good for the whole community who participate in the practice. So when Turner transformed the seascape in painting or W.C. Grace advanced the art of batting in cricket in a quite new way their achievement enriched the whole relevant community.
>
> (MacIntyre 1981: 178)

It might seem to follow from these claims about internal and external goods that, as it were, practices would do well to avoid contact with the latter altogether. But this would ignore the fact that practices cannot normally survive for long without being sustained by institutions, and that institutions necessarily involve the use of external goods. Chess, physics and medicine, for example, require institutions such as clubs, laboratories and hospitals; and these institutions depend in various ways upon money, power, status, and so on (ibid: 181).

Thus practices require institutions, but this makes them highly vulnerable to various forms of 'corruption' stemming from the use of external goods. To see why this is so, it may be helpful to identify a number of reasons why institutions – and hence external goods – are required to sustain practices.[4] First, there is the fact that most practices make demands upon material resources, which must somehow, therefore, be acquired, typically in competition with other demands upon them. Second, the rules and standards of the practice must be potentially enforceable: they must not only have 'authority' in an abstract sense, but must also be backed by some authoritative system of power, involving the use of various kinds of sanctions.

Finally, whilst the primary motivation of participants in a well-ordered practice may be directed towards internal goods, they are unlikely to be altogether indifferent to their acquisition of external ones – not only money, but also prestige and status, especially where these involve some form of public recognition or reward for their performance in the practice concerned.

But in each of these dimensions of 'institutional life', the role of external goods can easily develop in ways that are damaging to the practice. First, for example, the acquisition of material resources may come to be pursued as an end in itself, rather than as a means to further the ends of the practice, which may then turn out to conflict with what is required in meeting this new objective. Second, the institution's structure of power may come to take on a life of its own, and instead of serving to maintain the rules and standards of the practice, tend rather to subvert them. Third, and possibly as a result of either or both of the preceding, the system of external rewards for the practice's participants may come to diverge significantly from the judgements of their relative contribution and success made by reference to its standards. If this happens, participants may then experience serious 'strains of commitment' to the practice, its internal goods no longer providing sufficient motivation for them.

PRACTICES AND MARKETS

Given this account of practices, their institutional requirements, and their consequent sources of vulnerability, one can now consider how far they are likely to be damaged or undermined by being subjected to the kinds of forces operating in a free market economy. But before doing so it is worth noting that markets are by no means the only potential threat to the integrity of practices. For example, their subordination to the state, or indeed to any system that allocates external goods in ways that conflict with their own institutional requirements, may well be at least equally damaging.

I will begin by presenting an argument designed to show that the integrity of practices cannot be sustained when transferred to the market domain, where different firms compete with one another in selling their goods and services (the 'products' of their previously shared practice) to consumers.[5] But this argument will later be modified in response to an important objection.

There are two main features of the market that are relevant here.

222

First, competition in the market is oriented primarily towards the maximization of external goods, in the form of financial profits. The aim of such competition is not to further the development of a practice in ways that are then available to all of its participants, but rather to gain exclusive access to goods that are only contingently related (through the circumstances of the market) to its standards being met or developed. The logic of market competition implies that the success of one's competitors must be greeted with dismay, since it is inimical to one's own: at best it may provide ideas to exploit to one's own advantage, measured in external terms, rather than contributions from which one may learn, and which may enhance one's experience of the practice's internal goods. Competing producers are thus unable to regard themselves as sharing membership in a practice whose internal goods are held in common.

Second, success and failure in the market are supposedly determined by the relative ability of competing producers to satisfy the preferences of their potential consumers. Thus what counts as a 'good' product is judged by reference to the wishes and preferences that consumers happen to have, whether or not these are consistent with the practice's own internal standards; and when the two conflict, the market dictates who will be the victor. Markets are want-regarding, whilst practices are ideal-regarding – they give no weight or credence to 'uninformed' judgements, and typically regard themselves instead as involved in the 'cultivation' of these, and hence of the potential to appreciate their internal goods. Practices subordinate individual inclinations and wishes to the authority of their own criteria of judgement, whilst markets subordinate producers to the preferences of individual consumers. They therefore, *inter alia*, allow no 'free space' for the kinds of open-ended, reflective development characteristic of practices, which itself contributes to new conceptions of the human good.

Taken together, these two features of the market seem clearly inimical to the integrity of practices. One way of seeing this is by attending to the 'strains of commitment' that may be expected to be experienced by the members of a practice that is transferred to the market domain. For a variety of reasons, external goods will no longer tend to be distributed (either between competing groups, or between the members of each such group) in ways that map on to the judgements of performance made by reference to the practice's own standards. Further, the relative priority of internal and external goods, and their means–ends relationship, will be reversed; and the kinds of activity or performance leading to the achievement of external goods will often diverge from those leading to internal ones. Thus the continued commitment of participants to the standards and goals of the practice will require a potentially unsustainable degree of self-sacrifice on their part, measured in terms of external goods. Far from their previous altruism being threatened by egoism, it is only now that such altruism becomes necessary.

However, the preceding line of argument might well be thought to prove too much, at least if it is taken to imply that the characteristics of practices could never be displayed by firms operating in a free market economy. For intuitively, anyway, it seems that such characteristics are by no means always entirely absent; and correspondingly, that the account of practices provided earlier would not be altogether alien or unrecognizable to some of those involved in them. And if this is so, it may suggest that the preceding argument depends on too abstract a picture of markets, one that ignores the many significant differences that can exist between their more concrete, specific forms.

For example, competition for external goods may in some cases have a relatively low salience in the ways in which 'rival' producers conceive of the primary rationale for their activities, and they may correspond-ingly have a relatively strong sense of the bonds that unite them with other producers in a shared activity whose internal goods are held in common. Rather than aiming at strict profit-maximization, they may instead adopt some individual or collective version of 'earning a decent living'; and they may also be inclined towards some form of 'gentlemen's agreement' to limit competition with other producers. (Such behaviour is usually condemned by free market proponents, and depicted in a sinister light. But it might sometimes be better understood as a quite innocent or admirable expression of the desire to conduct economic life as a practice.)

Turning now to the relations between producers and consumers, one can note a number of reasons why the kind of conflict presented earlier, between consumer preferences and the standards of 'producer-practices', may not in fact arise. For whilst it is true that there is no pre-established harmony here, neither is there any pre-established discord. For example, consumers may, in some cases, exhibit a high degree of 'deference' towards producers, being quite willing to accept the 'authority' of the relevant practice's standards, and thus readily allowing their choices to be shaped by producers' judgements; or they may likewise be rather passive and undemanding, but this time because the whole activity of consumption has relatively little significance in their lives. Alternatively, there may be situations in which consumers and producers regard themselves more or less equally as members of a single practice, so that although the latter, unlike the former, actually earn their living through the practice, this distinction is, in other respects, seen as superficial or fortuitous. (It should not, after all, be assumed that only 'producers' can be members of a practice.)

However, although these points suggest that, under certain specific conditions, firms in a free market economy may be able to possess some of the characteristics of practices, such situations are inherently fragile or unstable. In particular, it requires only one reasonably powerful firm to, as it were, take seriously the aim of profit-maximization, for others to be forced to follow suit on pain of elimination from the contest. And if the changes thereby required are damaging to the practice, there is nothing that can realistically be done to protect it – the well-attested dynamic nature of market economies has, after all, a nasty habit of presenting people with unattractive options between which to choose.

Furthermore, it is arguable that at least some of the recent developments in both the organization of production, and the relations between consumers and producers, are likely to be inimical to the character of production as a practice. For example, the increasing role in commercial enterprises of financial control and marketing may militate against the priority that might otherwise be given to the internal goods associated with direct involvement in productive activities; and the shifts towards 'consumer-driven production' may indicate an increasingly active and non-deferential mode of consumption that challenges in various ways the privilege or authority of the producer (cf. Abercrombie, Chapter Nine). Indeed, it is significant that in areas such as private sector publishing and broadcasting, the criticisms that are often made of their growing 'commercialization' bear a striking resemblance to those made within non-commercial cultural practices, subject to similar changes. For this would suggest a common set of problems in the relations between market forces, at least in their contemporary forms, and the integrity of practices.

CONSUMER SOVEREIGNTY AND SUBJECTIVE VALUES

Suppose now that, for the kinds of reasons outlined previously, the forces operating in a free market economy will tend strongly to under-mine the character of, amongst others, cultural practices of the kind noted at the outset. It would none the less not follow from this that they have any claim to be supported or protected by public means. For it is one thing to argue that certain activities are best conducted outside the market domain, and quite another that public funds and resources should be provided to sustain them. In particular, it might instead be proposed that they should basically be ascribed the status of 'private' hobbies or pastimes, their resources being provided by whatever voluntary means happen to be available – like amateur sports, or bird-watching.

Such a proposal might be justified in the following way. The moral basis for the market is quite simple: produce what people as consumers show they wish to have, and one has a right to receive the ensuing external rewards (which themselves enable production to take place). But if one is unwilling to meet this requirement, on the grounds that to do so would distort the nature of one's preferred activity, one has no such right. There is nothing to prevent people engaging in such activities if they so choose, and deriving what satisfactions they may from the internal goods involved. But there is no obligation on the part of anyone else materially or otherwise to support them.

The issues raised by this response have an important bearing upon some well-known problems confronting certain kinds of socialist critique of the market, including Marx's. For there is obviously a close resemblance between Marx's conception of non-alienated labour, and MacIntyre's account of practices – a resemblance due partly to their shared Aristotelian ancestry.[6] Marx believed that production in communist society could both provide workers with the intrinsic satisfactions of such labour, and at the same time satisfy the needs of those who received its products. But it seems that no non-market mechanisms have yet been discovered by which both these aims can be simultaneously achieved; and hence the current attempts by many socialist theorists to develop models of an economic system that makes use of market mechanisms, but without capitalist property relations. However, such attempts still have to deal with the problem of boundaries between market and non-market domains, and thus also with justifying the provision of public resources for activities deemed unsuited to the market domain.

In broad terms, any such justification must presumably involve showing that such practices have a social value over and above the benefits accruing to their participants, and which cannot appropriately be judged by reference to consumer preferences: it must appeal to ideal-regarding rather than want-regarding principles. There are many ways in which this justificatory task might be performed. But rather than trying to survey or adjudicate between these, I shall conclude by focusing upon a particular difficulty that they are likely to face, especially in the case of cultural practices.

This difficulty is generated by what is arguably an increasingly marked feature of modern (or indeed post-modern) societies, namely the widespread acceptance of 'subjectivist' theories of value, according to which questions of a moral, aesthetic or political nature have no objective or authoritative answers. Judgements of value are, instead, regarded as the expression of individual opinions, tastes or attitudes, for which no rational justification can be provided – though these 'judgements' may sometimes happen to be shared by other individuals with similar inclinations. Nor is this subjectivist view confined to the elevated realm of meta-ethical theorists, be they existentialist, analytical, post-structuralist or otherwise. It seems also to be accepted in a good deal of everyday thought and action, as evidenced, for example, in the terms 'value judgement' and 'subjective opinion' being widely treated as more-or-less synonymous.

But there is a close relationship between subjectivist theories of value, on the one hand, and the criteria by which judgements are made in the free market, on the other.[7] For the latter depend ultimately upon the satisfaction of consumer preferences, 'whatever these may happen to be'; whilst according to the former, values are themselves essentially a matter of individual preferences. Hence, as it were, the market makes value judgements upon precisely the same basis (or rather, lack of basis) as the subjectivist proposes; and its ability to maximize aggregate want-satisfaction will thereby also maximize the provision of whatever has value, understood in subjectivist terms. (Of course it will not do so *justly* – but that is a separate issue, as noted earlier.)

This is not to say that the use of the market can only be justified by reference to a subjectivist theory of values. For it is one thing to claim that there is a value in satisfying people's preferences – a claim that might itself be justified on non-subjectivist grounds – and quite another that judgements of value are no more than the expression of preferences. Rather, the point is this: if a subjectivist theory of values is accepted, then the use of markets will provide one obvious means (though not necessarily the only one) of allocating material resources to the production of whatever is judged to be valuable.

This link between subjectivist theories of value and the market may itself be embodied in a specific interpretation of the concept of 'consumer sovereignty'. Consumers may be ascribed sovereignty not only in the sense that it is they who should 'rule' over producers, and hence that the success or failure of rival producers is to be determined by their ability to satisfy consumer preferences; but also in the additional sense that they are the sole and unchallengeable arbiters of value – that there are no further, objective or authoritative criteria by reference to which their own opinions and preferences can be assessed.[8]

There seems, then, to be a kind of natural alliance between value-subjectivism and the market, mediated and expressed by this particular understanding of consumer sovereignty. In the face of this alliance, it may prove difficult to justify non-market provision for activities whose value is claimed not to reside exclusively in their satisfaction of preferences – especially when, as is the case with cultural practices, they do not produce the kinds of goods and services, such as health care, about whose value most people are not in fact prepared to be subjectivists. And in order successfully to combat this alliance, it may thus prove necessary to articulate some plausible alternative to value-subjectivism.

One way in which this might be done is suggested by considering the implications of replacing public by market provision in a particular area of cultural practices, namely public service broadcasting – for example, news and current affairs programmes, documentaries and so on. This replacement might well take the form of a single channel devoted to such programmes, financed by subscriptions from those willing to pay for them; and what had previously been regarded as a service of public value would be seen instead as satisfying the preferences of a particular 'niche' audience. (No doubt this would be called an 'up-market' channel, thereby expressing a kind of commodified remnant of non-market, non-subjectivist values – just as 'high culture' comes to be redefined as an up-market leisure activity.)

But such a development could be criticized for its potentially damaging consequences for the operation of democratic political institutions, which depend, *inter alia*, on their citizens being suitably equipped to make well-informed and reflective decisions.[9] The judgements made by democratic citizens are not regarded, at least in

228

theory, as the mere expression of personal preferences, but as resulting from a certain kind of critical engagement with the issues involved in the political sphere. But this is something that requires the acquisition and exercise of a number of skills and capacities, and hence also the availability of a wide range of cultural resources that provide, as it were, the necessary basis for relevant forms of 'educative experience'. There is thus a crucial role for certain cultural practices in contributing to this process, whose significance is itself at odds with any purely subjective theory of values.

Thus at least in the political sphere one can see how the value of certain cultural practices might be viewed as partly residing in their contribution to the educative experiences involved in acquiring and exercising the ability to make genuine 'judgements' about values. But similar arguments might also be constructed in relation to other areas in which it seems equally important to provide people with the cultural resources for critical reflection: in particular, to enable them to determine what place in their lives is to be given to activities such as consumption itself. And it would be counterintuitive, to say the least, if the cultural practices contributing to the kinds of experience involved in coming to terms with *this* kind of question were themselves to be subordinated to the preferences of consumers in a free market economy.

NOTES

1 This problem of boundaries has been highlighted and explored by Michael Walzer (1983, esp. ch. 4), though my approach differs from his, and owes much to discussions with John O'Neill and Nick Abercrombie.

2 The distinctions and terminology introduced here, and their use in characterizing utilitarian arguments for the free market, derive from Brian Barry's *Political Argument* (1965: 38–47: see also his discussion of public funding for the arts).

3 Hence the tendency for professional bodies to present themselves as committed to an 'altruistic' ethic is generally misconceived: cf. Johnson 1972.

4 From this point on, and right through the following section of the chapter, I develop and apply MacIntyre's analysis of practices in ways that he might well not endorse.

5 The relations between markets, practices and institutions has an important bearing on the social organization of science: see Ravetz (1971), esp. pp. 273–89 on problems of 'quality control'.

6 Cf. Kamenka (1972), esp. pp. 110–17 on Marx's use of artistic production as a model for non-alienated labour. Throughout this

chapter I focus on those features of markets that are not dependent on the kinds of property relations peculiar to *capitalist* market economies.

7 This relationship is explored by MacIntyre in ch. XVII of his later book (1988); but my concluding remarks about democracy and citizenship depart from his views there.

8 Cf. the following claims about consumer sovereignty in a recent lecture by Sir Alan Peacock, chairman (*inter alia*) of the Scottish Arts Council – though these are significantly qualified later on in the lecture:

> This view implicitly rejects any notion that there is a hierarchy of tastes and preferences however this could be decided. It explicitly rejects the idea that the creative artist, the performing artist, or the informed aesthete can . . . have any special status in the community when it comes to the allocation of resources to the arts. (Peacock 1987: 3)

9 For a somewhat similar, but much more elaborate argument, see Keane (1989).

REFERENCES

Barry, B. (1965) *Political Argument*, London: Routledge & Kegan Paul.

Johnson, T. (1972) *Professions and Power*, London: Macmillan.

Kamenka, E. (1972) *The Ethical Foundations of Marxism*, London: Routledge & Kegan Paul.

Keane, J. (1989) 'Citizenship and the Freedom of the Media', *Political Quarterly* 60: 285–96.

MacIntyre, A. (1981) *After Virtue*, London: Duckworth.

MacIntyre, A. (1988) *Whose Justice? Which Rationality?* London: Duckworth.

Peacock, A. (1987) 'Cultural economics and the finance of the arts', Esmee Fairbairn Lecture, University of Lancaster.

Ravetz, J.R. (1971) *Scientific Knowledge and its Social Problems*, Oxford: Oxford University Press.

Walzer, M. (1983) *Spheres of Justice*, Oxford: Martin Robertson.

NAME INDEX

NAME INDEX

SUBJECT INDEX